Memory and Identity

This book examines the ways in which ghosts haunt and shape cultural identities and memory, considering the manner in which the fluctuations of such identities sometimes imply the rethinking or rewriting of the past.

Drawing on case studies in historical, political, literary and linguistic studies, it explores the narratives that produce imagined communities and identities and the places in which cultural identities are constructed through memory, asking how far these identities and memories disinherit or exclude otherness, and how far ghosts disturb orderly narratives, inviting multiple readings of the past. Thematically organized to consider the persistence of ghosts within present memory and identity, the creation of new identities through intertwining narratives of the past, and the reclamation of identities in postcolonial contexts, *Memory and Identity: Ghosts of the past in the English-speaking world* offers a multi-disciplinary examination of the concept of haunting.

Memory and Identity will appeal to scholars of sociology, anthropology, cultural studies and history with interests in memory and identity.

Linda Pillière is Professor of English Language and Linguistics at Aix-Marseille Université, France. She is the co-editor of *Standardising English: Norms and Margins in the History of the English Language* and *Standardisation and Variation in English Language(s)* and author of *Intralingual Translation of British Novels: A Multimodal Stylistic Perspective.*

Karine Bigand is Senior Lecturer in Irish Studies at Aix-Marseille Université, France. She has recently co-authored *Faces and Places. Northern Ireland, 1975–2020.*

Memory Studies: Global Constellations

Series editor: Henri Lustiger-Thaler, Ramapo College of New Jersey, USA and Ecole des Hautes Etudes en Sciences Sociales, France

The 'past in the present' has returned in the early twenty-first century with a vengeance, and with it the expansion of categories of experience. These experiences have largely been lost in the advance of rationalist and constructivist understandings of subjectivity and their collective representations. The cultural stakes around forgetting, 'useful forgetting' and remembering, locally, regionally, nationally and globally have risen exponentially. It is therefore not unusual that 'migrant memories'; micro-histories; personal and individual memories in their interwoven relation to cultural, political and social narratives; the mnemonic past and present of emotions, embodiment and ritual and finally, the mnemonic spatiality of geography and territories are receiving more pronounced hearings.

This transpires as the social sciences themselves are consciously globalising their knowledge bases. In addition to the above, the reconstructive logic of memory in the juggernaut of galloping, informationalisation is rendering it more and more publicly accessible and therefore part of a new global public constellation around the coding of meaning and experience. Memory studies as an academic field of social and cultural inquiry emerge at a time when global public debate – buttressed by the fragmentation of national narratives – has accelerated. Societies today, in late globalised conditions, are pregnant with newly unmediated and unfrozen memories once sequestered in wide collective representations. We welcome manuscripts that examine and analyze these profound cultural traces.

Titles in this series

https://www.routledge.com/sociology/series/ASHSER1411

Memory and Identity

Ghosts of the Past in the
English-speaking World

**Edited by
Linda Pillière and Karine Bigand**

Routledge
Taylor & Francis Group

LONDON AND NEW YORK

First published 2023
by Routledge
4 Park Square, Milton Park, Abingdon, Oxon OX14 4RN

and by Routledge
605 Third Avenue, New York, NY 10158

Routledge is an imprint of the Taylor & Francis Group, an informa business

British Library Cataloguing-in-Publication Data
A catalogue record for this book is available from the British Library

Library of Congress Cataloging-in-Publication Data
Names: Pillière, Linda, 1958- editor. | Bigand, Karine, editor.
Title: Memory and identity : ghosts of the past in the English-speaking world / edited by Linda Pillière and Karine Bigand.
Description: 1 Edition. | New York, NY : Routledge, 2023. | Series: Memory studies: global constellations | Includes bibliographical references and index.
Identifiers: LCCN 2022020187 (print) | LCCN 2022020188 (ebook) | ISBN 9781032012841 (hardback) | ISBN 9781032012865 (paperback) | ISBN 9781003178040 (ebook)
Subjects: LCSH: Collective memory. | Memory—Social aspects. | English-speaking countries—Social life and customs. | Narratives.
Classification: LCC HM1033 .M4537 2023 (print) | LCC HM1033 (ebook) | DDC 306.4—dc23/eng/20220729
LC record available at https://lccn.loc.gov/2022020187
LC ebook record available at https://lccn.loc.gov/2022020188

ISBN: 978-1-032-01284-1 (hbk)
ISBN: 978-1-032-01286-5 (pbk)
ISBN: 978-1-003-17804-0 (ebk)

DOI: 10.4324/9781003178040

Typeset in Times New Roman
by codeMantra

Contents

Figures

Contributors

Karine Bigand is a Senior Lecturer in Irish Studies at Aix-Marseille Université, France. Her research interests lie in how history, memory, identity and politics interact in contemporary Northern Ireland. Her more recent work has focused on cultural heritage and museums, the debate on dealing with the past and the impact of Brexit. She recently co-authored *Faces & Places. Northern Ireland, 1975–2020* (Editions Juillet, 2020) with French photographer Bernard Lesaing.

Charlotte Brewer is Professor of English Language and Literature at the University of Oxford and a Fellow of Hertford College, Oxford, UK. She has published widely on dictionaries and the *OED* and is currently co-editing the correspondence of the *OED*'s first chief editor, Sir James Murray, for publication in an online edition at the *Murray Scriptorium* (http://murrayscriptorium.org).

Tanvi Chowdhary is a PhD student at Ashoka University, India where she is working on early nineteenth-century English literature and the nature of fannish reappropriation in the West and in South Asia. She was a part of the Iowa Writing Program in 2019, and her creative work has been published in *Asterism* and *Multitudes*.

Marjorie Galelli is the Associate Director of the Center for Military, War, and Society Studies at the University of Kansas, USA. She has a PhD in military history, and her work focuses on military power and the relationship between the US military, the government, the media and the American people throughout the twentieth and early twenty-first centuries.

Anne Lesme holds a PhD in American Studies and lectures in English and communication studies at Aix-Marseille University, France. Her research interests lie at the crossroads of Childhood Studies and Visual Studies, and she is the author of *Photographier l'enfant pour changer la société: Images réformatrices de l'enfant pauvre aux Etats-Unis 1888–1942* (2019).

Kathy Luckett is Emeritus Professor in the Centre for Higher Education Development and currently works for the Institutional Planning

Department, University of Cape Town, South Africa. Her research interests are higher education policy around equity, access and language; sociology of knowledge and curriculum studies with a focus on the Humanities, Africana, decolonial and postcolonial studies and research methods that apply critical/social realism to educational evaluation.

Fiona McCann is Professor of postcolonial literatures at the Université de Lille and director of the research centre CECILLE (ULR 4074). She has published widely on contemporary Irish, South African, and Zimbabwean writing and is the author of a monograph *A Poetics of Dissensus: Confronting Violence in Contemporary Prose Writing from the North of Ireland* (Peter Lang, 2014) and the editor of an essay collection *The Carceral Network in Ireland: History, Agency and Resistance* (Palgrave, 2020).

Veeran Naicker is a Doctoral Candidate in the Department of Sociology at the University of Cape Town, South Africa. He has recently submitted his doctoral thesis, 'The Necropolitical Crisis of Racial Subjectivity in the South African Postcolony: Black Consciousness as a Technology of the Self and the Limits to Transformation'. His research interests include postcolonial studies, post-structuralism, psychoanalysis, critical theory and the intersections between histories of the Anthropocene, racism, patriarchy and capitalism.

Armelle Parey is Assistant Professor at the University of Caen-Normandie, France. She has recently edited *Prequels, Coquels and Sequels in Contemporary Anglophone Fiction* (Routledge, 2019) and co-edited *Adapting Endings from Book to Screen* (Routledge, 2020). She also co-edited *A.S. Byatt, Before and after Possession: Recent Critical Approaches* (PUN-Editions de Lorraine, 2017) and *Reading Ian McEwan's Mature Fiction: New Critical Approaches* (PUN-Editions de Lorraine, 2021). She is currently completing a monograph on Kate Atkinson's fiction.

Linda Pillière is Professor of English Language and Linguistics at Aix-Marseille Université, France. Her research expertise lies at the intersection of several fields, including stylistics, translation and sociolinguistics. Her monograph, *Intralingual Translation of British Novels: A Stylistic Multimodal Perspective* was published by Bloomsbury in 2021, and she has co-edited several volumes including *Standardising English: Norms and Margins in the History of the English Language* published by CUP in 2018.

Marie-Odile Pittin-Hédon is Professor of British Literature at Aix-Marseille Université, France. Her research focuses on twentieth- and twenty-first-century Scottish fiction. She is the author of *The Space of Fiction: Voices from Scotland in a Post-devolution Age* (Scottish Literature International, 2015), the editor of *Women and Scotland: Literature, Culture, Politics* (Presses Universitaires de Besançon, 2020) and co-editor of

Literature after the Devolution: Edges of the New (Edinburgh University Press, 2022).

John Potts is Professor of Media and Director of the Centre for Media History at Macquarie University, Sydney, Australia. He is the author of numerous books including *Ideas in Time: the* Longue Durée *in Intellectual History; The New Time and Space* and *A History of Charisma*. He has also edited or co-edited *Technologies of Magic: A Cultural Study of Ghosts, Machines and the Uncanny; The Future of Writing* and *After the Event: New Perspectives on Art History.*

Philip Rycroft was a civil servant in the United Kingdom for 30 years and worked both for the devolved government in Scotland and for the government in Whitehall. A major focus throughout his career was on constitutional issues, including devolution and the future of Scotland. He continues to work on these themes as a visiting fellow at the Bennett Institute for Public Policy at Cambridge University, UK and as an Honorary Professor at Edinburgh University.

Michael Stricof is a Senior Lecturer in American studies at Aix-Marseille University, France. His research focuses on post-Cold War American defense spending and its multifaceted influence on politics, identity and foreign policy. Previously, he was a visiting scholar at Georgetown University's School of Foreign Service.

Gilles Teulié is Professor of British and South African Studies at Aix-Marseille University, France. He has written extensively on South African history, including a book on the Afrikaners and the Anglo-Boer War (2000), another on racial attitudes in Victorian South Africa (2015) and a history of South Africa (2019). He is also the editor and co-editor of several collections of essays including *Healing South African Wounds* (2009), *L'Afrique du Sud : de nouvelles identités?* (2010) and *Spaces of History, History of Spaces.*

Sara Thornton is Professor of English at Université de Paris Cité, France where she co-directs the 'Cultural Intelligence and Innovation' Master's programme. She has published *Advertising, Subjectivity and the Nineteenth-century novel* (2009) on Dickens and Balzac, *Circulation and Transfer of Key Scenes in Nineteenth-Century Literature* (2010), *Persistent Dickens* (2012), *Dickens and the Virtual City: Urban Perception and the Production of Social Space* (2017) and *Comforting Creatures: Changing Visions of Animal Otherness in the Victorian Period* (2018).

Acknowledgements

We would like to thank the following libraries and institutions for giving permission to reproduce the images in this volume: the Library of Congress and the Museum of Fine Arts, Boston.

Our thanks also to all our colleagues in the seminar research group *Rémanence* of the Laboratoire de Recherche d'Etudes du Monde Anglophone (LERMA, Aix-Marseille University) for their fruitful discussions on ghosts, memory and identity over the past four years which have inspired us to produce this volume of essays. We are also very grateful to the production and editorial team at Routledge, and especially Neil Jordan for his advice, support and encouragement throughout the process.

Our warmest thanks go to all the contributors who have worked on this project despite the challenges of the pandemic and the difficult working conditions that followed. Finally, our grateful thanks to our families and partners whose support and patience were, as ever, invaluable in helping us complete this project.

Introduction
Memory and identity
Ghosts of the past in the English-speaking world

Linda Pillière and Karine Bigand*

This collection of essays represents the fruit of several years' reflection on the trope of the ghost as a concept for exploring memory and identity within the research seminar *Rémanence* (LERMA, Aix-Marseille University). The volume examines how ghosts haunt and shape cultural identities and memory, whether in a constructive or disruptive way, but also how the fluctuations of such identities sometimes imply the rethinking or rewriting of the past and inevitably haunt the future. Drawing on case studies in historical, political, literary and linguistic studies, the volume focuses on the inextricable connection between past, present and future, the narratives that produce imagined communities and identities (Anderson, 1983) and the places where cultural identities are constructed through memory (Nora, 1989). It investigates how far such representations of memories and identity disinherit or exclude otherness and how far ghosts disturb the orderly narratives and invite multiple readings of the past.

Ghosts have been haunting humanity studies ever since the publication (1993) and translation (1994) of Derrida's essay *Spectres of Marx: The State of the Debt, the Work of Mourning, and the New International*, the title of which is a direct reference to Marx and Engel's *Manifesto of the Communist Party* and the sentence 'A spectre is haunting Europe: the spectre of communism'. In his essay, which discusses the legacy of Marxism, Derrida coins the term 'hauntology' or *hantologie*. In French, the term is pronounced in nearly the same way as *ontologie*, or ontology, and this play on words enables Derrida to replace the philosophical study of being with the ghost or spectre, an entity whose very nature defies definitive knowledge:

> It *is* something that one does not know, precisely, and one does not know if precisely it *is*, if it exists, if it responds to a name and corresponds to an essence. One does not know: not out of ignorance, but because this non-object, this non-present present, this being-there of an absent or departed one no longer belongs to knowledge. At least no longer to that

DOI: 10.4324/9781003178040-1

which one thinks one knows by the name of knowledge. One does not know if it is living or if it is dead.

(Derrida, 1994, p. 5)

For Derrida, the ghost is a deconstructive, liminal figure that both is and is not, one that challenges neat binary oppositions and certainties, casting doubt on claims of objectivity and certainty and questioning accepted frames of reference and interpretation. Although Derrida's essay has been extremely influential, it is far from being the only theorization of the ghost. Colin Davis (2005) demonstrates that the concept of the phantom, as developed by psychoanalysts Nicolas Abraham and Maria Torok, has also played an important role in theories of hauntology (see Luckett and Naicker, Chapter 9 this volume).

It is therefore hardly surprising that the figure of the ghost has been examined by a number of disciplinary fields, such as international relations and commemorative practices (Auchter, 2014), trauma studies (Kaplan, 2005), studies on diaspora and postcolonization (Chassot, 2018), psychoanalysis (Abraham and Torok, 1994) and gender studies (Doubiago, 2016; McLeod, 2019). The concept of the ghost has even created new areas of study such as spectropolitics and spectrogeography (Maddern and Adey, 2008), leading some academics to even identify a 'spectral turn' in the humanities (Dziuban, 2019), although the accuracy of this term has been challenged by Maria del Pilar Blanco and Esther Peeren (2013a), who argue that a ghost does not turn, but returns.

One of the attractions of the ghost trope for memory and identity studies arises from its capacity to disrupt neat categorizations, its unstable character, inviting us to consider identity and memory as more fluid, as being continually constructed. Both memory and identity have often been likened to tangible objects: a memory can be lost, an identity stolen. However, more recent research, in psychology, sociology and sociolinguistics, has questioned this presentation of memory and identity as static, stable phenomena. In the words of Jenkins (2008, p. 17):

Much writing about identity treats it as something that simply is. Careless reification of this kind pays insufficient attention to how identification works or is done, to process and reflexivity, to the social construction of identity in interaction and institutionally. Identity can only be understood as a process of 'being' or 'becoming'. One's identity – one's identities, indeed who we are is always multi-dimensional, singular and plural – is never a final and settled matter.

The concept of hauntology, and the ghost trope, can therefore offer new insights into memory and cultural identity studies (Lincoln and Lincoln, 2015), both of which have multiplied in recent years, often linking in culture and heritage (Edensor, 1997; Johnston, 1999; Lahiri, 2003; Moore and Whelan, 2007; Erll, 2011).

Writing on memory, postmemory and identity, Eaglestone (2004, p. 74) points out that the relationship between memory and identity is an important philosophical question and that

> the way in which we remember plays a large role in constructing our identity (personal, social, communal), and in turn our identity shapes in no small way how we remember the past, cope in the present, and hope of expect the future.

He concludes (2004, p. 75) that 'identity without memory is empty, memory without identity is meaningless'. In the same vein of thought, the historical sociologist Jeffrey Olick (2003, p. 15) contends that 'memory is the central faculty of our being in time; it is the negotiation of past and present through which we define our individual and collective selves'. The trope of the ghost thereby offers a lens through which to view memory and identity for:

> The ghost forces us to confront and deal with the burden of the past and its unacknowledged spectres. In effect, summoning ghosts makes the present itself appear as not something solid, one-dimensional, or self-sufficient, but as something that is split and unstable, based on the suppression of other presents and voices, and, ultimately, spectral.
> (Lorek-Jezińska and Więckowska, 2017, p. 12)

The ability of the ghost to reappear, unannounced, to recall the past in the present also challenges and disrupts both the linear flow of time (Gordon, 2000; Bevernage, 2012) and the neat, stable compartmentalization of time into past, present and future (Ballif, 2013). Derrida (1994, p. 3) notes that 'haunting is historical, to be sure, but it is not it is never docilely given a date in the chain of presents, day after day, according to the instituted order of a calendar'. The ghost is thus both a *revenant* who inexorably returns, thus linking past to present, and also an *avenant*, announcing what will come and linking past and present to future.

Indeed, for del Pilar Blanco and Peeren (2013b, p.15) 'all history and memory may indeed be spectral in some sense, but one field of memory and identity studies where the trope of the ghost has played an important role is that of trauma studies'. For Abraham and Torok (1994), the traumatic past remains in the subconscious but, like a ghost, may erupt into the present moment. Auchter (2014, p. 36) remarks that 'during and after a traumatic event, traditional schemas of identification and representation are ruptured and fractured. Identities, spaces and times are thrown into disorder'.

The ghost can be a trope not just for individual memories but also for collective memories too. Memory, as a collective identity (Halbwachs, 1992) or as a cultural memory (Assmann, 1995), is also a social construct, and how we remember the past inevitably shapes our present and our identity. Tosh (1984, p. 3) argues that

> all societies have a collective memory, a storehouse of experience that is drawn on for a sense of identity and a sense of direction … To understand our social arrangements, we need to have some notion of where they have come from.

However, these representations of the past do not imply historical accuracy. As Jedlowski (2001, p. 30) points out, the past 'is constantly selected, filtered and restructured in terms set by the questions and necessities of the present'. Such selective memories then become stabilized and endowed with authority. The ghost challenges such collective memories, because it suggests that beneath the official account of events – the doxa – there is another story yet to be told. Derrida (1994, p. 46) argues that 'haunting belongs to the structure of every hegemony', and Gordon (2008), elaborating on Derrida, points out that haunting is inherent in every social and political order because it signals what has been forcibly evacuated from that order – as such it is an absence but also a 'seething presence'. It operates outside and beyond the doxa, defamiliarizing the past. For Richardson (2003, p. 25) ghosts 'operate as a particular, and peculiar kind of social memory, an alternate form of history-making in which things usually forgotten, discarded or repressed become foregrounded whether as items of fear, regret, explanation or desire'. Multiple narratives therefore exist, and to focus on one narrative is to inevitably exclude other versions. The ghost is therefore a useful trope in the contemporary revisiting of received narratives including, as it does, those voices 'we normally exclude or banish, or more commonly … what we never even notice' (Gordon, 2004, p. 24). As Potts (2009, p. 114) remarks

> Ghosts manifest the weight of the past, which can disturb the complacency of the present built on the repression of dark or guilty memories: ghosts represent the liberation of the repressed, unsettling a present that often prefers to forget the shame of the past.

By considering the ghosts of unheard voices, by seeking to include those who have been excluded, 'be they victims of wars, political or other kinds of violence, nationalist, racist, colonialist, sexist, or other kinds of exterminations, victims of the oppressions of capitalist imperialism or any other forms of totalitarianism' (Derrida, 1994, p. xix), an ethical dimension is introduced into memory and identity studies. Re-examining the past, to include these marginalized voices, implies seeing the past differently. Writing on the need for a change in the concept of sexual identity, Adrienne Rich argues that 'We need to know the writing of the past' but we need to 'know it differently than we have ever known it; not to pass on a tradition but to break its hold over us' (1972, p. 19). As the contributors in this volume illustrate, it is only by living with the ghosts that there can truly be 'a politics of memory, of inheritance, and of generations' (Derrida, 1994, p. xix).

The ghost can thus be seen as a justice-seeking figure, challenging the past, calling it to account, bringing 'to light travesties of justice that dispute the official record' (Weinstock, 2018, p. 209). This figure of the ghost as a redresser of wrongs is to be found in several of the chapters in this volume (see Potts, Chapter 3; Teulié, Chapter 9; Luckett, Chapter 8). Such ghosts may inspire fear as they constitute a subversive force that can 'destabilize discourses of power and knowledge and, with that, supposedly stable subject positions' (Wolfreys, 2002, p. 11). These ghosts thus challenge the doxa and the narratives of states and governments (see Stricof and Galelli, Chapter 7 and Teulié, Chapter 9, this volume).

The emphasis on the ghost's ability to disrupt linear time and introduce a different narrative or even multiple narratives should not blind us to the fact that spaces too are haunted and equally destabilized by the presence of ghosts. If the image of the haunted house immediately comes to mind, or the ghost town of the Far West, haunted spaces refer to more than just houses and buildings. The haunting of the Australian landscape by the ghosts of indigenous peoples is an important theme in Potts's chapter (see Chapter 3, this volume). Aboriginal religious belief has as its core principle the spiritual infusion of the land. The landscape and everything within it are believed to have been created by spirit-ancestors, who maintain a spiritual residence within the land. In this way, the ancestral past lives on in the present, apparent in the very land or 'country' traversed by Aboriginal peoples. The ways in which land and territories are still haunted by the 'physical and epistemological progeny of colonialism' is a theme to also be found in the fiction of the writers studied by McCann (see Chapter 11, this volume).

With the far-reaching implications of hauntology and the concept of the ghost in memory and identity studies, it might be tempting to apply the trope indiscriminately to all memory and identity studies. Such an approach runs the danger of ignoring the specificities of culture, geography and historical context. While ghosts may haunt various national myths, cultural traditions and identities in similar ways, 'they perform these roles … in narratives shaped by and reflecting specific historical contexts and concerns' (Weinstock, 2018, p. 214). We have therefore included in this volume studies that examine the concept of the ghost in relation to memory and identity from various sociocultural perspectives, and throughout the English-speaking world, from Europe to North America, from Asia (India) to Australia and inevitably the United Kingdom. Likewise, considering the recent influential role of the trope of the ghost in recent studies in the humanities, this volume adopts a cross-disciplinary approach and combines studies in lexicography, literature, visual arts, sociology, politics and history to offer a multiple disciplinary approach to the notions of memory and identity, from scholars across the world, all specialists in their fields. Finally, because the impact of ghost figures covers a broad spectrum, from disrupting spectres to structuring foundations, the volume is divided into three sections which explore various ways in which ghosts interact with memory and identity.

In the first section, 'Shackled Identities', the figure of the ghost is seen as persisting into present memory and identity, revealing how the past continues to shape the present and even to shackle it to past being or thinking, thus impeding progress. Bringing together studies in lexicography, visual arts, history and literature, this section illustrates how ghosts haunt the modern conscience.

In Chapter 1, 'Ghosts of the past and the *Oxford English Dictionary*', Charlotte Brewer focuses on a textual haunting: the ghostly presence of definitions written by other lexicographers many decades before that continue to manifest themselves in later editions of the *Oxford English Dictionary* (*OED*). Language is by its very nature sedimented 'through acts of identity' (Pennycook, 2006, p. 73), 'a vast collection of hand-me-downs that reaches back in time' (Hopper, 1998, p. 159). It should therefore cause little surprise that even dictionaries reveal such hauntings. Brewer's chapter looks particularly at the ghosts that are specific to the *OED*, institutional ghosts that reveal just how difficult it can be to shed cultural identities and values of the past. The examples studied underline the degree to which the dictionary's identity is shackled to remnants of Victorian and Edwardian culture.

Chapter 2, 'The invisible American shoeshine boy: creation and persistence of a ghostly icon' investigates how the idealized image of the shoeshine boy as depicted in popular paintings and photographs has persisted through time, fuelling the American myth of the country being a land of opportunity for all. Spanning almost one century, Anne Lesme's survey demonstrates how, despite the work of social reformers in denouncing the exploitation of child labour – notably in the photographs of Lewis Hine and the writings of the National Child Labor Committee, from 1908 to 1917 – the icon of the cheerful, resourceful shoeshine boy has haunted the American collective memory, comforting the collective consciousness that adversity is no barrier to success and thus reinforcing the American cultural identity and the rags-to-riches myth.

Chapter 3, 'Australian ghosts: representations of the past in Australia', takes the reader to another continent to examine the specific context of the colonial legacy in Australia, thus expanding further the concept of the ghostly presence that endures into the present to include both cultural and spatial dimensions. John Potts conducts his analysis of Australian ghosts within the context of dispossession and colonial displacement and within the additional setting of the Australian landscape, described by Europeans since the eighteenth century as eerie, spectral, weird – un-European, but seen through the eyes of the indigenous population of Australia, steeped in a culture where spirits inhabit the landscape. This dispossession results in a sense of guilt shared by white Australians for the past.

In Chapter 4, 'Ghosts from the future: post-apocalyptic narratives in Scotland and the displacement of memory', Marie-Odile Pittin-Hédon examines six post-apocalyptic novels written by Scottish authors John Burnside, Jenni Fagan and Louise Welsh. She offers an original take on the trope of the ghost by demonstrating how these novels, written between 2009 and 2017, may provide a window onto the present, with ghosts returning from the future to reassess the shackled identities and history of our current generations.

The second section, 'Multi-layered Identities', features studies in literature, politics and history to analyse how various ghosts from the past may serve to forge new identities and complexify traditional narratives. In the chapters gathered here, identity and memory are no longer stable or static: they become hybrid or multi-layered by integrating narratives of the past that had hitherto been silenced or where the past is revisited. In contrast with the first section, ghosts from the past contribute to change rather than immobility.

Chapter 5, 'Ghosting the Victorians in A.S. Byatt, Kate Atkinson and Michèle Roberts's neo-Victorian fiction', analyses the multiple layers to be found in neo-Victorian fiction of three contemporary writers. Armelle Parey examines how the Victorian past and the contemporary age establish

> a dual relationship by means of which the Victorians come to life in neo-Victorianism, and contemporary revisions of the Victorian past offer productive and nuanced ways of unlocking occluded secrets, silences and mysteries which return and reappear in a series of spectral/ textual traces.
>
> (Arias and Pulham, 2009, p. xx)

In Chapter 6, 'Whose past is it before us? The shaping of identity in Scotland's 2014 referendum on independence', Philip Rycroft considers the political arguments used by both sides in the 2014 referendum campaign and the shaping of identity in debates on Scotland's future. Although many of these arguments were based on the economic and social benefits to be gained from the Union or independence, the emotional case for or against independence played just as an important role. The chapter examines how various narratives rooted in the deep mythologies of Scotland and Britain's histories, informed and shaped the emotional charge of the independence campaign. Indeed, the Scottish conscience is haunted by multi-layered narratives that appeal to independence: the ghost of Knox, the romanticizing of the Jacobite movement and Gaelic culture, along with the grievance of the Highland clearances. Equally strong in its emotional appeal is the shared experience of conflict and Empire that calls for solidarity among the nations of the United Kingdom.

Chapter 7, 'Haunted by the Lessons of "the good war": post-Cold War contestation of World War II narratives', turns to explore the transition of an historical event, the Second World War, into the realm of the mythical.

In this instance, the ghost is an 'uncomfortable presence' (Ruitenberg, 2009; Bevernage, 2012), providing conflicting lessons in the 'collective remembrance' (Winter, 1998). Michael Stricof and Marjorie Galelli's chapter focuses on the multi-layered narratives of the Second World War in the American consciousness and how they were used by politicians to promote their own agenda, significantly influencing two instances of US international policy and the ensuing debates. On the one hand, the end of the Second World War and the subsequent Cold War were used as a cautionary tale to defend preserving defence budgets in the early 1990s; on the other hand, the 'ghost of Munich' and Europe's appeasement against a dictatorial regime were used by the Bush administration to justify fighting the Iraq War. Other counter-narratives also emerged in the ensuing debates, demonstrating that narratives are negotiated continuously and that while the State may seek to impose one narrative, other ghosts emerge. As Derrida and Stiegler (2002, p. 63) point out, a politics of memory 'is simply a politics of memory, a particular politics ... this politics is in transformation, and ... it is a politics'.

The third section of this volume, 'Reclaimed Identities', turns to sociology, history and literature to focus on how identities have been reclaimed in a postcolonial context. The figure of the ghost is often used to represent marginalized or repressed memories; for Weinstock (2004, p. 6), it is 'a symptom of repressed knowledge' that 'calls into question the possibilities of a future based on avoidance of the past', thus destabilizing socio-political hegemonies. Within the context of postcolonial studies, the concept of a repressed and silenced past has been both useful and problematic. Including these repressed and marginalized voices into the collective cultural identity frequently involves rewriting official representations of the past.

In Chapter 8, 'Haunting in a postcolony: race, place and intergenerational trauma on a South African campus', Kathy Luckett and Veeran Naicker investigate how far a spectral engagement with the colonial past and contemporary forms of coloniality can provide a basis for resistance politics in South Africa through a case-study on the RhodesMustFall student protest movement (2015–2017) at the University of Cape Town. As with the chapter by John Potts, this chapter relates the concept of hauntology and the ghost to a sense of place: an elite, historically white university in the South African postcolony.

In Chapter 9, 'First World War memorial ghosts and the reshaping of South African identity: remembering the SS Mendi in Delville Wood', Gilles Teulié also examines South African identity and the political dimension of haunting, by focusing on a different place: the Delville Wood museum in the Somme in France. Teulié demonstrates how the opening of a room dedicated to the sinking of the ship and, more broadly, to the role played by Black soldiers in the First World War contributed to reshaping South African identity and presented a 'new history'.

Chapter 10, 'Blyton's ghosts: childhood receptions in India and Britain', shows how Enid Blyton's fiction is haunted by a Victorian and imperial past and is reclaimed in various ways by past and present global generations. As in previous chapters, the emphasis is on the need to consider the trope of the ghost within a specific spatiotemporal and cultural context. Sara Thornton and Tanvi Chowdhary present two very different responses to Enid Blyton's literature for children: one from early 1970s England not so long after Blyton's death, and the other from India in the early 2000s. Both trace reactions to the different forms of hegemony and even 'manufacture of consent' (Gramsci, 1971) at work in the writing but at the same time reveal the construction of identity that Blyton's quite rigid moral universe paradoxically allows.

In Chapter 11, 'Decolonial poetics: ghosts of coloniality, capitalism, and care in contemporary anglophone literature', Fiona McCann analyzes three recently published literary works from a decolonial perspective. The three authors focussed upon in this chapter, Adam Dickinson, Mia Gallagher and Arundhati Roy, all raise essential questions about the manner in which the memory of a colonial past, and its continued role in modelling identities, haunts the present. In all three works, identities are reclaimed albeit in different ways and in doing so, all three authors suggest alternative modes of being which disrupt both identity and literary norms.

The aim of this collection is to offer individual case studies that will not only provide scholars and students with an enlarged vision of cutting-edge research in the field but also have the potential to promote further cross-disciplinary research.

Note

* Linda Pillière, Aix Marseille Univ, LERMA, Aix-en-Provence, France; Karine Bigand, Aix Marseille Univ, LERMA, Aix-en-Provence, France.

References

Abraham, N. and Torok, M. (1994) *The Shell and the Kernel.* Volume 1, Translated by N. T. Rand. Chicago, IL: Chicago University Press.

Anderson, B. (1983) *Imagined Communities: Reflections on the Origin and Spread of Nationalism.* London and New York: Verso.

Arias, R. and Pulham, P. (2009) *Haunting and Spectrality in Neo-Victorian Fiction: Possessing the Past.* Basingstoke: Palgrave Macmillan.

Assmann, J. (1995) 'Collective Memory and Cultural Identity', Translated by John Czaplicka, *New German Critique*, 65, pp. 125–133.

Auchter, J. (2014) *The Politics of Haunting and Memory in International Relations.* London and New York: Routledge.

Ballif, M. (2013) 'Historiography as Hauntology: Paranormal Investigations into the History of Rhetoric' in Ballif, M. (ed.) *Theorizing Histories of Rhetoric*. Cabondale: Southern Illinois University Press, pp. 139–153.

Bevernage, B. (2012) *History, Memory, and State-Sponsored Violence: Time and Justice*. London and New York: Routledge.

Chassot, J. (2018) *Ghosts of the African Diaspora: Re-Visioning History, Memory, and Identity*. Dartmouth, NH: UP of New England.

Davis, C. (2005) 'État Présent: Hauntology, Spectres and Phantoms', *French Studies*, 59(3), pp. 373–379.

del Pilar Blanco, M. and Peeren, E. (eds.) (2013a) *Spectralities Reader: Ghosts and Haunting in Contemporary Cultural Theory*. London, UK: Bloomsbury.

del Pilar Blanco, M. and Peeren, E. (2013b) 'Introduction: Conceptualizing Spectralities', in del Pilar Blanco, M. and Peeren, E. (eds.) *The Spectralities Reader: Ghosts and Haunting in Contemporary Cultural Theory*. London: Bloomsbury, pp. 1–27.

Derrida, J. (1994) *Spectres of Marx: The State of the Debt, the Work of Mourning, and the New International*. Translated by P. Kamuf. London and New York: Routledge.

Derrida, J. and Stiegler, B. (2002) *Echographies of Television*. Translated by J. Bajorek. Cambridge: Polity Press.

Doubiago, S. (2016) 'Algerian Feminist Methodologies of Recovery, Redress and Resistance in Assia Djebar's *La Femme Sans Sépulture* (2002)' in Wibben, A.T.R. (ed.) *Researching War: Feminist Methods, Ethics and Politics*. London and New York: Routledge, pp. 239–257.

Dziuban, Z. (ed.) (2019) *The "Spectral Turn": Jewish Ghosts in the Polish Post-Holocaust Imaginaire*. Bielefeld: Transcript Verlag.

Eaglestone, R. (2004) *The Holocaust and the Postmodern*. Oxford: Oxford University Press.

Edensor, T. (1997) 'National Identity and the Politics of Memory: Remembering Bruce and Wallace in Symbolic Space', *Environment and Planning D: Society and Space*, 15, pp. 175–194.

Erll, A. (2011) *Memory in Culture*. Translated by S.B. Young. Basingstoke: Palgrave Macmillan.

Gordon, A. (2008) *Ghostly Matters, Haunting and the Sociological Imagination*. Minneapolis: University of Minnesota Press.

Gramsci, A. (1971) *Selections from the Prison Notebooks*. Translated by Q. Hoare and G.N. Smith. London and New York: International Publishers.

Halbwachs, M. (1992) *On Collective Memory*. Translated by L.A. Coser. Chicago, IL and London: The University of Chicago Press.

Hopper, P.J. (1998) 'Emergent Grammar' in Tomasello, M. (ed.) *The New Psychology of Language: Cognitive and Functional Approaches to Language Structure Volume I*. Mahwah, NJ: Lawrence Erlbaum, pp. 155–175.

Hutcheon, L. (2013) *A Theory of Adaptation*. 2nd ed. New York: Routledge.

Jedlowski, P. (2001) 'Memory and Sociology: Themes and Issues', *Time and Society*, 10(1), pp. 29–44.

Jenkins, R. (2008) *Social Identity*. London and New York: Routledge.

Johnston, N.C. (1999) 'Framing the Past: Time, Space and the Politics of Heritage Tourism in Ireland', *Political Geography*, 18, pp. 187–207.

Kaplan, E.A. (2005) *Trauma Culture: The Politics of Terror and Loss in Media and Literature*. New Brunswick, NJ and London: Rutgers University Press.

Lahiri, N. (2003) 'Commemorating and Remembering the 1857 Revolt in Delhi and its Afterlife', *World Archaeology*, 35(1), pp. 35–60.

Lincoln, M. and Lincoln, B. (2015) 'Toward a Critical Hauntology: Bare Afterlife and the Ghosts of Ba Chùc', *Comparative Studies in Society and History*, 57(1), pp. 191–220.

Lorek-Jezińska, E. and Więckowska, K. (2017) 'Hauntology and Cognition: Questions of Knowledge, Pasts and Futures', *Theoria et Historia Scientiarum*, XIV, pp. 7–25.

Maddern, J.F. and Adey, P. (2008) 'Editorial: Spectro-geographies', *Cultural Geographies*, 15(3), pp. 291–295.

McLeod, L. (2019) 'Investigating "Missing" Women: Gender, Ghosts, and the Bosnian Peace Process', *International Studies Quarterly*, 63(3), pp. 668–679.

Moore, N. and Whelan, Y. (eds.) (2007) *Heritage, Memory and the Politics of Identity: New Perspectives on the Cultural Landscape*. Aldershot: Ashgate.

Olick, J. (ed.) (2003) *States of Memory: Continuities, Conflicts, and Transformations in National Retrospection*. Durham, NC: Duke University Press

Pennycook, A. (2006) *Global Englishes and Transcultural Flows*. London and New York: Routledge.

Potts, J. (2009) 'Rough Justice and Buried Country: Australian Ghosts' in Joseph-Vilain, M. and Misrahi-Barak, J. (eds.) *Postcolonial Ghosts*. Montpellier: Presses Universitaires de la Méditerranée, pp. 113–124.

Rich, A. (1972) 'When We Dead Awaken: Writing as Re-Vision', *College English*, 34(1), pp. 18–30.

Richardson, J. (2003) *Possessions: The History and Uses of Haunting in the Hudson Valley*. Cambridge, MA: Harvard University Press.

Ruitenberg, C. (2009) 'Education as Séance: Specters, Spirits, and the Expansion of Memory', *Interchange*, 40, pp. 295–308. https://doi.org/10.1007/s10780-009-9097-0

Tosh, J. (1984) *The Pursuit of History*. London: Pearson Education Limited.

Weinstock, J.A. (2004) 'Introduction: The Spectral Turn' in Weinstock, J.A. (ed.) *Spectral America: Phantoms and the National Imagination*. Madison: University of Wisconsin Press/Popular Press, pp. 3–17.

Weinstock, J.A. (2018) 'The American Ghost Story' in Brewster, S. and Thurston, L. (eds.) *The Routledge Handbook to the Ghost Story*. New York and London: Routledge, pp. 206–214.

Winter, J. (1998) *Sites of Memory, Sites of Mourning: The Great War in European Cultural History*. Cambridge: Cambridge University Press.

Wolfreys, J. (2002) *Victorian Hauntings: Spectrality, Gothic, the Uncanny and Literature*. Basingstoke: Palgrave.

Part I
Shackled identities

1 Ghosts of the past and the *Oxford English Dictionary*

Charlotte Brewer

Ghosts reveal the impossibility of escaping the past. Their eerie and often surprising presence, decades or more after one thought the world (or an institution, or a dictionary) had changed, illustrate how hard it is for cultural entities to shed former identities and invent themselves anew. Their continued existence, however manifested, illustrates how past ways of making, being, and thinking continue to shape – and sometimes to shackle – their equivalent forms in the present. The multi-faceted concept of the ghost can help us investigate not only physical or material aspects of an entity, but also intellectual and ideological ones. It is a particularly fruitful concept to apply to the *Oxford English Dictionary* (*OED*). First embarked on in the late 1850s, and eventually published (in its first edition) between 1884 and 1928, this was a quintessentially Victorian undertaking in its confident assumption that it would be possible to chart the history of the English language in its entirety. It remains a monumental and lasting achievement in historical lexicography, and in its current new-minted reincarnation, it is regarded as the single most authoritative record of the vocabulary of English.

Today's version of the *OED* looks very different from the multi-volume first edition of 1928, which in its re-issued 1933 version (with a first supplement) weighs over 70 kilos and occupies around 1.2 metres of shelf space. Since 2000, the dictionary has taken the form of an online website to be found at www.oed.com, a resource that could only have been dreamed of 50 years ago and was certainly unimaginable in 1884, when the first printed instalment of the *OED* was published. One of the most conspicuous characteristics of this new online version is its claim to authority: every page is labelled 'The definitive account of the English language'. Equally notable is its use of features only available in an electronic medium. Users can browse the dictionary's contents much as one might a traditional print dictionary, but they are also invited to explore and search the online entity in entirely new ways. It is now possible to identify and (potentially) analyse many of the different elements across the dictionary as a whole, not just entry by entry, including date of first use, quotation source, region of use, language of origin, subject, or editorially assigned labels (e.g. *allusive, colloquial and slang,*

DOI: 10.4324/9781003178040-3

derogatory, etc.), along with other features. The front page prominently displays the date of the latest quarterly update, listing words and senses which have just been recorded in the dictionary for the first time and linking to interactive graphics, video guides, and electronic aids for researchers. Clicking on these resources yields an impressive harvest of newly coined and/or newly researched words and senses such as *Brexit, Covid-19, lockdown, superspreader, ze* (the gender-neutral form for the third person singular pronoun), *cancel culture, keyboard warrior*, and many others. One might well ask what ghosts of the past could possibly linger here – but it turns out that there are many.

This chapter sets out to identify some of these lingering apparitions of the past. To understand how and why they haunt, or fetter, today's ultra-modern form of the dictionary, we need first to review some of the main characteristics of the first edition and second to explore the *OED's* own institutional history, in both cases focussing on categories of vocabulary which have turned out to be particularly problematic. The chapter then turns to look at the dictionary's representation of female-authored quotation sources, whose ghosts haunt by their absence rather than their presence, indicating that a Victorian and Edwardian mindset continues to shackle this aspect of the *OED*. It concludes with three recommendations for laying the ghosts to rest.

The first edition of the OED

We should begin by considering the special feature of the initial nineteenth-century *OED* project, its historical approach to vocabulary. The English language – like every other natural language – is rooted in the past and has changed and developed over time, and the originators of the dictionary set out in the late 1850s to document the history of every word used in English from the late medieval period to the present day. For the first time in the history of English lexicography, all entries were to be based on verifiable documentation of historical usage, in the form of quotations from texts witnessing every period of a word or sense's use. The lexicographers (and their hundreds of public-spirited volunteers) collected this evidence from a wide range of sources – historical, literary, philosophical, theological, drawn from the sciences as well as the arts, relating to commerce, professional activities, crafts, industry, sports, and so on – from 1150 and earlier up to the present day. Five million quotations were assembled for the first edition, of which around two million were printed in the dictionary itself (Craigie and Onions, 1933, p. v). The *OED* is grounded in these quotations, and it is this revolutionary characteristic which made and makes the dictionary such an authoritative and comprehensive source of information on the history and development of vocabulary in English.

The most obvious ghosts in the dictionary, therefore, are the past uses of language to be found in the banks of quotations, often huge, which fill entry after entry. As Virginia Woolf wrote, 'Words, English words, are full of echoes, of memories, of associations – naturally. They have been out and about, on people's lips, in their houses, in the streets, in the fields, for so many centuries' (Woolf, 1937, p. 868). The first editor of the *OED*, Herbert Coleridge (grand-son of the poet), thought that '"Every word [in the diction- ary] should be made to tell its own story" – the story of its birth and life, and in many cases of its death, and even occasionally of its resuscitation' (Coleridge, 1860, p. 72) and each entry begins with an account of the etymol- ogy of a word, detailing its past relationships with other languages, before documenting its usage from Old English (if applicable) to the present day. Given that so many words have changed over time and usage, past senses float like ghosts over present ones – but to a liberating or enabling effect, rather than a confining one. The *OED* entry for the word *ghost* itself shows that the word was used from the earliest Old English texts onwards to mean 'the soul or spirit', a sense that lingers on today in the occasional continued use of the term 'Holy Ghost' in Christian theology. The founders of the *OED* were well aware of the powerful presence of such ghosts, using a vari- ety of different metaphors to express their sense of the connections between the past and present that such words enable. One of the most famous, R. C. Trench, observed that 'language is the amber in which a 1,000 precious words have been safely embedded and preserved', developing the essayist R. W. Emerson's notion of 'fossil poetry' (itself later quoted in the diction- ary under *fossil*):

> just as in some fossil, curious and beautiful shapes of vegetable or ani- mal life...are permanently bound up with the stone, and rescued from that perishing which would otherwise have been theirs, – so in words are beautiful thoughts and images, the imagination and the feeling of past ages, of men long since in their graves.
>
> (Trench, 1851, pp. 4–5)

These are the ghosts inherent in the language itself, often evident in Eng- lish's non-phonetic spellings which reflect past forms of a word as well as its previous meanings.

Just as interesting, however – though often much less benign – are the ghosts specific to the *OED* itself, that is to say, ghosts which tell us about the *OED*'s *own* history, or in other words about the dictionary as a cul- tural as well as linguistic entity. It is these institutionally inflected ghosts on which the chapter concentrates, whose origin and whose presence – or absence – is harder for the dictionary-user to detect, but who continue to exert a strong influence over the dictionary's content.[1] Whether read online or in its earlier print versions, the *OED* displays such hugely impressive quantities of scholarly information that it is hard to get under its skin, as it were, and identify the assumptions, biases, and inconsistencies that went into its making, side-by-side with the formidable scholarship of successive generations of lexicographers. But no work can be independent of the culture of its time, and the *OED* is no exception: the first edition of the dictionary reflected a range of beliefs and positions typical of its day, many of which are still anachronistically apparent in the dictionary we consult today.

First and foremost among these was the view that language both shaped and reflected a culture's history, so that in mapping the evolution of the English language, the *OED* seemed also to tell the story of a nation. The nationalist role of the *OED* had been a major element in the dictionary's conception and became a source of pride both for the lexicographers and the public more generally. Its founders were well aware of the German writer and philologist Friedrich Schlegel's dictum: 'the care of the national language I consider as at all times a sacred trust and a most important privilege of the higher orders of society', and in their *Proposal...for a New English Dictionary* (1859), the Philological Society issued an appeal to 'Englishmen', observing

> it is abundantly clear, that England does not possess a Dictionary worthy of her language; nor, as long as lexicography is confined to the isolated efforts of a single man, is it possible that such a work should be written. We do but follow the example of the Grimms, when we call upon Englishmen to come forward and write their own Dictionary for themselves.
>
> ([Philological Society], 1859, p. 8)[2]

This new nationalist project had both internal and external aspects. As we have seen, the use of quotations as its principal evidentiary source was a revolutionary feature of the *New English Dictionary*, but these quotations were drawn disproportionately from some sorts of sources rather than others. Shakespeare dominated the final work, with over 33,000 quotations alone, followed by the Bible, a thirteenth-century historical work in verse (*Cursor Mundi*), Walter Scott, Milton, Chaucer, Dryden, Dickens, along with some major periodicals and newspapers (*Philosophical Transactions of the Royal Society, The Daily News*) and many other writers in the traditional Victorian canon, only a tiny number of them women. Such quotation choices point to the predominating view of the time that 'great writers' past and present – in this case, principally male poets and novelists – play a key role in the history and development of a national language. As the later editor of the contemporary American *Century* dictionary put it in 1867:

> A great body of literary works of acknowledged merit and authority, in the midst of a people proud and fond of it, is an agent in the preservation and transmission of any tongue, the importance of which cannot be easily over-estimated.
>
> (Whitney, 1867, p. 23; see further Brewer, 2020a)

That *OED* entry for *ghost*, therefore, like countless others, is studded with quotations from great writers of the past and present: Langland (three quotations), Spenser (two quotations), Shakespeare (four quotations), Hobbes, Defoe, Tennyson, and Ruskin, among many others, illustrating the life history of *ghost* from Old English up to 1970, with the bulk of quotations concentrated in the nineteenth century. Almost all illustrate British English alone, and almost all are from male authors (the entry has 95 senses altogether, of which 7 refer to non-UK use; it contains 253 quotations, of which 8 are from female authors). As discussed in the final section of this chapter, the dictionary's huge numbers of citations from such culturally specific authorities certainly help their words and phrases to linger on in ghost-like form years after their first utterance – although most modern-day lexicographers do not now regard literary writers as pre-eminently important witnesses to the use and transmission of English, or male users of language as more valuable than female ones, aiming instead to draw on a more balanced range of sources, whether geographically or socio-linguistically.

The external dimension of the *OED* project lay in its depiction – explicit or implicit – of England and English's role in the world more generally (see Mugglestone, 2012). In this respect, it should be seen in relation to the Victorian armies, companies, and explorers mapping and taking control of nations and territories around the globe. In fact, the chief editor of the first edition, J. A. H. Murray (1837–1915), once used what we would now regard as a disturbing image of imperialist territorial exploration, with correspondingly destructive implications, to describe his work, telling a London Philological Society meeting in 1884, 'I feel that in many respects I and my assistants are simply pioneers, pushing our way experimentally through an untrodden forest, where no white man's axe has been before us' (Murray, 1884, p. 509).

Unapologetically Anglo-centric, Murray (himself a Scotsman) was nevertheless fully aware of the geographical range of the English language (Murray, 1977, p. 193). The widespread penetration and dominance of English reflected the language's imperial scope and cultural value, both in the British colonies of the time (e.g. South Africa, India, Australia) and in former colonies and other territories nearer home (e.g. America, Ireland, and Scotland). Murray repeatedly encouraged volunteer readers to send in words from these territories and others and took care to record and label them in the gradually emerging dictionary instalments, but he treated the variety written and spoken in England as the central source (as the *ghost* entry exemplifies). The linguistic characteristics of this variety, along with the typical cultural characteristics of its users, were never articulated in full (not surprisingly given that modern linguistics was then in its infancy, and sociolinguistics not yet born), but every so often one can spot the editors' underlying assumptions about both. For example, in applying the descriptive label 'well known' to a word or sense, the editors revealed their expectation

that users of the dictionary would share (or wish to share) the language preferences of well-educated and relatively prosperous residents in Britain. So
anchor, to mean 'anchoress' – a female semi-recluse, motivated by religious
beliefs – was explained in the first edition of the *OED* as 'well known in
the book-title *Ancren Riwle*' (an abstruse work in Early Middle English),
while *champagne* was said to be 'a well-known wine'. A *charley*, i.e. a small
triangular beard, was 'well-known in the portraits of Charles 1 and his contemporaries'; the *Dunciad* was explained as 'the name of a well-known poem
by Pope' (though Pope was not identified as a famous eighteenth-century
English poet); one of the senses of *thrift* was defined as a 'well known sea-
shore and alpine plant'.

Other cultural assumptions to be found in the first edition of the *OED* are
more disturbing, notably those relating to race, ethnicity, religion, gender,
and sexuality. The use of terms like 'uncivilized' or 'savages' to describe
non-Western peoples and their practices, disparaging references to Jewish people and to people of colour, and the description of same-sex desires
and practices as 'unnatural', were not remarkable or controversial at the
time; they reflected the prevailing social consensus in late Victorian and
early Edwardian England or Britain, however unequally formed and intrinsically discriminatory. Countless entries – or their absence – mirror historical facts, social sensibilities, or a state of knowledge since transformed, for
example the definition of *clergy* as 'the body of men set apart by ordina-
tion for religious service in the Christian church', or the omission of entries
for four-letter words on the one hand or the chemical element *radium* on
the other. Today, we would unhesitatingly identify some of the first-edition
treatments of vocabulary as completely unacceptable (e.g. the definition of
white man as 'a man of honourable character such as one associates with a
European (as distinguished from a negro)'), while seeing others as offensive,
insensitive, euphemistic, prudish, dated, or in one way or other inappropriate for today's readership.[3] The existence of such terms in a work compiled
from the 1860s to the 1930s is unsurprising. Along with the many positive
features of the dictionary, they reflect the scholarship and the cultural men-
tality of the day in historically invaluable ways. However repugnant a small
proportion of the dictionary's content is today, the first edition of the *OED* is
an unmatched record of the views, beliefs, attitudes, and state of knowledge
not only to be found in English language studies of the late nineteenth and
early twentieth centuries but also in the innumerable disciplines and activities whose vocabulary is recorded in its pages.

One of the main aims of today's *OED* is to entirely re-cast the linguistic and cultural assumptions of its parent and to update its Victorian and
Edwardian content. Despite major revision and rewriting, however, and
despite the transformed medium of communication with the reader, ghosts
from the various stages of the dictionary's past have proved difficult to
extirpate. Of those four 'well known' definitions reported above, for example, two have disappeared – the allusion to the book-title *Ancrene Riwle*, the

characterization of *champagne* – but two still remain, in entries published online in December 2020 (*thrift*) and March 2021 (*charley*). And it is easy to come across definitions like the following for *slang*, also published in March 2021: 'The special vocabulary used by any set of persons of a low or disreputable character; language of a low and vulgar type'. It is hard to imagine any linguist in the last 50 years finding this formulation acceptable. It makes a value judgement both on the users of this vocabulary ('of a low and disreputable character') and on the vocabulary itself ('of a low and vulgar type'); moreover, it is not linguistically accurate: ever since the publication of *Webster's Third New International Dictionary* in 1961, which played an important role in the *OED*'s own twentieth-century history, it has been widely recognized that users of all demographics use slang (Brewer, 2007, 167–168; Coleman, 2012). In fact, as the definition's own choice of vocabulary suggests – 'low' to mean 'lower class' is an obsolescent if not obsolete usage – it is an unaltered reproduction of the first-edition definition, originally published in 1911. In other words, this definition is a ghost from the past, or as Trench put it in the passage already quoted, it represents the 'imagination and the feeling of past ages, of men long since in their graves'. But while we can welcome such language preserved for posterity in the *OED*'s illustrative quotations, it is a surprise to find it in the definitions, especially unidentified as such. The words of 'men long since in their graves' are nevertheless here and there repeated, without any warning to the reader, in many instances elsewhere (it is impossible to search for them, the dictionary-user simply happens on them here and there). A more disquieting example is the phrase 'woman of loose character', used in the definitions for the nouns *buer, flap, flirt, kitty, kittock, Tib, vizard*, all last updated between June 2019 and December 2020. In each case, the definitions are carried over without change from the respective first-edition entries (or in the case of *buer*, the second-supplement entry). Manifestly, they imply an editorial disparagement of sexually active women which is quite out of place in an up-to-date dictionary of English (such attitudes were and continue to be commonplace, it goes without saying, but they are not now reproduced without comment in today's dictionaries). At the same time, however, the definitional phrase 'woman of loose character' has been removed from various other entries in which it originally occurred (e.g. *slut*, first published in 1912), and in general, it seems that many other definitions for sexually active women (e.g. *harlot, whore*, etc.) have been successfully re-written to remove any implication that today's editors share the pejorative views connoted by the use of such words.

The *OED*'s own editorial history

To understand how and why such ghosts of the first edition here and there survive in these surprising ways in today's online *OED*, we need to look into the dictionary's own institutional and editorial history. This has been complicated, to say the least. Given the length of time that first edition had taken to compile and publish – 44 years from first to last instalment – the early parts of the dictionary were out of date by the time the last appeared. The hasty publication of a 'scratch' supplement in 1933, along with the re-issue of the first edition, could not adequately redress this problem, but the *OED* project had consumed such huge quantities of money and energy that its publishers Oxford University Press (OUP) were reluctant to contemplate a further update until the late 1950s (Brewer, 2007, pp. 60, 131–151). Balking at the prospect of an entire revision at this point, OUP instead commissioned a second supplement, which confined itself almost entirely to new twentieth-century words and senses and left the parent dictionary virtually untouched (Burchfield, 1972–1986; see Brewer, 2007, pp. 130–212). By the mid-eighties, when this four-volume work was completed, another pressing issue was looming: the expiry of copyright ownership over the first-edition text and the need to prevent other publishing companies exploiting OUP's intellectual property. The publishers decided to protect their commercial interests and preserve the *OED* as 'a national monument and intellectual resource', by merging the second supplement with the original first-edition text and marketing the result as a 'second edition' of the dictionary (Weiner, 2009, pp. 378–379). However, this was not a new edition in the commonly understood sense of the term; that is, it was not a revised or updated version of the earlier edition. The first edition was reproduced in the second in almost unaltered form, and only 5,000 truly new entries, less than 1% of the original total, were spliced in together with the second-supplement additions. Despite its 1989 publication date, therefore, very nearly all the content in *OED2*'s entries had already appeared in print, in most cases between 60 and 100 years earlier.

To create *OED2*, OUP joined forces with the computer company IBM. The content of the first edition and second supplement was tagged and digitized, and the two separate works digitally merged into a seamless entity. This was an innovative project for its day and established the digital basis of all future forms of the *OED*. But it also established a dangerous precedent: the mashing together of dictionary entries deriving from wholly distinct editorial periods and processes – that of 1884–1928 with that of 1972–1986 – without making this clear to the unsuspecting user (Brewer, 2007, pp. 212–237). Shackling new technology to old scholarship in this way is what first unleashed the institutional ghosts in the *OED*.

Using *OED*'s own figures, we can work out that around 86% of *OED2*'s entries were in fact 'ghosts' – i.e., first-edition entries (see *OED Online* (n.d.), 'Dictionary Facts', which reports that *OED1* contained 252,200 entries and *OED2* contained 291,500 entries). However, these ghosts varied widely in character. A small number of particularly offensive ones were tackled by the editors straightaway, though as these have never been identified it is impossible to draw up a complete list. They include the entry for *white man* quoted above, re-written in *OED2* to expunge the denigration of the supposed character of Africans or those of African descent, as well as that for *canoe*, defined in 1888 as 'A kind of boat in use among uncivilized nations ... any rude craft in which uncivilized people go upon the water', with an accompanying reference to 'savages'. Here, *OED2* re-cast the entry altogether, deleting the term *savages* along with a comparison between 'civilized' and 'uncivilized' use, and referring instead to 'primitive societies' in comparison with 'Europe, North America, etc.'. Elsewhere, a bracketed insertion was added to the definition for *jury* to allow for the inclusion of women ('a company of persons (orig. men) sworn to render a verdict ...'), and homophobic definitions for terms relating to sex between women (e.g. *Sapphism, tribade*) were reformulated and references to 'unnatural' relations and 'vice' deleted. Unsurprisingly, however, given the speed and urgency with which the second edition of *OED* was produced, these spot excisions and rewritings were inconsistently carried out and did not begin to address the major problem, namely that the bulk of the 1989 second edition was (to quote a review published by the Philological Society itself) 'a magnificent work of nineteenth-century scholarship clothed in late twentieth-century technology...old wine in a very new jar' (Algeo, 1990, p. 150).

No one knew this better than the publishers and editors themselves. In 2000, after long preparation, a newly assembled team of lexicographers – led by *OED2* compilers John Simpson and Edmund Weiner – began online publication of quarterly instalments of an entirely revised version of the original *OED*, the first ever to have occurred in its long history. This third edition (*OED3*; see Simpson and Proffitt 2000–) is today nearly half-way through its task, while being simultaneously engaged in keeping abreast of all new usages appearing in the English language (hence its remarkably swift record of vocabulary related to Covid-19).[4] Up to 2010, the ghosts were to some extent kept at bay. This was because the website presented the outdated version of the dictionary (in the form of *OED2*) and the slowly emerging new version (the third edition, or *OED3*) in two separate versions, each independently electronically searchable. The ghosts were thus relatively safely relegated to an online presence which – if misleadingly dated 1989 (the date of publication of *OED2*) – was manifestly not the most recent updated version of the dictionary to be found.

Most unhappily, this clear distinction between new scholarship and old disappeared in 2010. The relaunched website of that year reverted to a hybrid form even more confusing than that of *OED2* (Brewer, 2013). The two pre-2010 online versions of the dictionary were run together, making it impossible to differentiate between the different dates of publication of the various entries through electronic searches. Even worse, alphabetically sequential revision of entries was also abandoned, so that users can no longer guess from the initial letter of a word whether its corresponding entry has been updated or not. In consequence, institutional ghosts have flooded back into the dictionary, but in a bewildering variety of forms, some innocent, some offensive, some absurd – or a mixture of these characteristics.

Some entries are almost exactly as published in the first edition between 1884 and 1928, like the noun *banter*. Notwithstanding the date assigned by the website ('latest version published online March 2019'), this entry can be confidently (and disappointingly, given the word's interesting modern currency) identified as a ghost: the clue is both the quaint wording of the definitions, which begin 'Wanton nonsense talked in ridicule of a subject or person... good-humoured raillery, pleasantry...a merry jest', and the date of the quotations, the most recent of which is dated 1880. It is difficult to estimate how many entries are left in this state, though they include the 'loose women' ones we have already looked at along with that for *clergy*.

Other entries represent a mixture of editorial stages, for example *dinner*. The first definition begins, 'The chief meal of the day, eaten originally, and still by the majority of people, about the middle of the day (cf. German *Mittagsessen*), but now, by the professional and fashionable classes, usually in the evening'. This remarkable formulation was published in 1896, but turned into a ghost perhaps as early as 1911 (the first edition of the *Concise Oxford Dictionary*, which appeared that year, said simply 'Chief meal of the day, whether at midday or evening'; Fowler and Fowler, 1911). But the 1896 *OED* definition continues to be found in a version published online in April 2020 which has quotations dated as recently as 2009. Clearly, the lexicographers have re-visited the entry, but left that definition untouched. Random searching of the dictionary suggests that hundreds, perhaps thousands, of entries, exist in this state (such as *slang*).

Still other ghosts have been wrestled to the ground by the lexicographers almost as soon as they become ghosts, for example in the entry for *marriage*. This was originally published in 1905 and revised in 2000. In 2013, UK legislation changed to permit same-sex marriage and almost immediately – the date is not recorded – the entry was updated to reflect that change (though as of May 2021 the entry for *marry* continues to specify *husband* and *wife*).

Most recent predictions of *OED3*'s completion have named the date 2040, and we can hope that by that date, all first-edition ghosts will have disappeared, although the lexicographers must constantly keep an eye on all its entries to ensure that they do not subsequently turn into ghosts, owing to contemporary changes of one sort or another (a possibility successfully warded off in the case of *marriage*, if not *marry*). Certainly, huge numbers of ghosts have disappeared as the revision has progressed – and of course, it should be noted that the removal of offensive or seriously outdated material across the dictionary as soon as possible must have been one of the reasons why the lexicographers abandoned alphabetically sequential revision. The lexicographers' access to OUP's own Oxford English Corpus, a multi-billion-word corpus, helps identify and deal with many of these ghosts, since it enables the *OED* to keep track of recent changes in vocabulary use – those relating to pandemics and consequent societal changes, for example – and ensure that its definitions are as representative and accurate as possible (see further *OED* Editorial 2020).

Ghost-hunting: presences and absences (particularly female ones)

Personal browsing of *OED Online* by the author of this chapter, necessarily unsystematic given the impossibility of electronic identification of such material, suggests that the dictionary editors have been particularly alert to racist ghosts, arguably the most offensive residue of the first-edition *OED*. Rewriting definitions referring to people of colour, and marking demeaning and derogatory vocabulary relating to race with appropriately descriptive labels, occurred very early on in the *OED3* revision (notably, the entry for the *n*-word was re-written numerous times). *OED3*'s commitment to extending the geographical range of the Englishes recorded in its pages, bringing many overseas varieties into its fold from historical as well as present-day sources, has constituted a parallel form of attempted ghost-beating, designed to tackle the Anglo-centric nature of the original Victorian enterprise already discussed – though the fascinating discussion in Williams (2021), which characterizes new editorial work on World Englishes as 'a palimpsest, drawn over layers of successive images of English' dating back to the first-edition *OED*, suggests that previous versions – or ghosts – of the dictionary will never be entirely laid to rest.

More recently, the editors have turned their attention to homophobic ghosts: while the term 'unnatural' to describe same-sex practices and desires was not uniformly removed from entries till after 2010, a relatively exhaustive sweep of entries was undertaken in 2017–2018 (Brewer, 2013; Dent, 2018). They also appear sensitive to non-binary constructions of gender: thorough research has been carried out on the history of gender-neutral terms such as the non-gender specific pronoun *ze* and the more recent use of singular pronoun *they* (see sense 2, added soon after September 2019 as recorded in Brewer, 2020b). By contrast, they are relatively insensitive to (some) issues of male-female sexism, as indicated in the preservation of the 'loose women' definitions already noted, and the absence of any recognition that generic *he* (i.e. to refer to females as well as males) is both outdated and potentially offensive.[5]

Failure to identify a salient characteristic of a word is a sort of negative ghost, and absences can be just as important – and as haunting – in dictionaries as presences. The first edition notably excluded some four-letter and other sexual words from its pages, after extensive discussion between Murray and various correspondents; terms for birth control were also excluded with apparently less discussion (or at any rate, it has yet to come to light); *lesbian* was excluded from the first Supplement after a minimal exchange of editorial memos; all these omissions have since been rectified (Brewer, 2007, pp. 48–50; Mugglestone, 2007; Turton, 2020). But women in particular have not fared well in terms of presence in the *OED*. After the digitization of *OED2* in 1989, it became possible to quantify and analyse their absence, whether manifested by the strikingly low proportion of female

to male pronouns in the dictionary's text or the equally striking low proportion of female- to male-authored quotations, so that by the time work
started on the *OED3*, the editors announced that 'women's writing' (along
with other neglected texts and genres) was receiving special attention in the
new edition's reading programme (Fournier and Russell, 1992; Brewer, 2012;
OED Online n.d. 'Reading Programme'). But the implied promise has not
been kept. Today's *OED Online* website publishes a regularly updated list
of the 1,000 most quoted sources in the dictionary; as of April 2021, in proportions similar to those characterising the list since it was first published
in 2010, it records the names of just 28 female authors. This is a staggering
discrepancy for a dictionary which is based on the evidence provided by
its quotation sources and calls itself 'The definitive account of the English
language'.

Over the early centuries of English covered by the *OED*, women produced
far fewer texts than men, whether in published or unpublished forms. Part
of the explanation for the minimal citation of their works, therefore, is the
comparative paucity of evidence, particularly over the period in which
the first edition was produced, when far fewer historical texts by women
had been edited and published. But these proportions changed as women's
access to literacy and education improved. By the end of the eighteenth and
into the nineteenth century, women had established an active presence in
many fields of writing, including those most prominently recorded by the
OED such as novels, poetry, and journalism. Recent research on a database
of over 16,000 titles in Victorian fiction has found that of the 15 most published authors over 1837–1901, 11 were women (Bassett, 2020).

On linguistic grounds, there was (and is) no reason to differentiate
between women's and men's writings as suitable evidence for the history
and development of the language. But the linguistic and cultural climate
in which the first edition of the *OED* was compiled was markedly different
from that of today. As we saw earlier, literary texts were seen as central to
the creation and preservation of the national language which the *OED* was
committed to recording, and male literary geniuses, notably Shakespeare,
were by far the most favoured individual quotation sources for the parent
dictionary. Dozens of male writers were quoted in far greater numbers
than their female equivalents, for example Chaucer, Milton, and Dryden
(c. 9,000–12,000 quotations each), not to mention Walter Scott (c. 15,000),
and Tennyson and Dickens (both c. 7,000–8,000). This compares with just
over 3,000 quotations for the most quoted female author in the first edition,
George Eliot, followed by Frances Burney (c. 2,000), and by Harriet Marti-
neau, Mary Braddon, and Elizabeth Barrett Browning (all around 1,500; see
further Brewer, 2019b).

The historically and culturally determined preferences of the first-edition
OED can be understood. It is far harder to understand their continuance,
after 20 years of revision, into today's third edition. The English language
has always been used by women as well as by men. It is inconceivable that

women will not have played an important role in its history and development and their texts should therefore be represented for both linguistic and cultural reasons (as argued in Brewer, 2012 and elsewhere).

But here too, it should now go without saying, the ghosts are at work, whether as presences or absences. The repeated hybridization of the dictionary means that even half-way through the revision, all those unrevised entries and their quotations – and lack of female-authored quotations – continue in the dictionary much as when first published. And even in the revised entries, quotations from male authors continue to predominate, as can be seen from their continued unchallenged dominance of the 'top 1,000' list of most quoted sources. This striking phenomenon is due to the fact that the third-edition editors have found it impossible to jettison the first edition's huge numbers of quotations from Shakespeare, Milton, Chaucer, Dryden, Pope, and all the rest. Nearly half-way through the *OED3* revision, therefore, it looks as if the Victorian cultural canon is still dictating the outline shape of linguistic documentation in the *OED*.

In the meantime, the most quoted female writer in today's *OED* is still George Eliot, 92nd on the 'top 1,000' list, followed by two other female novelists, Frances Burney (141st) and Jane Austen in (241st). In December 1879, a writer signing herself M. G. Lewes wrote to J. A. H. Murray to confirm that she wished 'always to be quoted as George Eliot', thanking him 'for [his] courteous solicitude on this point' (see Brewer and Turton, 2021, pp. 275–276; the letter is included in Brewer and Turton, 2022). It is irresistible to wonder whether Eliot's continued predominance as a female-authored source in the *OED* today is due at least in part to her insistence on a male pseudonym: male ghosts seem to be more robust than female ones.

Conclusion

What can the *OED* do to unshackle itself from the apparitional remnants of Victorian and Edwardian culture, still evident in so many entries? Twenty years from now, when the *OED3* revision is complete, many of these institutional ghosts – in particular the outdated definitions – will have disappeared from *OED Online*. But this is a long time to wait. Instead, the publishers could do three things straightaway: first, gather together the thousands of new and revised entries into a single entity; second, increase the number of quotations from female-authored texts; and third, make available the earlier digitized editions of the dictionary. Users would then be able to consult the newly emerging dictionary, free from the fetters of the past, and gain a just sense of the contribution being made by the *OED*'s twenty-first-century scholarship to the history of vocabulary in English – based on evidence sourced from the writings of women as well as those of men. And the institutional ghosts would return to their rightful places in their original publications, preserving its invaluable historical record while unshackling today's version of the *OED* from their haunting influence.

Notes

1 A lexicographically specific use of the term *ghost*, undiscussed here, should also be noted. The term *ghost-word* was coined by W. W. Skeat (contributor to and close associate of the first-edition *OED*) in 1886 to refer to words 'which have no real Existence, being mere coinages due to the blunders of printers or scribes, or to the perfervid imaginations of ignorant or blundering editors'. The lexicographers took pleasure in identifying and exposing such errors, as for example the term 'belt of paternosters', derived from a seventeenth-century misreading of Old English, described as 'one of the most grotesque blunders on record' (*OED* entry for *belt*, n. 1). See further Read (1978); Brewer and Turton 2022 (Letter 851109A).
2 See further Brewer (2019a), Momma (2013, pp. 96–136).
3 Valuable recent discussions of the first-edition *OED*'s treatment of such terms include Turton (2020) and Mugglestone (2012, 2013 and 2007).
4 At the time of writing, the most recent editorial report on the progress of the third edition of the *OED* is https://public.oed.com/blog/the-oed-2021/ (accessed 3 May 2021).
5 Collins (2010) shows conclusively that generic *he* is now rarely used.

References

Algeo, J. (1990) 'The Emperor's New Clothes: the Second Edition of the Society's Dictionary', *Transactions of the Philological Society*, 88, pp. 131–150.

Bassett, T.J. (2020) 'At the Circulating Library: A Database of Victorian Fiction 1837–1901'[online]. Available at: http://victorianresearch.org/atcl/index.php (Accessed: 4 May 2021).

Brewer, C. (2007) *Treasure-house of the Language: The Living* OED. London: Yale University Press.

Brewer, C. (2012) '"Happy Copiousness"? *OED*'s Recording of Female Authors of the Eighteenth Century', *Review of English Studies*, 63, pp. 86–117.

Brewer, C. (2013) '*OED Online* Re-launched: Distinguishing Old Scholarship from New', *Dictionaries*, 34, pp. 101–126.

Brewer, C. (2019a) 'Patriotism', *Examining the* OED [online]. Available at: https://oed.hertford.ox.ac.uk/historical-background/oed1-intellectual-climate/patriotism/ (Accessed: 4 May 2021).

Brewer, C. (2019b) 'Top Female Sources', *Examining the* OED [online]. Available at: https://oed.hertford.ox.ac.uk/quotations/outline/fe-male-sources/top-female-sources/ (Accessed: 4 May 2021).

Brewer, C. (2020a) 'Literature and the Nation', *Examining the* OED [online]. Available at: https://oed.hertford.ox.ac.uk/historical-background/oed1-intellectual-climate/literature-and-the-nation/ (Accessed: 4 May 2021).

Brewer, C. (2020b) 'Keeping Up with Contemporary Dictionaries', *Examining the* OED [online]. Available at: https://oed.hertford.ox.ac.uk/topics/dictionaries/#contemporary (Accessed: 4 May 2021).

Brewer, C. and Turton, S. (2021) 'Aggravated Mischief: Editing and Digitizing the Papers of Sir James Murray', *Dictionaries*, 42, pp. 259–280.

Brewer, C. and Turton, S. (2022) 'Murray's Scriptorium. A Pilot Digital Edition of the Correspondence of J. A. H. Murray' [online]. Available at: https://murray-scriptorium.org (Accessed: 13 February 2022).

Burchfield, R.W. (1972–1986) *Oxford English Dictionary Supplement*. 4 vols. Oxford: Clarendon Press.

Coleman, J. (2012) *The Life of Slang*. Oxford: Oxford University Press.

Coleridge, H. (1860) 'A Letter to the Very Revd. the Dean of Westminster' (dated 30 May 1860), in Appendix to *On Some Deficiencies in our English Dictionaries*. 2nd edition. London: John W. Parker & Son, pp. 71–78.

Collins Dictionaries (2010) 'The Development and Use of Gender Language in Contemporary English – A Corpus Linguistic Analysis' [online]. Available at: https://www.thenivbible.com/wp-content/uploads/2015/02/Collins-Report-Final.pdf (Accessed: 4 May 2021).

Craigie, W.A. and Onions, C.T. (1933) 'Preface', in Murray, J.A.H., Bradley, H., Craigie, W.A. and Onions, C.T. *The Oxford English Dictionary*. Supplement. Oxford: Clarendon Press, pp. v–vi.

Dent, J. (2018) 'Release Notes: The Formal Language of Sexuality and Gender Identity', *OED* blogpost, 29 March. Available at: https://public.oed.com/blog/march-2018-update-release-notes-formal-language-sexuality-gender-identity/ (Accessed: 4 May 2021).

Fournier, H.S. and Russell, D.W. (1992) 'A Study of Sex-role Stereotyping in the *Oxford English Dictionary* 2E', *Computers and the Humanities*, 26, pp. 13–20.

Fowler, H.W. and Fowler, F.G. (1911) *The Concise Oxford Dictionary of Current English*. Oxford: Clarendon Press.

Momma, H. (2013) *From Philology to English Studies: Language and Culture in the Nineteenth Century*. Cambridge: Cambridge University Press.

Mugglestone, L. (2007) '"Decent Reticence": Coarseness, Contraception, and the First Edition of the *OED*', *Dictionaries*, 28, pp. 1–22.

Mugglestone, L. (2012) 'Patriotism, Empire and Cultural Prescriptivism: Images of Anglicity in the *OED*' in Percy, C. and Davidson, M.C. (eds.) *The Languages of Nation*. Bristol: Multilingual Matters, pp. 175–191.

Mugglestone, L. (2013) 'Acts of Representation: Writing the Woman Question in the *Oxford English Dictionary*', *Dictionaries*, 34, pp. 39–65.

Murray, J.A.H. (1884) 'Thirteenth Annual address of the President to the Philological Society', *Transactions of the Philological Society*, 19 (1882–1884), pp. 501–600.

Murray, J.A.H., Bradley, H., Craigie, W.A. and Onions, C.T. (1933) *The Oxford English Dictionary*. (Vols. I–XII, Supplement). Oxford: Clarendon Press.

Murray, K.M.E. (1977) *Caught in the Web of Words: James Murray and the Oxford English Dictionary*. New Haven, CT and London: Yale University Press.

OED Editorial (2020) 'Using Corpora to Track the Language of Covid-19: Update 2', *OED* blogpost, 15 July [online]. Available at: https://public.oed.com/blog/using-corpora-to-track-the-language-of-covid-19-update-2/ (Accessed: 4 May 2021).

OED Online (n.d.) 'Reading Programme' [online]. Available at: https://public.oed.com/history/reading-programme/ (Accessed: 4 May 2021) [Originally published online as Preface to The Third Edition of *OED*, March 2000].

OED Online (n.d.) 'Dictionary Facts' [online]. Available at: https://www.oed.com/page/facts/loginpage (Accessed: 4 May 2021).

[Philological Society] (1859) *Proposal for a Publication of a New English Dictionary by the Philological Society*. London: Trübner.

Read, A.W. (1978) 'The Sources of Ghost Words in English', *Word*, 29, pp. 95–104.

Simpson, J.A. and Proffitt, M. (2000–) *OED Online*. 3rd edition. Available to subscribers at https://www.oed.com.

Simpson, J.A. and Weiner, E.S.C. (1989) *The Oxford English Dictionary*. 2nd edition. Oxford: Clarendon Press.

Trench, R.C. (1851) *On the Study of Words: 5 Lectures*. London: Parker.

Turton, S. (2020) 'The Confessional Sciences: Scientific Lexicography and Sexology in the *Oxford English Dictionary*', *Language & History*, 63, pp. 214–232.

Weiner, E. (2009) 'The Electronic *OED*: The Computerization of a Historical Dictionary' in Cowie, A.P. (ed.) *The Oxford History of English Lexicography*. Oxford: Oxford University Press. Vol. 1, pp. 378–409.

Whitney, W.D. (1867) *Language and the Study of Language*. New York and London: Scribners.

Williams, D.-A. (2021) '"Alien" vs. Editor: World English in the *Oxford English Dictionary*, Policies, Practices, and Outcomes 1884–2020', *International Journal of Lexicography*, 34, pp. 39–65.

Woolf, V. (1937) 'Craftsmanship', *The Listener*, pp. 868–869.

2 The invisible American shoeshine boy

Creation and persistence of a ghostly icon

*Anne Lesme**

This chapter examines how visual arts inform us about the power of what has become an iconic image of street children in the United States – the independent cheerful shoeshine or bootblack boy. The shoe shiner's trade developed in the wake of urbanization in the second half of the nineteenth century and it could be found at every corner of the busy streets of New York and other industrialized American cities. But while the shoeshine or bootblack boy's presence was ubiquitous in the city and popular imagination along with stories and novels, such as Horatio Alger's best-seller, *Ragged Dick or Street Life in New York with the Boot Blacks*, his true nature remained invisible. What interested the writers, illustrators, painters and photographers who portrayed city life at the time (1870–1948) was mainly an idealized image. Looking back at these representations, one can see that they are closely connected with the values and social norms which prevailed in the Gilded Age (1870–1900), namely, resourcefulness, diligence and hard work. The idea, or one might say the fantasy, that a young shoe shiner could rise from poverty and reap the allegedly inevitable rewards associated with living according to these values and norms was strongly suggested by writers and storytellers and reinforced by visual representations.

When studied from the 1870s to the 1940s, a time span of almost a century, this iconic image seems to be frozen in time. Over time, the image came to create a sense of identity for many in the United States while simultaneously acting as a disruptive spectre for reformers who sought to deconstruct the rags-to-riches myth in an attempt to protect children from being exploited in the workplace. The icon thus became not just an image removed from reality but also a ghost casting a dark shadow over the prospects of poor children in America. In the absence of any reliable development in the narrative and with no visual representations of the shoeshine boy in the later stages of his life, the character is trapped in childhood, never growing old. Relentlessly optimistic, he is the hero of multiple narratives with the same tropes. What is lost in this iconic image of the shoeshine boy as an embodiment of the American dream is the *real* shoeshine boy. It is paradoxical that although one finds so many representations of him, the real boy and his true living conditions remained largely invisible.

DOI: 10.4324/9781003178040-4

This chapter will first analyse the origins and main characteristics of the representation of the shoeshine boy in the nineteenth century.[1] It will then examine how, in the 1910s and the late 1920s, photography and texts were specifically used by reformers of the Progressive era, who attempted to change the public's perceptions about the realities experienced by poor children in America, since very few boys, if any, ever rose from the rags of shoe shining to riches. It will finally consider how the narrative of the iconic shoeshine boy persisted into the late 1930s and 1940s to the point of his becoming a ghost-like figure, whose identity is shackled in the past.

The making of an icon

The representation of the bootblack or shoeshine boy can be traced back to the nineteenth century: it is deeply rooted in paintings of the second half of the century but even more so in Alger's influential best-selling novel *Ragged Dick or Street Life in New York with the Boot Blacks* (1868), which, in turn, also influenced the visual culture of the time. The street trade soon came to be the emblem of resourceful and independent children ready to rise from a ragged, homeless life to a respectable position in society. We only find the depiction of male children: there are no shoeshine girls. Girls were rarely included in the depiction of street waifs due to the implicit link between working on the streets and prostitution.[2] The shoeshine trade fully developed in the era of urbanization and industrialization in America, along with the mass production of shoes and products to clean them, and with the emergence of a white-collar class who worked in offices and, contrary to agricultural workers or factory employees, had to wear clean, shiny shoes.

The fact that shoeshine boys worked hard did not prevent them from also becoming romanticized figures. In Europe, the pictorial representations of shoe shiners oscillate between, on the one hand, the evocation of hard work bordering on exhaustion, and on the other, the portrayal of a form of freedom, of energy, but also sometimes of gentleness. The forerunner of the shoeshine boy first occurs in an etching by Joseph Wagner (1706–1780) entitled *The Shoe Black, engraved by Wagner* (1739). The boy is wearing rags but he is dedicated to his work, carrying his tools and looking carefully and seriously at the viewer. The etching cannot be deemed picturesque as it does not seek to be attractive or charm its viewers. It was not until the second half of the nineteenth century that this street trade, most often practised by children in Europe, became a real motif in European art. The British artist and illustrator Charles Keene, who worked in black and white, drew a *Study of Shoe Black* between 1850 and 1890. The French painter Jules Bastien-Lepage, closely associated with the beginning of the Naturalism movement, portrayed a *London shoeshine boy* in 1882 leaning casually on an urban pillar placed on the pavement, his legs crossed, his head resting on his right hand, his left hand in his pocket. There is a sense of freedom and an even nonchalance in this pose. The child is not working; he is probably waiting for a customer, but he could also be in a contemplative state. By contrast, John Thomson's *Independent Shoe Black* (1877) is hard at work and very diligent but his facial and gestural expression is also gentle. He represents one of the different trades of *Street Life in London*, published the same year by Adolphe Smith who wrote essays on local workers and street dwellers accompanied by 36 photographs taken by the Scottish photographer John Thomson. In this precursor of social documentary photography, the author does not seek to conceal the hardships of the trade for independent boot-blacks, who were often fined or arrested for working without a licence. Paradoxically, these representations suggest that the shoeshine trade can be associated with both dilettantism and hard work.

In the United States, the portrayal of street children and trades in visual and literary media was contemporary with the era of mass urbanization and the wave of immigration from the 1830s and 1840s. Different kinds of representations can be observed. Claire Perry, an art historian and curator, distinguishes three categories: some artists, for instance David Gilmour Blythe, depicted street children as innately vicious, bearing responsibility for their own misery with moral and physical defects; others depicted poor children as passive but worthy to be reformed since they were seen as victims of adverse circumstances (Henry Inman, Nathaniel Currier); and finally, a category, including John George Brown and Jacob Riis, represented 'the waif as a go-getter whose ambition and ability were honed by adverse fortunes' (Perry, 2006, p. 115). The shoe shiner clearly belongs to the final category. A positive image of the boy emerged in the United States, more so than in England, which may be connected with the American work ethic: the boy worked very hard and this inspired admiration more than pity. This perspective suggested that a child who had suffered hardship in this way might be better prepared for adulthood than one who had been supported by a financially stable family. Thus, America's relative lack of social hierarchies (at least on the surface) had found an icon. While the hierarchical social systems prevalent in Europe tied people to their social class and rank, America was the land of opportunity for the hard-working street child, who would rise from rags to riches. This was indeed the implicit promise to be written on the tablet of the Statue of Liberty delivered to New York in 1886: 'Give me your tired, your poor, your huddled masses yearning to breathe free, the wretched refuse of your teeming shore. Send these, the homeless, tempest-tost to me, I lift my lamp beside the golden Door.'

By the mid-century, the portraits of shoeshine boys had increased in popularity, as illustrated in a painting by American artist George Henry Yewell entitled *The Bootblack* in 1852. But it was in the turmoil of industrialization that followed the American Civil War that street trades, many of them held by children (newsboys, bootblacks, messengers, etc.), became unwitting supporters of *laissez-faire* capitalism. Two very popular artists contributed to the success of the shoe shiners: the painter, John George Brown, and the novelist, Horatio Alger. Their works acted as moral reminders of the values of the middle class, which was then becoming an emblem of entrepreneurialism and resourcefulness, promoting hard work as an ethos.

Brown, a prolific genre painter originally from England, portrayed newsboys and bootblacks as rosy-cheeked cherubs who prospered on the street. It is noteworthy that his idealized depiction of street urchins adapted the British genre painting style to American subjects. Brown earned the sobriquet of 'Boot-Black Raphael' after the Civil War. His fascination with his subject is closely related to his modest origins: 'I do not paint poor boys solely because the public likes such pictures and pays for them, but because I love the boys myself, because I was once a poor boy' (Perry, 2006, p. 137). Even with torn clothing, his subjects appeared clean, well-fed and healthy. There is no sign of the wretched conditions in which shoeshine boys lived. Rather, what Brown brings forth is their determination and gentleness.

Brown underlines their ethos of hard work, humility and solidarity, as in *Sympathy* (1885b). Their seriousness and diligence are also evident in *Jersey Mud* (1887), whereas *Tuckered Out* (1888, Figure 2.1) depicts their exhaustion after work. Meticulous and highly detailed, the painting *Tuckered Out* portrays an exhausted bootblack boy at the end of the day, sitting on a wooden stool, leaning against a wall. It is intended to be realistic but the artist does not conceal the romanticized nature of his representation. The boy has shiny curls and rosy cheeks. His mouth is half open, conveying a feeling of vulnerability. Brown's sleeping boy is not unlike some of Jacob Riis's Street Arabs (a term used for homeless young people) taken in New York's Lower East side in the early 1890s (Riis, 1890). At the time, Riis, a journalist and social reformer, photographed children in the street to document their poor living conditions and plead for social reforms. The alleged dangerousness of the young boys, denounced by the American philanthropist Charles Loring Brace a few years earlier in *The Dangerous Classes of New York* (1880) is neutralized by sleep through Riis's lens. The values of solidarity and friendliness is emphasized, as in Brown's *A Jolly Lot* (1885a) or *A Tough Story* (1886).

In the latter, a very young barefoot bootblack, sitting on his shoe shine box, is telling a story to three of his dusty co-workers. The central motif is storytelling, a widespread practice among young street workers, even if it meant inventing fictitious origins as in John Morrow's novel *A Voice from the Newsboys* (1860). These portrayals play with the public's expectations and participate in turning shoe shiners into icons. In Brown's *A Tough Story* the tale is told visually and achieves an almost improbable synthesis between the values of work and play, in some of the poorest categories of society.

Alger's most famous novel, *Ragged Dick*, features a poor but honest shoe shiner, Dick, who is emblematic of New York street urchins living in the poorest parts of the city. This synthesis is also what contributed to the success of *Ragged Dick*, and other dime novels by Alger, whom Brown acknowledged to be a major source of inspiration. In this respect, visual culture and

Figure 2.1 J.G. Brown, *Tuckered Out – The Shoeshine Boy*, circa 1888. Painting
© [c. 1888] Museum of Fine Arts, Boston.

literature appear to be closely connected. Alger portrayed street traders in
his many novels as rugged individualists whose essential good character led
to inevitable success in life. The omniscient narrator does not hesitate to
intervene several times in the novel to pass judgements about his characters
and to guide or even direct the reader's understanding. From the very first
chapter, entitled 'Ragged Dick is Introduced to the Reader,' the tone is set.
Despite his extravagant lifestyle of betting and smoking expensive cigars,
the eponymous hero is generous with his fellow sufferers, sharing his guilty
pleasure of smoking with them. These positive qualities are underlined by
the narrator who clearly shows his empathy for the boy:

> I don't consider him a model boy. But there were some good points
> about him nevertheless. He was above doing anything mean or dishon-
> ourable. He would not steal, or cheat, or impose upon younger boys, but
> was frank and straight-forward, manly and self-reliant. His nature was
> a noble one, and had saved him from all mean faults.
>
> (Alger, 1867, p. 8)

All these qualities of honesty, independence and sense of initiative guar-
anteed a respectability that opened up the possibility of climbing the
social ladder, albeit modestly. The hero ends up working in an office, and
thanks to this new position, he can conform to middle-class standards.
Dick's unwavering optimism may seem excessively romanticized but Alger
reminded his readers that his characters and stories were drawn from real
people and situations. Alger's and Brown's works implicitly reassured the
middle class that poor city children could improve their social status if
they truly wanted to succeed. Brown even said once that most of the street
children he painted had grown to become successful businessmen (Gail,
2011, p. 129).

In 1882, Italian-born writer Luigi Donato Ventura (1845–1912) published *Peppino*. The tale, originally published in French, is a transcribed version of a (supposedly) real-life experience. The author, adopting the persona of his alter ego Mr Fortuna, narrates his difficult beginnings as a writer and chronicler in New York City. He explains, sometimes in a paternalistic tone, how he befriended a shoeshine boy, an Italian like himself, whose generosity, vivacity and honesty were remarkable:

> The boy's intelligence was very alert: in spite of his brusqueness he was respectful and polite... Peppino is proud of his aristocratic friendships and says that he owes his acquaintance with the good doctor to me, while I congratulate myself on having met Peppino, a rare specimen of honesty in the world of childishness.
>
> (Ventura, 1889, pp. 25, 65)

Finally, in *Street Types of Chicago* (1896), Sigmund Krausz tried to define different urban categories through the Kodak photographs included in the book. Rather than taking photos on the streets, he had his subjects pose in his studio and created what he termed 'Character Studies' of average urban Chicagoans in the 1890s. Sigmund Krausz's prose conforms to the previous representations of the shoeshine boy: he holds them in much higher esteem than other street trades. He does not conceal the bootblacks' shortcomings, but insists that these are due to their high spirits and not to a morally condemnable vice: 'The bootblack, no matter what nationality, is always good-humored, fond of mischief and practical joking. Though he dearly loves to fight he does not do it out of viciousness, but simply in an exuberance of spirits seeking an outlet' (Krausz, 1896, p. 182).

The bootblack thus became an icon, more so than any other street trades, notably newsboys or newsgirls and messengers. This was largely due to the public's reading of popular literature and to the success of widely circulated picturesque paintings and illustrations. Through his example, the public understood that if you work hard, you will climb the social ladder and be rewarded. The shoeshine boy was not unlike the character from a social fairy tale, a tale with moral lessons like many traditional ghost stories. As such, the icon of the shoeshine boy served as a moral reminder. He is haunting for good reasons: the belief in a better future, in keeping with the spirit of the times, becoming more and more embedded in American history and collective memory. But unlike in fairy tales, the shoeshine boy is not the hero of a story. With time, the true and diverse nature of the boys tended to be replaced by a more static, shackled identity, a new iconic status substituting itself for the reality it claimed to embody. But what about the real state of affairs regarding this street job? The following section will focus on the icon of the shoeshine boy ended up resisting the power of rational explanation even better than any other trade.

An icon confronted to reality and reforms: resistance, permanence and evolution

Many historical sources (Bremner, 1971; Trattner, 1970) remind us that the romantic image of the successful working child belongs to the mythology of modern times. He is perceived as a true urban hero who earns a living through entrepreneurship and lives a cheerful and financially satisfying life, often helping a widowed mother or a sick parent. In fact, very few children actually prospered thanks to the street trades, and the popularity of their representation in the American collective memory does not match the conviction of the early twentieth century reformers who tackled the thorny problem of the young working poor. To these reformers, the discrepancy between fact and fiction was not just obvious, it was profoundly disturbing and frustrating. Indeed, the complexity and diversity of the shoe shining trade was not perceived despite the evidence, figures and arguments that they provided.

As early as 1905, Myron E. Adams, a social worker and Baptist minister, delivered this laconic formula about the shoeshine boy: 'The public sees him at his best and neglects him at his worst' (Adams, 1905, p. 437). Historian Walter Trattner summarizes the prevailing mood in American society on the eve of the first campaigns of the National Child Labor Committee (NCLC), which targeted young street workers: newspaper sellers, shoeshine boys, delivery boys and messengers. When confronted with stories or representations of children working in factories or in mines, recoiling at the evil of these wasted, sacrificed lives, people became increasingly outraged and inclined to push for social change. However, when it came to children working on the streets – shoe shiners, newsboys and others – the general public did not see much of a problem. The children carried out their work 'in the 'healthful open air,' as rugged individuals starting on the road toward success' (Trattner, 1970, p. 110). Instead of perceiving their plight, people continued to feel a combination of fascination and admiration toward them. Perhaps they believed that, just as in the stories they read and the images they saw, these boys were actually nobly helping to support their family, and redeeming poverty, the city and society.

In 1903, in an article published in *McClure's Magazine*, 'Waifs of the Street,' Ernest Poole highlighted the competitive struggle between children in street trades and the hard-working conditions. He tried to bring to their senses those who insisted on considering street trades as the prelude to a dazzling social ascension within a mythicized capitalistic system:

Out of the thousands of messenger boys only a very small per cent become operators. Few bootblacks come to have stands of their own. All are constantly pushed on by the thousands of newcomers, and the street gives later work to only a small per cent [sic] of these thousands.

> Newsboys do not become reporters. An editor of one large New York daily told me he knew of not a single instance.
>
> (Poole, 1903, p. 43)

Reformers, many of them women working together in settlement houses, temperance unions and trade unions, made the elimination of child labour a priority. In Chicago, Florence Kelley (1890) called street trading 'white child slavery' and targeted newsboys and bootblacks as needing care and support.[3] Contrary to popular belief, relatively few newsboys or bootblacks were orphans. Most lived with one or both parents and worked in the street as part of a family business, often accompanied by siblings and monitored by relatives. They typically started to work between the age of five and ten. Their earnings accounted for up to 20% of a household's income, and this gave them some autonomy and considerable status within their family. Few continued in the trade after the age of 15, but some boys, particularly African American boys, stayed on longer simply because there were no better jobs for them. The ethnicity of boys usually reflected the ethnic composition of a city's working class, with the newest and poorest arrivals tending to dominate the trade. Thus, shoeshine boys up to the 1880s were mostly of Irish origin, while the children of southern and eastern European immigrants, mainly Italian and Greek, were the main other groups.

In 1904, to coordinate their effort, activists formed the National Child Labor Committee (NCLC), a private, non-profit-organization, which aimed at promoting 'the rights, awareness, dignity, well-being and education of children and youth as they relate to work and working.' In 1907, the Committee was chartered by an act of Congress with a board of directors composed of prominent Progressive reformers (Jane Addams, Florence Kelley, Edward T. Devine and Lillian Wald). If street trading was seen by many as the solution to youth homelessness, poverty and delinquency, it was soon considered as a major problem for the Committee. In 1908, the NCLC hired Lewis Hine, a sociologist and photographer who documented child labour over the next decade to support the organization's efforts to end or regulate the practice of child labour. However, he took few photographs of bootblacks (about 50) compared to newsboys (almost 800) or those working in the mill (1,815), in agriculture (733), in canneries (301), in tenement home industry (265) or even in glass factories (150) and coal mines (265). By the time Hine started to document the bootblack business, it had undergone many changes. David Nasaw's well-researched and richly detailed narrative explains how the business was the first of the street trades to undergo radical changes at the turn of the century. An era in the history of bootblack children was drawing to a close. Greek and Italian adult immigrants came to work with the children in the central business districts. They soon erected shoeshine stands on the streets, in saloons, in railroad terminals and on the ferries, benefiting from the growing numbers of white-collar workers in need of shoe shining. Within the space of a few years, those barons had succeeded in monopolizing the downtown market. According to a confidential report to the New York Child Labor Committee in 1903, 'the business of blackening boots has become so concentrated and systematized that it can now be described only as an industry' (Nasaw, 1985, p. 188).

The days of the shoeshine boy walking the streets carrying his equipment were thus becoming a ghost of the past. In New York City, Italian immigrants controlled the new market and the traditional Irish bootblack had almost disappeared. Elsewhere, Greek immigrants were predominant in building bootblack parlours in cities where young Greek immigrant boys worked for them in very harsh conditions. The boys worked from six in the morning until nine or ten at night, slept in overcrowded, unventilated rooms rented by their *padrones* and had very little to eat, sometimes only bread and olives or cheese. They were poorly paid and all the tips they earned went to the *padrone*. The child labour reformers, judging the situation to be one of the most preoccupying, did what they could to end the importation of children and act in favour of those who were already working in an attempt to free them from this form of exploitation. But they were confronted with the boys' unwillingness and usual refusal to testify against their *padrones*. By Greek standards, the boys were far better treated in the United States than in the slums they had fled in their home country, and some of them even managed to go to night school (Nasaw, 1985, p. 188).

As a result of new legislation and the increasing number of bootblack parlours and stands, many independent workers were forced out of business, sometimes with imported boys. *The Biography of a Bootblack* (Corresca, 1902), describes how this new mafia-like system operated. Nasaw mentions how Child Labour investigators in Tennessee and North Carolina found out how African American boys shoe shining after school and during the week-ends and holidays were actually working for adults operating parlours downtown. The children who continued to be independent had no other choice than to gather outside saloons and railroad terminals, begging to shine or they had to seek more remote locations that were not so profitable for adults.

Despite these major changes, the shoeshine boys were still on the street and they were still being photographed, whether by Hine in the 1900s to 1920s (Figures 2.2–2.4) or by photographers of the Farm Security Administration[4] in the early 1940s (Figure 2.5). However, photographs of shoe shiners are rare in comparison to photographs denouncing child labour in other trades. Moreover, according to the archives consulted on the photographs published at George Eastman House and the Library of Congress in Washington, when these photographs of shoeshine boys do exist, they seem to have been kept in the shadows as they remained unpublished for the most part.

For example, *Greek Bootblacks in Indianapolis,* taken by Lewis Hine in 1908 (Figure 2.2), which seems to illustrate the aforementioned elements of the subjugation of children to *padrone* law, was never published in the documents edited by the NCLC (pamphlets, articles in the reviews *The Charities*

Figure 2.2 L.W. Hine, *Greek Bootblacks in Indianapolis,* 1908. Photograph © [1908] Library of Congress, Washington D.C.

and the Commons, The Survey) or in newspapers.[5] Was it because the reformers had the greatest difficulty in curbing this mafia-like mode of operation due to the prevailing law of silence, which prevented children from testifying? Direct testimonies to make the image more explicit were not available. Moreover, pictures never stood alone in progressive rhetoric, they needed a textual and statistical arsenal to guarantee their legitimacy and guide the reading of the reader/viewer.

One photograph of Greek bootblacks was nevertheless published in the Progressive magazine *The Survey* (Figure 2.3). The cliché was not taken in the United States but in Greece, while Lewis Hine was working for the Red Cross in Europe (1917–1919).

A very short text denouncing the abolition in 1917 of the laws passed in 1912 which regulated child labour in Greece is written as a long caption, but it does not seem very powerful compared to the appeal of the photograph. The iconic qualities of the picture are all in display here: industrious and smiling, the shoe shiner looks at the lens – he looks at us and seems to be happy. The picturesque character of the Greek boy dominates. Likewise, many clichés taken by Hine remain haunted by a vision of the past. When we look at Tony in his traditional pose (Figure 2.4), the *punctum* of the photograph (what attracts the viewer, according to Roland Barthes, 1980, p. 73) is undoubtedly the boy's smile. Almost 20 years later, the same observation can be made about a photograph taken by Marjorie Collins for the Farm Security Administration (Figure 2.5).

Whatever the written arguments of the reformers, the image of the nineteenth century shoe shiner is still present: 'Photographic rhetoric is nothing other than the transfiguration of one figure into the other, which at the same time enchains, entrains and cancels all possible narrative elements'[6] (Derrida, 2013, p. 267). The shackled narrative of the shoeshine boy continued with Tony in the 1920s, then with the two Stanleys of the 1930s and 1940s.

Figure 2.3 L.W. Hine, *A Greek shiner on his native heath (Athens)*, 1919. Photograph © [1919] The Online Books Page, University of Pennsylvania.

Figure 2.4 L.W. Hine, *Tony, a 12-year-old bootblack at his station in Bowling Green, New York City*, 1924. Photograph © [1924] Library of Congress, Washington D.C.

Figure 2.5 M. Collins, *Baltimore, Maryland. Shoeshine boy*, 1943. Photograph © [1943] Library of Congress, Washington D.C.

The shoeshine boy as a liminal figure, a ghostly presence frozen in time

Although individual workers were losing their independence to organized groups, and the shoe shiner's trade was no exception to this, the iconic images of boys continued to prevail in popular culture. The folklore of the friendly, brave, straightforward shoe shiner brought joy to people; in stories or representation of street life, he was a source of comfort, as 'friendly' as benevolent ghosts can be.

In the late 1930s, these ghostly images arrived in American homes through magazines and popular periodicals which fulfilled expectations by telling and showing inspiring stories and heroes. In August 1938, the magazine *Look* published a photo-story entitled: 'The Shoe Shine Boy: The True Story of a Boy Who, at 10, is His Family Chief Support.' At the time, a photo-story or a photo-essay (very popular in *Life* and *Look* magazines, created in 1935 and 1936) were visual storytelling, with an average of six or nine pictures on a double page accompanied by texts resulting from a shooting script.[7]

In this photo-story, readers could follow bootblack Stanley Martin around New York City, going about his day. Although he was followed and photographed by *Look*'s reporters, he 'is not posing' for this 'true genuine documentary story.' Against the backdrop of the Great Depression, the boy's father has been out of work for a long time. In addition to being a homemaker, his mother does small jobs, thus enabling her family to leave the city from time to time to breathe the fresh country air. Most importantly, the family embraces the values of hard work and independence and refuses to rely on 'social welfare.' For the past two years (since he was eight), Stanley has been attending night school, starting at nine in the evening, that is after his full day of work. In the story, one can see that after arriving back home dishevelled, he changes into shirt and tie and carefully combs his hair before doing his homework on the dining room table. The story is edifying and exemplary.

A strong work ethic and the values of independence, honesty and cheerfulness in the face of adversity dominate the storytelling. Not only does Stanley earn his own money and educate himself, he also already supports his family. In a world turned upside down in the aftermath of the 1929 crisis, a period marked by financial and ethical failure (a father unable to provide for his family), the shoeshine boy redeems not just his family but the whole of society, including the public who read his story, by demonstrating the unbreakable power of the human spirit. As a beacon of morality, he's haunting for good reasons.

The same narrative, linking the past with a present that follows a major crisis (the 1930s) or war (World War II) is later adapted cinematically. In 1946, *Shoeshine*, by Italian director Vittorio de Sica, was released and met with popular success. Two years later, it was the first foreign movie to receive an award in the United States: the *Honorary Award*, the precursor of the Academy Award. In 1947, a promising young reporter, Stanley Kubrick, published a photo-story in the magazine *Look* tapping into the same vein, the shoeshine boy: 'The Adventure of Mickey in New York City or A tale of a shoeshine boy.' The boy who lives in a deprived area is introduced as a celebrity: 'This photo narrates the daily life of Mickey, a handsome twelve-year-old from Brooklyn, already sure of himself, who works as a shoeshine boy after school to help support his younger brothers and sisters' (Crone and Wirth, 2011, p. 62). Although in his case the day starts with school and finishes with work, the parallel with the storytelling of *Look* magazine is striking. History is repeating itself and the representation of the shoeshine boy. Robert Hariman and John Lucaites underline how much: 'Copying, imitating, satirizing, and other forms of appropriation are a crucial sign of iconicity, and more so than we realized at first' (Hariman and Lucaites, 2007, p. 37). Twenty-one pictures serve to create a complete narrative with a protagonist who, like Stanley in 1938, is posing according to the stage directions given to him: Mickey making pocket money by shoe shining, gambling, going to the movie theatre, doing his homework later on but also playing sports and finally releasing doves from a roof (Lesme, 2019, p. 203). This last shot conveys a very romantic feeling of freedom. And the cinematic nature of this photo-story demonstrates the early talent of a reporter who would become a world-famous artist.

Rainer Crone underlines how much 'Kubrick's pictures appear to make the transcendent perceptible in the seemingly ordinary' (Crone and Wirth, 2011, p. 18), a direct reference to the irrational characteristics that can be found in ghost stories. Meanwhile, throughout the successive representations of the shoeshine boy, it is obvious that, in the collective imagination of the American nation, the shoe shiner remains the eternal child. What he becomes is never mentioned or discussed. If he is supposed to climb from rags to riches, this rise to wealth is never portrayed. Like a ghost, he is trapped in one age, never changing, yet passing from one generation to the next, from one era to the other, from the nineteenth century to the twenty-first, almost untouched, as if frozen in time.

Conclusion

By examining paintings, illustrations and photographs, as well as novels and films, this chapter offers an analysis of how the iconic image of the shoeshine boy persisted despite the reformists' arguments against the harsh reality of child labour. The ubiquitous shoeshine boys, or bootblacks, were dynamic and useful workers, real participants in the bustling life of New York City, Chicago, Philadelphia and other cities. They became an urban type, a typical subject for popular journal illustrators and genre painters who were searching the city for picturesque themes. Periodicals provided news stories and entertainment to the middle class, and while they were expected to express popular taste, they also had a crucial role in affecting the cultural appetites of the day. With time, the shoeshine boy became the icon of a certain America, a fantasy, through which the urban middle class could nostalgically 'remember' its beginnings, as well as measure the distance covered since. They felt reassured by the resourceful child who faced adversity with such unbreakable hope and cheer.

There was an understanding about America being a young, new country which required its people to devote their best energies to its economic development. Thus, given how the shoeshine boy's life was represented by popular media, the job could be deemed fitting for a boy whose family needed the supplemental income in challenging circumstances, and it could even teach him certain useful survival skills. Even those who were employed but felt trapped in the rat race could still fantasize about the boy's life, his freedom and independence in particular, when they watched him rest or chat idly while waiting for customers. America had created a work-oriented rather than a leisure-oriented culture, in which the fantasy of the shoeshine boy resonated very well. Not only was it very deeply embedded in people's imagination but it was also necessary to the way they led their daily lives. It should be no surprise then that people clung to this image even when confronted with the reformists' arguments and with photographs documenting the real lives of real shoeshine boys.

In the light of the appalling realities of the life of poor working children in the city and of their gloomy prospects, which the reformists observed and recorded, the myth seems completely incongruous. The prevailing version of the shoeshine boy's story disregarded his suffering and exploitation and did not correspond to the realities of his life. The reformists, and particularly the NCLC, understood that they needed to transform, shift and clarify the public's preconceived ideas about individual entrepreneurship and to confront these ideas with realities. In several cases, they were able to demonstrate that organized mafia-like groups were actually reaping all the benefits. Even then, the boys themselves remained silent and refused to testify. They embraced the image that was so prejudicial to them and continued to hang on to it for dear life.

Reformers failed to alter the public's perceptions and alert them to the urgency of the shoe shiner's situation despite their strong arguments backed by facts and supported by photographs. It seemed as if people would not let go of the fascination that this romanticized character exerted over them. And even Hine's photographs continued to show a kind of ambivalence, rooted in his sympathy for the know-how of the shoe shiner. The rise of photo-stories with *Look* and *Life* and the cinematic storytelling of the young Kubrick for *Look* magazine show that the shoeshine boy continued to haunt the streets of American cities through their narratives. Through the consistent retelling of the bootblack's legend, the image of the shoeshine boy never disappeared, shackled to his iconic status of an eternal ghost-like, never aging child.

Notes

* Anne Lesme, Aix Marseille Univ, LERMA, Aix-en-Provence, France.
1 Since many elements of American cultural and visual arts are informed by their counterparts in England, this study will occasionally take on a transnational quality.
2 When they were represented, impoverished girls were either in a situation of being rescued and protected or in situations where their virtues were explicitly not endangered (very young age, selling flowers, newspaper girls, etc.).
3 At the time Florence Kelley was writing, in 1890, many boys still gained their independence thanks to their trade. They also formed unions and mounted strikes (1870, then 1880 or 1899) that allowed them to express their voice and be partly successful in their demand for better pay and working conditions.
4 The Farm Security Administration (FSA) was a New Deal agency created in 1937 to combat rural poverty during the Great Depression in the United States.
5 The archives of Lewis Hine in George Eastman House have retained a copy of the media in which his photographs were published and the author of this chapter made an exhaustive research on the photographs published in *The Survey* between 1908 and 1909.
6 Original quote: « La rhétorique photographique n'est rien d'autre que la transfiguration d'une figure dans l'autre, ce qui à la fois enchaine, entraine et annule toute narrativité possible » [trans. mine].
7 Roy Stryker's shooting scripts offered a very comprehensive look at all of the possible ways that you could photograph a subject.

References

Adams, M.E. (1905) 'Children in American Street Trades', *The Annals of the American Academy of Political and Social Science*, 25(3), pp. 23–43.

Alger, H. (1867) *Ragged Dick, or Street Life in New York with the Boot-blacks*. New York: Signet Classics, 2005.

Barthes, R. (1980) *La chambre claire. Note sur la photographie*. Paris: Seuil.

Brace, C.L. (1880) *The Dangerous Classes of New York and Twenty Years' Work among Them*. New York: Wynkoop & Hallenbeck.

Bremner, R.H. (ed.) (1971) *Children and Youth in America: A Documentary History. Vol. II 1866–1932*. Cambridge, MA: Harvard University Press, pp. 601–666.

Corresca, R. (1902) *The Biography of a Bootblack: Rocco Corresca, The Independent*, 54, 4 December [online]. Available at: http://www.digitalhistory.uh.edu/voices/social_history/1bootblack.cfm (Accessed: 4 October 2021).

Crone, R. and Wirth, W. (eds.) (2011) *Stanley Kubrick: visioni e finzioni 1945–1950*. Catalog a cura di Rainer Crone e Wouter Wirth. Reggio Emilia: Giunti.

Derrida, J. (2013) *Penser à ne pas voir: écrits sur les arts du visible, 1979–2004*. Paris: La Différence.

Gail, A. (2011) *Birmingham Museum of Art: A Guide to the Collection*. London: Giles.

Hariman, R. and Lucaites J.-L. (2007) *No Caption Needed. Iconic Photographs, Public Culture, and Liberal Democracy*. Chicago, IL: University of Chicago Press.

Hine, L.W. (1919) 'The Child's Burden in the Balkans: A Photo Story', *The Survey*, 42, 6 September, pp. 813–817.

Kelley, F. (1890) '" White Child Slavery" in "White Child Slavery: A Symposium,"' *Arena*, 1, pp. 89–603.

Krausz, S. (1896) *Street Types of Great American Cities*. Chicago, IL and New York: The Werner Company.

Lesme, A. (2019) *Photographier l'enfant pour changer la société: Images réformatrices de l'enfant pauvre aux Etats-Unis 1888–1942*. Paris: L'Harmattan.

Morrow, J. (1860) *A Voice from the Newsboys*. [online]. Available at: https://archive.org/details/avoicefromnewsb00morrgoog (Accessed: 6 February 2022).

Nasaw, D. (1985) *Children of the City: At Work and At Play*. Garden City, NY: Anchor Press/Doubleday.

Perry, C. (2006) *Young America: Childhood in 19th Century Art and Culture*. New Haven, CT: Yale University Press.

Poole, E. (1903) 'Waifs of the Street', *McClure's Magazine*, 21(1), pp. 40–44.

Trattner, W.I. (1970) *Crusade for the Children; A History of the National Child Labor Committee Reform in America*. Chicago, IL: Quadrangle Books.

Ventura, L.D. (1889) *Peppino*. New York: W.R. Jenkins.

Picture and art work

Bastien-Lepage, J. (1882) *London Shoeshine Boy* [online]. Available at: https://www.heritage-print.com/london-shoeshine-boy-1882-artist-19050511.html (Accessed: 11 November 2021).

Brown, J.G. (1885a) *A Jolly Lot* [online]. Available at: https://en.wahooart.com/@@/8XXJ78-John-George-Brown-A-Jolly-Lot (Accessed: 11 November 2021).

Brown, J.G. (1885b) *Sympathy* [online]. Available at: https://commons.wikimedia.org/wiki/File:John_George_Brown_-_Sympathy_(1885).jpg (Accessed: 4 October 2021).

Brown, J.G. (1886) *A Tough Story* [online]. Available at: https://artsandculture.google.com/asset/a-tough-story-john-george-brown/ZwF11QehrVrtZA (Accessed: 11 November 2021).

Brown, J.G. (1887) *Jersey Mud* [online]. Available at: https://www.cutlermiles.com/jersey-mud-john-george-brown (Accessed: 11 November 2021).

Brown, J.G. (c. 1888) *Tuckered Out – The Shoeshine Boy* [online]. Available at: https://collections.mfa.org/objects/33832 (Accessed: 4 October 2021).

Collins, M. (1943) *Baltimore, Maryland. Shoe Shine Boy* [online]. Available at: www.loc.gov/item/2017849682/ (Accessed: 4 October 2021).

Hine, L.W. (1908) *Greek Bootblacks in Indianapolis, Ind. Witness, E.N. Clooper.* Indianapolis, Indiana [online]. Available at: www.loc.gov/item/2018673702/ (Accessed: 4 October 2021).

Hine, L.W. (1919) *A Greek Shiner on His Native Heath (Athens)*, in 'The Child's Burden in the Balkans', *The Survey*, 42(6), 6 September, p. 814.

Hine, L.W. (1924) *Tony, a Twelve-Year-Old Bootblack at His Station in Bowling Green, New York City. He Says He Makes from $2. to $3. a Day Regularly.* New York, New York State [online]. Available at: www.loc.gov/item/2018678683/ (Accessed: 4 October 2021).

Riis, J. (1890) *Street Arabs in Sleeping Quarters* [online]. Available at: https://collections.mcny.org/CS.aspx?VP3=DamView&VBID=24UP1GRP7R36P&PN=2&WS=SearchResults&FR_=1&W=1536&H=664#/DamView&VBID=24UP1GRMWTBEI&PN=1&WS=SearchResults (Accessed: 11 November 2021).

Thomson, J. (1877) *The Independent Shoe-Black* [online]. Available at: https://www.nationalgalleries.org/art-and-artists/10724/independent-shoe-black (Accessed: 11 November 2021).

Wagner, J. (1739) *The Shoe Black, Engraved by Wagner* [online]. Available at: https://www.meisterdrucke.fr/fine-art-prints/Jacopo-after-Amiconi/567225/La-chaussure-noire, -grav%C3%A9e-par-Wagner, -1739.html (Accessed: 11 November 2021).

Yewell, G.H. (1852) *The Bootblack* Oil Painting. Accession no. 1933.8. Collection of The New-York Historical Society.

3 Australian ghosts

Representations of the past in Australia

John Potts

This chapter considers the distinctive characteristics of Australian ghost stories, as representations of the Australian past. The analysis of Australian ghosts is conducted within the historical context and legacy of three traumatic episodes in the history of the country: the dispossession and attempted erasure of Indigenous people by European settlers from 1788; the establishment of the European settlement as a penal colony and the ensuing colonial settlement of the continent. This often brutal past has ensured the prevalence of suffering and 'bad deaths' which permeates Australian ghost stories, rife with narratives of displacement, trauma and injustice. Australian ghost stories emerged from a context of European unease and estrangement within a vast, dry and forbidding continent. Even the surrounding landscape was experienced by Europeans in the eighteenth century as eerie, spectral, weird – un-European – with distinctive flora including the variety of eucalyptus tree known as the 'ghost gum'. The prevalence of themes of displacement and dispossession in Australian ghost stories suggest an undercurrent of guilt or shame in Australian culture since European settlement, and a legacy of anxiety and unease.

This chapter begins with a theoretical presentation of the ghost as a sign of the past in the present and of the role of ghost stories in filling in some of the silences or diverging interpretations about Australia's traumatic history. It analyses how ghosts and ghost stories present both in Aboriginal and colonial folklore and folk memory, revealing how Australia is a haunted land, shackled to its uneasy past.

Ghost as past

In the essay 'The Idea of the Ghost' (Potts, 2006), I developed the idea that the ghost is a representation of the past as it endures in the present. The ghost performs cultural work as it functions in folklore, in oral story-telling, in human imaginations, thereby keeping alive a memory of the past. A ghost is an immaterial presence haunting the living; and to be haunted by a ghost is to be haunted by the past.

DOI: 10.4324/9781003178040-5

There are minor exceptions to this rule of ghost-lore: these are the ghosts of the present (known in paranormal circles as 'crisis apparitions') and ghosts of the future (known as 'harbingers'). But in the great majority of cases, ghosts are representations of the past, most commonly in the form of deceased individuals, located geographically in the places where those individuals once lived – or died. Again, there are exceptions to this rule of the ghost as individualized immaterial presence: these exceptions include collective ghost-formations such as ghost armies; and even non-human phantoms such as ghost-ships or ghost trains, traveling along their former routes. Yet, the most common type of ghost activity is the haunting of a site or territory by a deceased individual, often a former resident or occupant of that space.

A ghost is a site-specific popular memory, a means for a community to preserve the knowledge of those who once lived there, or of that which once happened there. A common theme of all ghost narratives is that of the bad or unjust death. A narrative of justice attends those ghosts that return to avenge wrongs perpetrated on them. A ghost may be thought to haunt the place – such as a prison or fortress – where that person suffered and died unjustly, thus preserving the memory of injustice. Ghosts manifest the weight of the past, which can disturb the complacency of the present built on the repression of dark or guilty memories: ghosts in this regard can represent the liberation of the repressed, unsettling a present that often prefers to forget the shame of the past.

In her study of ghosts in ancient and medieval sources, Christa Tuczay identified the theme of the improper or bad death as the generator of unhappy ghosts throughout history. Tuczay notes that the importance of proper burial rites was upheld throughout the ancient world, and that 'the greatest shame' ensued from a failure to observe those rites (Tuczay, 2004, p. 100). The returning ghost is a manifestation of that shame: the ghost haunts those who have failed to properly conduct the deceased individual's rite of passage to the afterworld. Tuczay remarks that if a death were considered dishonourable or unlucky, this impropriety was believed to prompt the return of the deceased as a ghost. Tuczay finds that this concept is 'found in the Western world from antiquity to the Middle Ages and is still reflected in contemporary urban legends' (Tuczay, 2004, p. 107).

In Chinese culture, the concept of the 'hungry ghost' attests to the respect for ancestors and extended family within that culture. Hungry ghosts are the unhappy ghosts of the deceased who have no direct descendants to make sacrifices to them. This unfortunate breakdown in the social respect shown for ancestors can yield a malevolent ghost, which may manifest its displeasure by visiting persistent illness on living family members. Such unhappiness besetting both the living and the dead can be averted by ghost adoption or marriage, so that the unhappy ghost is provided with descendants who will recognize it as an ancestor in sacrificial rituals. The practice of appeasing hungry ghosts testifies to the enduring respect for ancestors and sense of obligation to the past within Chinese culture (Potts, 2006, p. 81).

The ghost is a manifestation of the conviction that the past persists in some form within the present. This idea remains strong despite the forces of progress and rationalization within modernity. In the twentieth century, the philosopher Henri Bergson asserted that the present is actually 'the invisible progress of the past gnawing into the future', enduring in consciousness (Bergson, 1919, p. 194). The composer Igor Stravinsky claimed that 'real tradition' is 'a living force that animates and informs the present' (Stravinsky, 1970, p. 57). Most famously, William Faulkner wrote in his 1951 play *Requiem for a Nun*: 'The past is never dead. It's not even past' (Faulkner, 1975, p. 73).

Ghost stories – and the very belief in ghosts – represent various means of keeping the past alive. Haunted houses maintain the memory of former occupants in the minds of the living. Ancestral ghosts vividly preserve the memory of ancestors within families. Territorial ghosts haunting the sites of their fatal accidents serve as memorials and as warnings of dangers implicit in those sites. Ghosts of the unburied or suicides preserve the memory of unhappy lives. Vengeful ghosts perform post-mortal acts of justice. Ghosts appearing to loved ones, or summoned by mediums, function as benevolent memories of the deceased (Finucane, 1982; Tuczay, 2004). These and many other inflections of the ghost keep memories of the past alive in the present.

Past spoken and written

Ghost stories have taken print form, published as short stories or novels, adapted into films. But ghost stories were first told by a story-teller to a group of avid listeners; indeed this continues to be a common experience, as children listen – spell-bound and terrified – to a story-teller of ghost narratives. As a form of folk memory, ghost stories are oral accounts of the past's persistence in the present; this oral memory differs from the written representation of the past also known as history.

History is the narration of past events; it is both a literary genre – deploying the literary technique of narrative – and a discipline whose aim is the objective and truthful account of past events and processes. In the nineteenth century, the discipline of history entrenched methods – such as the reliance on written documents as evidence – meant to facilitate objective and truthful narrations of the past. But the illusions of objectivity and 'truth' in historiography were shattered by wide-ranging critiques in the second half of the twentieth century, most notably in Hayden White's *Metahistory* (1973).

For White, history is not the objective ordering of an empirically recorded past; rather, it is a literary mode founded on rhetorical forms, the most important of which are emplotment and narrative. White (1973, p. 7) identified the various 'narrative tactics' by which historians construct their stories; he also asserted that none of these stories is any more 'true' or valid than others. This relativist refutation of a universal truth to be found in history opened the way for later critiques of official national histories, which seek to build a national identity based on a specific political construction of the past. White criticized these historical narratives, spanning colonial acts of dispossession of native peoples, as representing a 'specifically Western prejudice', through which 'the presumed superiority of modern, industrial society can be retroactively substantiated' (1973, p. 2).

The 'history wars' staged in many Western nations from the end of the twentieth century have involved the contesting of national identity and national history. Orthodox 'text-book' histories and official narratives have been challenged by alternative constructions of national history in a post-colonial context; this jostling of ideas and narratives of history has been one expression of the politics of memory.

In Australia, the history wars focused on the determination by revisionist historians to fully acknowledge the often violent dispossession of Aboriginal peoples by European settlers; this revisionist view of Australian history has been rejected by conservative historians – and conservative politicians. Among the revisionist historians of the left were Henry Reynolds and Robert Manne; prominent conservative historians included Keith Windschuttle and Geoffrey Blainey. Key texts in the debate were Reynolds' book *Why Weren't We Told?* (2000) and Windschuttle's 2002 book *The Fabrication of Aboriginal History*. Blainey coined the pejorative phrase 'black armband view of history' in 1993, a criticism of revisionist histories later adopted by conservative Prime Minister John Howard.

In 1968, the anthropologist W.E.H. Stanner, in his Boyer lectures initially broadcast on ABC Radio Australia, referred to the 'Great Australian Silence' in Australian history. For Stanner, this silence concerned the dispossession of the Indigenous people and their consequent ongoing suffering. Official histories up to that point had recounted the 'discovery' of Australia by Captain Cook in 1770, and the foundation of the British colony in 1788 – including acts of exploration, pioneering and land appropriation – as positive, even heroic, achievements. But subsequent historians took up the challenge identified by Stanner to fill the great Australian silence in its history.

Revisionist histories also sought to include an Aboriginal perspective, in which colonization was regarded as invasion by a European power. This invasion involved violent and murderous frontier conflict with First Nation inhabitants of the continent, and the dispossession of Aboriginal people from the land which they held sacred. While this account of settlement as invasion has been resisted by conservative historians, the historical attempt to eliminate the Indigenous race and culture by other means in the twentieth century has been thoroughly documented.

The 1997 national report to the Australian parliament *Bringing Them Home*, concerning the Stolen Generation, described the forced removal of

Aboriginal children from their families by Federal and State government agencies in the period from around 1905 to the 1970s. These children, many adopted by white families, were expected to assimilate into white society, while it was believed, even by state authorities, that 'the demise of Aborigines was inevitable' (Turcotte, 2009, p. 90) – that is, the Indigenous race was expected to die out. In 2008, the Australian Prime Minister, Kevin Rudd, made an official apology to Aboriginal people for the removal of children from families in the twentieth century.

The contested interpretations of Australian history – including the appraisal of colonization as invasion – have been reflected in the history wars of literary history. The oral memory represented in spoken ghost stories also reflects this turbulent past and the various interpretations of that past.

Aboriginal ghosts

In one important respect, it is inappropriate to use the term 'ghost' in considering Aboriginal beliefs and the spiritual connection of Aboriginal people to the land. Whereas European cultures preserve the idea of the ghost as a supernatural, immaterial entity – even in a largely secular age when religion has lost much of its former influence – Aboriginal religious belief had as its core principle the spiritual infusion of the land. The landscape and everything within it is believed to have been created by spirit ancestors, who maintain a spiritual residence within the land. In this way, the ancestral past lives on in the present, apparent in the very land or 'country' traversed by Aboriginal peoples.

W.E.H. Stanner (1969, pp. 44–45) attempted to explain the spiritual connection of Aboriginal people to the land, but admitted that it was impossible for Europeans to understand the strength of this connection:

> No English words are good enough to give a sense of the links between an aboriginal group and its homeland. Our word 'home', warm and suggestive though it may be, does not match the aboriginal word that may mean 'camp', 'hearth', 'country', 'everlasting home', 'totem place', 'life source', 'spirit centre' and much else all in one...

Stanner went on to indicate the devastating effect on Indigenous peoples when they were dispossessed of their country:

> When we took what we call 'land' we took what to them meant hearth, home, the locus of life, and everlastingness of spirit...every group structure was put out of kilter; no social network had a point of fixture left.

The Indigenous belief in spirit ancestors whose presence could be felt in the surrounding landscape was narrated by story-tellers, handed down as an oral tradition through generations. The spirit-world was also given visual representation in art, which generally served a ceremonial purpose for the benefit of the social group.

Some appreciation of the Aboriginal belief in the spiritual dimension of their land can be gained from a study of traditional Aboriginal painting. Wally Caruana (2003, p. 10) has written of the significance of art for Aboriginal people: 'Art is a means by which the present is connected with the past and human beings with the supernatural world'. Caruana notes that this art, practised for tens of thousands of years, 'activates the power of ancestral beings'; it also 'expresses individual and group identity, and the relationships between people and the land'. The land is thought to be infused by the power of the past, in the form of spirit ancestors who both created the landscape and exist within it.

A traditional Aboriginal painting may depict the country or territory known to a particular social group; but this visual depiction operates on two levels. A painting may denote physical features of that territory such as trees, dunes or waterholes, or it may represent traces of the spirit ancestors within the landscape. Indeed, one pictorial figure may represent both levels at the same time. The painting may be considered a map of the territory, but not in the Western sense of map as cartography. The painting is best understood as a spiritual map, in that it encompasses both the physical and metaphysical characteristics of the land, both its present and its past. Thus, a concentric circle may represent a camp or waterhole; but it may also symbolize the spiritual portal by which the ancestral spirit comes up through the earth. Straight or meandering lines may denote water courses or lightning; they may also trace the previous paths of spirit ancestors or other supernatural beings.

The Aboriginal belief system holds that the land is saturated with spiritual presence. The most important spiritual presence is that of the spirit ancestors but there are many other forms of spirit, some of which approximate the ghosts, fairies or demons of European culture. The mimi spirits, for example, were believed to once take human bodily form, at the time when they taught Aboriginal people the skills of hunting, cooking and painting. The mimis then transformed their shape, becoming extremely thin and elongated – so thin that they need to hide in rock crevices to avoid being blown away by wind. These fairy-like spirits are depicted in some of the oldest Aboriginal rock paintings – dating back 50,000 years – in Kakadu and Arnhem Land. Min min spirits – manifest as balls of light – are another distinctive spirit-formation in Aboriginal mythology.

Other spirit-creatures are less benign. Aboriginal myths narrate the fearsome activities of numerous demons, ghosts and ogres roaming the continent. These spirit beings are often described as hairy, tall, sometimes cannibalistic. The mamu spirits, thought to occupy a region of the Western Desert, are fierce fanged cannibal creatures, whose function in Aboriginal narratives may well be to warn children against venturing into dangerous territory (Nicholls, 2014). These monstrous spirit beings come close to the form of the malevolent ghost in European culture, although 'ghost' is a rather feeble descriptive term to cover the extraordinary range of spirit-beings populating Aboriginal myths.

Following the invasion of the continent by European colonists, ghosts and haunting took on new meanings in Indigenous culture. In his 2006 book *The Other Side of the Frontier: Aboriginal Resistance to the European Invasion of Australia,* Henry Reynolds argued that in many instances, the pale-skinned British arriving in huge ships were mistaken for long-dead Aboriginal ancestors returning to the land. In his essay 'First Nations Phantoms & Aboriginal Spectres', Gerry Turcotte (2009, pp. 95–96) cites Reynolds' research, proposing that the mistaking of 'the white invader body' for a returned spirit ancestor led to 'both overly generous and at times hostile encounters' with whites by First Nations people.

While the white colonists were mis-recognized as spirits – or ghosts – from the ancestral past, Indigenous people themselves soon became spectral presences in the European imagination. White settlers failed to understand or even recognize the rich and ancient Aboriginal culture, and Indigenous ownership of the land was never acknowledged in the form of treaties. Worse, policies to 'dematerialise the first inhabitants' (Turcotte, 2009, p. 95) were enacted by the colonizers: these policies included the massacre of Aboriginal people, most notably in Tasmania; and, later, the 'Stolen Generation' practice of removing Aboriginal children from their families.

This twentieth century policy had a devastating impact on Indigenous families, even if the stolen child eventually returned to its original family. Turcotte quotes the testimony of Zita Wallace, who was taken from her Eastern Arunda family at the age of eight, but managed to return to her home community ten years later:

> I know definitely, with Eastern Arunda people, in our culture when a child is taken away, or lost, or dies, they're not ever allowed to mention that child's name again. So here I am popping up, and so are other children, and we're supposed to be dead. My mother turned around and wouldn't accept me. She just straight out said, 'You're a spirit child. You're not my daughter, you're a spirit child'. And just wouldn't accept me…'comminja', which means I'm past, I'm of the past, I'm not here…
>
> (Turcotte, 2009, p. 97)

The child stolen by whites has become a ghost or spirit child, but one consigned to the past, sealed off from the present. Zita Wallace was only able to overcome this alienation from her own family after ten more years of initiation rituals, enabling her to return to her traditional culture. Immersion within the Indigenous culture – from which she had been forcibly removed – allowed her to shed her spectral identity, so that she was accepted again as a member of her family and culture.

Colonial ghosts

In her essay 'No Longer Malleable Stuff', the Indigenous (Wiradjuri) writer Jeanine Leane seeks to puncture the claims to universality often projected by the 'white imagination'. The expression of white culture, she writes, 'imagines itself as limitless – boundless, colourless, neutral and universal' (Leane, 2020, p. 11). In the Australian context, the white imagination has projected itself into the writing of Australian history. Until recently, the white construction of Australian history offered 'a view from a window which has been carefully placed to exclude a whole quadrant of the landscape' (Stanner, 1969, p. 25). White Australia constructed an image of itself, and of its history, that excluded Indigenous inhabitation of the continent, Indigenous knowledge, culture and custodianship of the land, even Indigenous history.

Remarkably, the European imagination had exercised itself in inventing a fantastic *Terra Australis Nondum Cognita* (Southern Land Not Yet Known) well before the landing of Captain Cook's *Endeavour* in 1770. Turcotte (2009, p. 95) describes the invention of an imagined Antipodean space by Europeans as 'a long legacy of explorers and commentators speculating upon and then outright inventing it, as well as peopling it with monstrous presences well ahead of the continent's actual discovery'. Tragically however, when they actually arrived on the continent in 1770 and 1788, British colonists completely failed to see the Aboriginal culture permeating the Great Southern Land.

The Europeans were only able to recognize culture in the form of written texts and constructs such as buildings; because the First Nations peoples transmitted their cultural knowledge orally, and because they enjoyed a semi-nomadic lifestyle, cultivating the land through means of mobile fire-stick farming, the extraordinarily rich Aboriginal cultures left no visible traces for Europeans to appreciate. For the European invaders, the great southern continent was *terra nullius* – understood as owned by no-one, 'and therefore available for imperial consumption without resort to treaties of any kind' (Turcotte, 2009, p. 96). By defining the continent as null or blank, the colonizers implicitly nullified the Indigenous presence, consigning it to only a spectral, ghost-like presence on the land.

This shockingly blinkered view from a European window has been transformed in recent years, as a growing number of Indigenous voices have been heard – articulating Aboriginal knowledge, culture and history while also offering an alternative perspective on white settler culture. Leane is strident in her accusation that 'theft is culturally ingrained in the modern nation of Australia':

> The invading British diaspora began their history here as thieves of all things Aboriginal, and this intergenerational mentality extends beyond land to all aspects of settler life, and cuts across all facets of modern Australian life and culture. White Australian settler culture is nothing without theft.
>
> (Leane, 2020, p. 12)

This theft 'of all things Aboriginal' also entailed a failure – or refusal – to recognize Aboriginal culture, even the prior Indigenous inhabitation of the land. Colonization in this sense involved an act of erasure of Aboriginal presence and identity.

In their book *Postcolonial Ghosts*, Mélanie Joseph-Vilain and Judith Misrahi-Barak (2009, p. 16) identify colonization as 'a ghostly presence', because 'it turns native peoples and cultures into spectres which haunt both their descendants and those of the conquerors/settlers'. They identify two types of post-colonial ghosts: 'native ghosts looking for recognition or revenge' and 'colonizers' ghosts manifesting the collective guilt of the victors of history'. This sense of white collective guilt for the sins of colonization has been articulated by many Australian writers, often using the language of ghosts and haunting. In her essay 'The Haunting of Settler Australia: Kate Grenville's *The Secret River*' (2009), Sheila Collingwood-Whittick (2009, p. 125) quotes the Australian poet Judith Wright, who declared in 1981 that Australia 'is a haunted country'. Collingwood-Whittick (2009, p. 128) also quotes Ken Gelder and Jane Jacobs, who wrote in 1998 that the process of reconciliation is 'to bring the nation into contact with the ghosts of its past'.

Early Australian settler ghost stories have been collected in a number of compendium volumes; some of these narratives concern the haunting of European society by deceased Indigenous people. In his collection *Australian Ghost Stories*, Frank Cusack includes 'The Black Wraith of Yarralumla', a ghost story dated to the 1840s. In this story, a young Aboriginal man is a tracker, accompanying a white man. The two are attacked by bushrangers seeking a valuable diamond held by the white man. The bushrangers kill the Aboriginal man, who attempted to protect his 'master'; they bury the body under a large deodar tree. Cusack notes that an unsigned document found at Yarralumla, near Canberra, purports to record as fact the murder of the Aboriginal man; the ghost tale of the 'black wraith' emerged as folklore, embellishing the act of murder with a post-mortal haunting. This ghost story describes manifestations of the 'sombre wraith' at the deodar tree, site of the murder; the ghost appears to be 'seeking the lost diamond' (Cusack, 1967, pp. 37–38).

Other Australian ghost stories record, in folkloric terms, the intersection of Indigenous culture and the early colonial experience – in many instances a violent, fatal clash. Some nineteenth century ghost stories describe the interaction of European interlopers – explorers or prospectors – with Aboriginal sacred sites, including burial sites commemorating massacres. Gelder collected numerous stories of this type in *The Oxford Book of Australian Ghost Stories*. In one story – 'The Red Lagoon' – dated 1899, a white bullock driver is disturbed in his sleep at a tranquil lagoon by a bloody vision of a massacre and retribution at that site (Gelder, 1994, pp. 139–141). The lagoon is 'red' because it is a site-specific ghostly memory of murderous conflict, in which local Aboriginal people have been massacred.

In 'The Evil of Yelcomorn Creek', another story from 1899, a white opal prospector and an Aboriginal guide rest at a site called 'Ghost's Glen' (Gelder, 1994, pp. 142–151). A spectral, despairing sound of 'Coo-ee' is heard in the night; this ghostly noise is described as 'a dreadful cry...moaning and writhing away through the air' (p. 150). The white man realizes he has stumbled on an Aboriginal burial site, which he perceives as a taboo, frightening zone. He is unnerved by this glimpse of Aboriginal ancestral dead, realising that he is 'meddling with things beyond my knowledge' (p. 151). He flees the site, abandoning his search for opals.

One of the interesting aspects of 'The Evil of Yelcomorn Creek' and similar Australian ghost stories is that they belie the notion of *terra nullius*, that the land was blank before European colonization. It was assumed by the European invaders that the Aboriginal people had left no imprint on the land – but the ghost stories concerning Aboriginal burial sites and spiritual presence tell a different story. The white trespassers onto Aboriginal sacred sites are made vitally aware of Indigenous presence – and history – on the land. In these ghost stories, the spiritual charge invested in sites like 'Ghost's Glen' functions as more than a marker of territory; it repels the trespassers with the force of terror. Understood in European terms as a haunting, this Indigenous spiritual force banishes the Europeans and their material, pecuniary interests, such as prospecting.

These ghost stories, initially recounted by settlers to an audience of other settlers, convey the idea of European trespass onto Aboriginal land, a concept not implicit in the doctrine of *terra nullius*. The stories have a moral dimension, setting limits on the rapacity of Europeans' land-grabs and their hunt for valuable minerals and natural resources. The ghost stories acknowledge the violent episodes of colonial frontier wars with Indigenous inhabitants, even if the official Australian history of the time did not. In acknowledging sacred Aboriginal sites and their spiritual force, they reveal the Indigenous relationship to the land, previously unseen through colonizers' eyes.

In demonstrating the falsity of the 'blank land' principle, the stories acknowledge the facts of dispossession; in this way, they disclose white settlement as 'fundamentally unsettled' (Gelder, 1994, p. xi). They incorporate the spirits of Aboriginal ancestors into the ghost folklore of settler society, thereby including Indigenous history – if only as a manifestation of white guilt – in the representation of the past as narrated in Australian ghost stories.

A haunted land

There is one other factor lending a distinctive quality to Australian ghost stories: the landscape itself. Australia is a dry continent, with vast deserts occupying much of the interior. The Australian bush is harsh and unvaried by comparison with European forest. The most common tree of the

Australian bush is the eucalyptus or gum tree, an extremely water-resourceful and resilient form of flora. The eucalyptus tree is able to flourish in a dry climate and able to survive ferocious bushfires by shedding charred exterior bark. Of the more than 200 varieties of eucalyptus tree, the most striking is the 'ghost gum', a white vertical shaft adept at reflecting moonlight and catching the eye at night.

The eerie effect of ghost gums at night imbues the landscape with a spectral hue, as described in the nineteenth century ghost story 'The Evil of Yelcomorn Creek'. The narrator of this story finds even the Australian bush troubling. He describes the flora of 'Ghost's Glen' in ghostly, frightening terms: 'every white-waisted gum shot its shadow straight down until it looked as if there was a whole army of ghosts watching the pool' (Gelder, 1994, p. 150). Here, the eucalyptus trees take on the character of a legion of ghosts guarding the waterhole, creating a forbidding sight for the European trespasser.

From the beginning of European settlement, the Australian landscape troubled the settlers due to its stark difference from the English countryside. Turcotte describes one of the earliest paintings of the colony, painted by Thomas Watling (a convicted forger) in 1794. Watling was given the difficult task of transforming the 'unpicturesque landscape of Australia' into a landscape painting 'comprehensible to his majesty' (Turcotte, 2009, p. 98). The painter attempted this feat by including visual features familiar to the British monarch, such as naval officers wearing wigs accompanied by a British wolfhound, while the landscape was softened to approximate the English countryside. Many early colonial paintings superimposed memories of English meadows and lush fields onto the drier and harsher Australian land.

The Great Southern Land soon revealed a suite of dangers to the colonists: venomous snakes and spiders, sharks and crocodiles in the tropical north. The European Australian imagination, mainly exercised from the coastal fringe as colonies grew around the continent, regarded the interior of the country – the outback – with foreboding and distrust. In the nineteenth century, explorers perished in the outback, the most famous failed exploration being the 1861 expedition of Burke and Wills when both explorers died. The European explorers possessed little or no bushcraft and were oblivious to the First Nations experience, which amounted to 60,000 years living on the continent, drawing sustenance from the land – in many cases within the interior.

European Australian culture preserves a mystique, even a fear, of the outback, which is thought to be a zone where humans beings can simply disappear. Joan Lindsay's 1967 novel *Picnic at Hanging Rock* (later adapted into a film and TV series) depicts the disappearance of schoolgirls at the mysterious rock formation in Victoria: it is as if the girls were swallowed by the rock. Real life disappearances in the outback have jostled with fictional representations in the public imagination: in 1980, a baby girl named Azaria

Chamberlain vanished in the Northern Territory. Her mother Lindy was initially found guilty of murder, amid unfounded public speculation that the name Azaria meant 'sacrifice in the wilderness'. Lindy Chamberlain was eventually exonerated when it was proven that Azaria had been taken by a dingo, an Australian wild dog.

In one respect, the European experience in Australia is one of alienation within the land it has colonized. It is not surprising, therefore, that settler ghost stories are often located in the outback or country towns. Dry lakes within the interior, some like Lake Mungo empty for 15,000 years, possess an other-worldly character, their beds dried and exposed to the air. Lake Gardiner in South Australia is reputed to be haunted by the ghost of the failed explorer Ernest Giles (Bull, 2006, p. 98). It is as if the doomed ambition to chart the land has found fitting memorial in a desiccated lake.

Inland plains, traversed by pioneer tracks and then modern roads, are in some cases thought to be haunted. Timothy Bull, in his book *Haunted and Mysterious Australia*, nominates the Monaro Plain in New South Wales (NSW) as a flat stretch of terrain thought to be populated by ghosts hovering off the ground beside the road (Bull, 2006, pp. 48–49). Fictional ghost stories mingle with purported ghost sightings in the public imagination. Frank Cusack reports that in 1957, seven people, including a journalist, claimed to see an apparition on an isolated road near Warrandyte in Victoria. This ghost was described as vapourish, 2 metres tall, silvery-yellow and floating 1 metre off the ground. When a car passed through it, the ghost was described as dissipating above the car, then re-appearing and drifting off into the bush (Cusack, 1967, pp. 176–177). This spectre seems to have absorbed the desolate silence of the landscape itself.

Many abandoned settler towns – 'ghost towns' – are thought to be haunted. Ghost towns attest to the fragility of attempts at civilization in inhospitable territory, known as 'the back of beyond' or the 'middle of nowhere'. Perhaps the ghost inhabitants of these ruined towns serve as remembrance of previous, failed habitation; perhaps they simply provide the ruined environs with some citizens. One Tree Hotel, near Hay in NSW, was once a staging post for Cobb and Co; it is now reputed to be haunted by 'mysterious balls of light' (Bull, 2006, pp. 46–47). The outback Queensland town of Boulia is well known for its 'bouncing balls of unexplained light' (Bull, 2006, pp. 87–89). This haunting phenomenon is known as the Min Min light, after the Aboriginal min min spirits; this is one instance of European and Indigenous cultures finding common expression, as both have believed this site to possess supernatural habitation.

The harsh and forbidding Australian landscape – at least as experienced by the European colonizers – provided an effective context for many of the early settler ghost tales. It should not be forgotten that the settlement established at Sydney in 1788 was a penal colony. The brutal conditions for the first convicts were reflected in the harsh surrounding landscape in ghost stories.

An element of profound injustice attended the lives of convicts transported for life from their homes in England, in many cases for extremely trivial crimes. Convicts were sentenced to seven years in the penal colony of NSW for offences such as stealing a piece of cloth or food. The irrational and disproportionate punishments meted out for these minor crimes were compounded by the reality of a seven-year sentence in the colony: after serving the sentence, it was extremely unlikely that a freed convict could earn the money for a ship's passage back to England. The sentence, in other words, was in effect a life sentence; even more cruelly, such a sentence often meant separation for life of a convict from his young family in England.

A prevailing current of injustice, then, pervaded the colony. Some of the earliest ghost stories emanating from the Australian colonies reflected this sense of injustice, cruelty and suffering. Cusack identifies as 'Queensland's oldest ghost story' a narrative concerning a sadistic commandant named Logan, in charge of the Queensland prison settlement in the 1820s (Cusack, 1967, pp. 124–127). This tale demonstrates a slippage between fact and fiction, including the fact that Logan administered such extreme punishment to one prisoner that the convict died. The fictional colouring of the narrative proceeds as the tale of a haunting: the deceased convict returns as a ghost, tormenting the commandant on his solitary horse rides exploring the bush. The ghost resolutely clings to commandant and horse, terrifying the otherwise fearless military man. Shortly afterwards, the commandant – in real life – disappeared in the bush; he was later found mutilated and beaten to death. The ghost story aspect of the narrative returns with the claim that Logan's body was found near the site where he first encountered the convict ghost. The rough justice incorporated in this early colonial ghost narrative expresses elements of brutality and suffering, characteristic of convict life.

Many of the roads, bridges and walls constructed in the early settlement were built with convict labour. These sites often have ghost stories attached, concerning convicts cruelly overworked or tortured to death. Convicts also built the prisons intended to contain them; these buildings invoke harrowing ghost stories. St Helena Island, a penal colony in Queensland, was known as the 'hell-hole of the Pacific' for its harsh regime; the prison is said to harbour audible moans of the deceased (Bull, 2006, pp. 147–149). Port Arthur in Tasmania, a prison site of brutal punishment and murder, opened in the 1830s; ghosts of deceased convicts were reported to haunt the premises from the 1870s (Bull, 2006, p. 105). These haunted prisons and other sites of cruelty may be regarded as a means – conveyed in folk memory – of preserving a trace of injustices suffered inside the buildings.

Australian ghost stories often involved themes of injustice and retribution, even in post-convict life. The widely known nineteenth century ghost narrative of Fisher's Ghost was a narrative addressing a bad – or unjust – death within settler society. Fisher, an ex-convict who was the first man to attempt to make paper in NSW, mysteriously disappeared in 1826. According to the ghost story, the deceased Fisher manifest as an apparition, dressed as when alive, pointing to a spot on the ground. When this spot was dug up, Fisher's corpse was discovered; it was also clear that he had been murdered. Once the murderer – who had committed the deed to appropriate Fisher's assets – was brought to justice, Fisher's ghost disappeared (Cusack, 1967, pp. 1–3). Narratives such as that of Fisher's Ghost invoke a supernatural force to ensure justice in the mortal world, representing the power of the past to rectify the present. The bad or unjust death that has provoked the haunting must be righted for the ghost to cease its activity.

Australian history, then, in the form of folklore and folk memory, is rife with ghosts. Narratives of ghosts emanating from Aboriginal burial sites mark those sites in a form of folk historical record. Other ghost stories testify to the suffering and injustices of a penal settlement. Ghost stories representing both Indigenous and convict histories within colonial Australia depict forms of shackled identities. Set in the context of an eerie landscape, Australian ghost stories tell narratives of dispossession, guilt, injustice, bad deaths and retribution: all contained in the form of the ghost story that haunts modern-day Australia. It has been argued by proponents of national reconciliation that Australian ghosts will only be put to rest when the guilt of Aboriginal dispossession is overcome through a full political act of reconciliation, in which the sins of the past may be overcome and eventually forgiven. On the other hand, Australian ghosts – as records of horrific deeds in the past – may never be forgotten, as they bear the truth of that sequence of events known as history.

References

Bergson, H. (1896) *Matter and Memory.* Translated by N.M. Paul and W.S. Palmer. London: George Allen & Unwin, 1919.

'Bringing Them Home'. (1997) Sydney: Human Rights and Equal Opportunity Commission [online]. Available at: https://humanrights.gov.au/our-work/bringing-them-home-report-1997 (Accessed: 22 September 2021).

Bull, T. (2006) *Haunted and Mysterious Australia.* Sydney: New Holland.

Caruana, W. (2003) *Aboriginal Art.* London: Thames & Hudson.

Collingwood-Whittick, S. (2009) 'The Haunting of Settler Australia: Kate Grenville's *The Secret River*' in Joseph-Vilain, M. and Misrahi-Barak, J. (eds.) *Postcolonial Ghosts.* Montpellier: Presses Universitaires de la Méditerranée, pp. 125–142.

Cusack, F. (ed.) (1967) *Australian Ghost Stories.* Melbourne: Heinemann.

Faulkner, W. (1975) *Requiem for a Nun.* New York: Vintage. [First published 1951].

Finucane, R.C. (1982) *Appearances of the Dead: A Cultural History of Ghosts.* London: Junction Books.

Gelder, K. (ed.) (1994) *The Oxford Book of Australian Ghost Stories.* Melbourne: Oxford University Press.

Joseph-Vilain, M. and Misrahi-Barak, J. (eds.) (2009) *Postcolonial Ghosts.* Montpellier: Presses Universitaires de la Méditerranée.

Leane, J. (2020) 'No Longer Malleable Stuff', *Overland*, 241, pp. 11–18.

Lindsay, J. (1975) *Picnic at Hanging Rock.* Melbourne: Penguin. [First published 1967].

Nicholls, C.J. (2014) '"Dreamings" and Place –Aboriginal Monsters and their Meanings', *The Conversation*, 30 April. [online]. Available at: https://theconversation.com/dreamings-and-place-aboriginal-monsters-and-their-meanings-25606 (Accessed: 21 May 2021).

Potts, J. (2006) 'The Idea of the Ghost' in Potts, J. and Scheer, E. (eds.) *Technologies of Magic: A Cultural Study of Ghosts, Machines and the Uncanny.* Sydney: Power Publications, pp. 78–91.

Reynolds, H. (2000) *Why Weren't We Told?* Melbourne: Penguin.

Reynolds, H. (2006) *The Other Side of the Frontier: Aboriginal Resistance to the European Invasion of Australia.* Sydney: UNSW Press.

Stanner, W.E.H. (1969) *The Boyer Lectures, 1968.* Sydney: ABC.

Stravinsky, I. (1970) *Poetics of Music in the Form of Six Lessons.* Cambridge: Harvard University Press.

Tuczay, C.A. (2004) 'Interactions with Apparitions, Ghosts, and Revenants in Ancient and Medieval Sources' in Houran, J. (ed.) *From Shaman to Scientist: Essays on Humanity's Search for Spirits.* Lanham: The Scarecrow Press, pp. 97–126.

Turcotte, G. (2009) 'First Nations Phantoms and Aboriginal Spectres: The Function of Ghosts in Settler-Invader Cultures' in Joseph-Vilain, M. and Misrahi-Barak, J. (eds.) *Postcolonial Ghosts.* Montpellier: Presses Universitaires de la Méditerranée, pp. 87–112.

White, H. (1973) *Metahistory.* Baltimore, MD: Johns Hopkins University Press.

Windschuttle, K. (2002) *The Fabrication of Aboriginal History Volume One: Van Diemen's Land 1803–1847.* Sydney: Macleay Press.

4   Ghosts from the future

Post-apocalyptic narratives in Scotland and the displacement of memory

Marie-Odile Pittin-Hédon*

In a 2011 interview, the Scottish writer John Burnside identifies the challenge facing writers and creative artists: 'I still refuse to accept that this way of living is inevitable – and I have one useful tool, Imagination, with which to continue the mental fight' (McCarthy, 2011, p. 26). The goal he sets for artists is to help shape our 'way of living' and not be content with a status quo which is unacceptable to him. His works, and those of many of his contemporaries, reflect this challenge. This chapter examines the recent spate of post-apocalyptic narratives to come out of Scotland and the disjuncture such narratives reflect. John R. Hall insists that apocalypticism arises most forcefully 'when the *present* historical moment is experienced as the ending of the old order and the passage to a new beginning' (Hall, 2009, p. 2) or even more broadly whenever previously 'taken-for-granted understandings of 'how things are' break down' (Hall, 2009, p. 3). This chapter examines precisely the way the present order is challenged in narratives that set the present apart as an object of 'historical' study, either from the future or from other displaced positions that also put the connection between past, present and future to the test. It focuses on six apocalyptic or post-apocalyptic novels, Burnside's *Glister* (2008) and *Havergey* (2017), Jenni Fagan's *The Sunlight Pilgrims* (2016) and Louise Welsh's post-apocalyptic *Plague Times* trilogy *A Lovely Way to Burn* (2014), *Death is a Welcome Guest* (2015) and *No Dominion* (2017), all of which interrogate the social, political or climate disjuncture at work in the present by linking it with a not-so-remote – possibly dystopian – future. In their own ways, they conjure up ghosts from the future to create a defamiliarized vision of identity which is then projected onto our world, our notions of who we are and what we are turning the world into, what 'way of living' we are enforcing. In that sense, the novels are related to Derrida's ethical questioning of what it is to live, which he presents at the outset of *Spectres of Marx*, explaining that 'I would like to learn/teach (*apprendre*) how to live, finally' (Derrida, 1994, p. xvii). The dilemma raised by Derrida is that we cannot know how to live in the present because our lives are not over, while we cannot know how to live when life is over either, because death is not within life. So ethics, or knowing 'how to live, finally' is located in a place that is both life and death, or between

DOI: 10.4324/9781003178040-6

life and death, in spirits or ghosts. In post-apocalyptic novels, the ghosts are situated in an in-between that, interestingly, has seen the future, the post-life/ death moment and are reporting back to the present they have left. All six novels, by being (post)apocalyptic, enact the hauntology postulate, with their main characters, John the Pilot (*Havergey*), Leonard (*Glister*), Stella, Constance and Dylan (*The Sunlight Pilgrims*) and Stevie and Magnus (Welsh's trilogy) acting effectively as ghosts from the future.

Both *Havergey* and *The Sunlight Pilgrims* are set in the future, a very near future in Fagan's novel, which describes a world that has frozen over, and 2050 in *Havergey,* Burnside's examination of the concept of Utopia in a post-apocalyptic environment. *Glister*, though not explicitly set in the future, shows a post-apocalyptic industrial wasteland in which poverty, disease and environmental catastrophes have become the received, unquestioned cultural conditions of everyday life, even to the point that the disappearance and murder of local children becomes mundane and familiar. Welsh's novels examine both the onslaught of the catastrophe when a deadly virus threatens to wipe the earth clean of humans, and the near future, the pandemic's aftermath in the last instalment, which follows the life of a group of self-styled 'survivors' who have taken refuge on the Orkney islands seven years after the pandemic.

All those novels, looking at the present from the vantage point of the future, hinge upon the displacement of memory, the reassessment of identity and history and on the notion of liminality in a world characterized by what historian François Hartog (2012, p. 13) calls presentism, an interminable present that has absorbed past and future. Poised as they are between then and now, between the future and the present, but also between life and death, the novels present a ghostly characteristic quite divorced from the ghost story and its conventional generic features.

The ghost story with its revenant story and the conventional motive of vengeance or protection of one's kin is indeed a constitutive element of Scottish folklore and beyond that, of Scottish identity which has an affinity with the supernatural. Very early on, in the seventeenth century, it was associated with religious guilt as well as with the wilderness of the Scottish countryside, before becoming very popular in the nineteenth century. It is also associated with a very prolific witchcraft literature, a famous example of which is Robert Burns's *Tam O'Shanter*, and with Northern folklore involving selkies and kelpies (creatures from the sea coming to steal humans from the world of the living). In a Scottish context, the ghost story therefore borrows from the spooky story (and the associated theme of hallucinations) as well as a very early interest in the fantastic and the Gothic.[1]

In the six novels, the theme of the return of the ghost or rather more generally the concept of spectrality can be seen not as a return of Scottish ghost stories or as a reactivation of ghoulish narratives of the Mackenzie Poltergeist or the Mysteries of Glamis kind (see Robertson, 1996), but in the sense of granting visibility, of 'exploring and illuminating phenomena' (del Pilar Blanco and Peeren, 2013, p. 2). To start with, none of the novels feature actual ghosts in the conventional sense of the term, since the ghostly characteristic is provided by the visitation from the future. All therefore share a reflection on historicity at a time when Scotland is focused on its own and on British history, and more specifically on the exploration of the present as seen from the future, of what led us to this 'state of living,' with a particular emphasis on the current environmental crisis, all six novels being based on ecological disasters.

In *Apocalyptic Discourse in Contemporary Culture*, Monica Germanà and Aris Mousoutzanis insist on the link between the current global situation and the relevance of apocalyptic and post-apocalyptic motifs to characterize it:

> While the world as we know it has never been free of conflict, pandemics, or natural disasters, such events have been recurrently read as apocalyptic, which, to refer to the two principal meanings of the word apocalypse, reflect the perception of such climactic events both as terminal (e.g., pointing to the end) and revelatory (e.g., disclosing some kind of truth).
>
> (Germanà and Mousoutzanis, 2014, p. 1)

On the other hand, Frank Kermode, in *The Sense of an Ending* (1967), points to an aspect that is crucial in the analysis of Burnside's, Fagan's and Welsh's novels. Discussing postwar literature, Kermode (2000, p. 30) argues that 'the End itself ... loses its downbeat, tonic-and-dominant finality, and we think of it, as the theologians think of Apocalypse, as immanent rather than imminent. Thus ... we think in terms of crisis rather than temporal ends'. Framing the apocalypse in terms of crisis enables us to see post-apocalyptic novels as a renegotiation of a notion used by John Burnside to characterize the present moment, the notion of 'juncture' which, as Ben Davies (2020, pp. 7–8) emphasizes, marks both a space of joining and a time of crisis. All the novels analysed in this chapter are poised at the point of juncture. They present the crisis as a variety of interconnected questions, an eco-crisis, a crisis of memory and representation as well as a political and historical crisis. According to Davies, Burnside's texts 'ask the reader to see and think differently' (2020, p. 4), a judgment that can be extended to Fagan's and Welsh's novels, which conjure up the ghostly to bring the readers to the brink of their existence – or the heart of the crisis – and ask them to reassess the way they relate to their own place in space and time. The novels ask us to inhabit the crisis, the immanent apocalypse in an attempt, to quote Burnside again, to 'refuse to accept that this way of living is inevitable'.

'[T]his is where the future begins: in the forgotten, in what is lost' (Burnside, 2009, p. 1)

In novels of the apocalypse, the problem of time is linked both to a displacement of history and to the impossibility of memory. *No Dominion* emphasizes the fact by placing its 'survivors' in a position that disqualifies history as a valid part of their lives and an understandable source of knowledge:

> History stretched behind them, an infinite past. Literature was fathomless and music had the power to evoke emotions better left buried. It was hard to know where to start and so they let the landscape around them take charge.
>
> (Welsh, 2017, p. 2)

Setting aside for the moment the interesting and very Burnsidian statement that when history ceases to operate, one can only fall back upon the land, which replaces problematic temporality with permanence, what this indicates is that time has ceased to function for the survivors. Memories are reduced to the status of ghostly apparitions, as they 'only truly came alive when [the children] were asleep, surfacing in dreams that woke their households and vanished upon waking' (Welsh, 2017, p. 1). The survivors locked in a presentist temporal framework, the collapse of the idea of progress in the twentieth century, means that we can no longer see history as future-oriented, as a process which can be altered by human actions. For Leonard in *Glister:*

> There *is* no afterlife because there *is* no after. It's always now, and everything –past and future, problem and resolution, life and death – everything is simultaneous here, at this point, in this moment.
>
> (Burnside, 2009, p. 2)

The other novels, though not as radical as *Glister* here, all question the effect of the everlasting present: in *No Dominion,* the result of the apocalypse is a societal and political crisis, with the protagonists reduced to exploring the territories outside of the island only to discover that the communities they find there are only versions of political organizations of the past that have all failed dramatically, therefore validating Hartog's hypothesis of the present that has engulfed past and future. In *The Sunlight Pilgrims*, the world is heading towards an ecological catastrophe that, in the manner of the giant iceberg heading for the coasts of Scotland, cannot be averted. *Glister* and *Havergey* both stress that the ecological crisis has finally rendered human efforts irrelevant. In all the novels, there seems to be no 'after' in any real sense, even if their open endings allow for moderate optimism. What is stressed instead is humans' lack of agency, the powerlessness of the protagonists to do anything to avert the final catastrophe. Leonard again:

> The bad people win and the rest pretend that they haven't noticed what's going on, to save face. It's hard to admit that you're powerless, but you have to get used to the idea.
>
> (Burnside, 2009, p. 81)

Here, what is fatalistically emphasized is the epistemological fracture created by the fact that the world is no longer a common world, a fact which makes it impossible for us to find meaning in our relation to it. Michaël Fœssel (2012, pp. 15–19) calls that an incapacity to 'faire monde'. For Jean-Paul Engélibert (2020), this incapacity is accompanied by a crumbling of order, an important addition which restores a political dimension to a crisis which is *essentially* political. This is made obvious in all the novels: in *Havergey*, the catastrophe that hits the world is called 'The Collapse'; *No Dominion* presents a world which resorts to the classic return to pre-industrial, pre-civilization political systems (feudalism, clannism, religious sects); *Glister* introduces a remote political power characterized by its corrupt nature (embodied in one villainish local industrial tycoon turned political leader); *Havergey* briefly attempts the anarchist route in a pedestrian pastiche of an anarchist play, while in *The Sunlight Pilgrims,* a feeble government appears in extremis only to prove how ineffective it is faced with the upcoming apocalypse. The collapse of all systems is summed up by a lawless character from *No Dominion*:

> 'We've heard tales of tribes forming, territories being claimed. I'd hoped some kind of order was reasserting itself.'
> Belle's expression was grave. 'There is some kind of order, but not the kind I'm guessing you were hoping for.'
>
> (Welsh, 2017, p. 64)

The bleak conclusion one can draw from the Collapse, or the collapse of order as depicted in all six novels is, as Engélibert (2013, p. 179) states, the human propensity to recreate mechanisms of domination, in the process creating a dynamic that leads to a fatalistic resignation to a re-instatement of order. As Leonard puts it in the quotation above, 'you have to get used to the idea'. In such a bleak context, memory and history are displaced in a ghostly re-enactment of the collapse of order.

Ghosts from the future: post-apocalypticism and the indictment of the present

The presentist vision that is conveyed in the novels takes the shape of an uncertain temporality in which the future colonizes the present, turned into an unchangeable past. Instead of agency, the novels foreground liminality, in the shape of many ghostly figures which come to occupy the narratives. Soon after the onset of the Sweats pandemic in *A Lovely Way to Burn* (Welsh, 2014, pp. 272, 316) and *Death is a Welcome Guest* (Welsh, 2015, p. 104), zombie-like victims people the streets of London; in *Havergey*, characters long dead make their appearance in the story through the Archive, a miscellany of letters, documents, reports and journals; the Moth Man in *Glister*, whose role it is to accompany the young men through death, is also one such eerie figure. Liminality is also conveyed by a light and darkness symbolism: *The Sunlight Pilgrims,* as indicated by its title, is a novel about looking for light, the one condition of survival (Fagan, 2016, p. 51); in *Havergey,* the Collapse is also known as 'the dark times', the time when 'the world went dark' (Burnside, 2017, p. 37). Finally, liminality is best represented by 'the Portal' in *Glister,* which serves, like the various ghostly figures, as a conceptual metaphor in the sense of a discourse, a system of producing knowledge (see del Pilar Blanco and Peeren, 2013, pp. 1–2), here a vehicle that can carry the readers across time, criss-crossing present, past and future in an attempt to represent as well as go beyond presentism.

In all our novels, the consequence of presentism and of the collapse of order, takes the shape of an indictment of the present – the NHS and its inability to stem the spread of the deadly virus in *A Lovely Way to Die,* but also its soul-destroying wilful ignorance of the plight of transgender people told that their case will have to wait until 'really' sick people have been attended to in *The Sunlight Pilgrims* (Fagan, 2016, p. 203), transphobia (*The Sunlight Pilgrims*), ruthlessness and violence, the descent of the civilized world into chaos (*Plague Times* trilogy). But the most severe indictment is that of the damage humans are doing to the environment – the Anthropocene motif – , which gives the apocalypse an ecopolitical dimension. *Glister,* described by Burnside himself as 'an environmentalist's book' and 'an ecocritical book' (Davies, 2020, p. 134), depicts a world where the traces of industrial pollution transform 'the poison wood' (Burnside, 2009, p. 16) and the whole of the Innertown into a world of death:

> You could see evidence wherever you looked of the plant's effects on the land: avenues of dead trees, black and skeletal along the old rail tracks and access roads; great piles of sulphurous rocks where pools of effluent had been left to evaporate in the sun.
>
> (Burnside, 2009, p. 11)

In *The Sunlight Pilgrims,* a character named 'Crisp Man' describes climate change as an act of terrorism:

> We're a race of zombies fucking the earth into oblivion. Fucked-up. Beheading people like it's Bingo! Look, Mum, see me on the internet with this bloke's head in my hand and a big-fucking-knife! Say cheese! Woo hoo. It's fucking trigger-happy time mate. That shit's a medieval bloodbath.
>
> (Fagan, 2016, p. 18)

But, of course, it is in *Havergey* that one finds the most sustained and uncompromising attack on the way we have wreaked destruction on the earth: it contains a chapter-length diatribe against wind turbines, concluding with the words 'Oh! The stupidity of it all!' (Burnside, 2017, p. 155), and identifies the damage done to the land as the single reason for the Collapse:

> The unbearable shame of what we'd done and were continuing to do to the land, to the oceans, to other species, to — well, everything.
>
> (Burnside, 2017, p. 27)

As a result, the ghosts from the future bring back to the present a vision of the world that is seen as a deadly open trap: the world, in *A Lovely Way to Burn*, is poised on the brink of a chasm:

> suddenly she felt as if the wakening streets around her were an illusion that might be peeled back any time, to reveal another, shadow world that could suddenly drag you under without a by-your-leave.
>
> (Welsh, 2014, p. 127)

Only the wide-open darkness that awaits Stevie here, and also John the Pilot after the Collapse, is of our own doing. It is the world that none of the characters can relate to, a collapse of order, and an affront to memories from the future.

Restoring time

What the novels are doing, therefore, is to underline the limits of presentism by showing that humans have little or no control over a political, social and historical environment that, having absorbed past, present and future, has taken on the static, unproductive shape of crisis. This is particularly obvious in Welsh's trilogy, which resorts to another genre – that of crime fiction – to try and shake off the apathy of the presentist postulate. All three novels are about a murder which Stevie and Magnus, together or separately, try to solve. The conventions of crime fiction, which rely on the linearity of time for the detective to solve the murder, is an attempt to jumpstart the apocalyptic world and restore temporality. However, their desperate attempts to travel in space (in London, from London to the North and then from Orkney to Glasgow) result in a restoration, not of chronology in the usual sense of the term, but in a different perspective on immanence. For Engélibert (2020, p. 245), the immanence of the apocalypse also makes it possible to restore history within presentism, because it shows an apocalyptic present, meaning a present that is determined by its own end. It is what Georgio Agamben (2005, p. 62) calls the time that remains, or 'messianic time', when he claims that:

> What interests the apostle is not the last day, it is not the instant in which time ends, but the time that contracts itself and begins to end … or if you prefer, the time that remains between time and its end.

The very postulate on which Welsh's trilogy is based, helped by the introduction of the genre of the thriller, is that of the contraction of time: Stevie, in *A Lovely Way to Burn,* contrasts the meaningless finality of death by the Sweats to her boyfriend's murder, which 'might be unravelled' (Welsh, 2014, p. 112), and she engages in a race against the contraction of time represented by the spread of the pandemic. In *The Sunlight Pilgrims,* the time that remains is represented by the government's desperate attempts to neutralize the approaching iceberg, and by the placing of the entire narrative within that interval in time. *Havergey,* on the other hand, is based on the reverse postulate, which in fact comes to the same idea of foregrounding messianic time to supersede apocalyptic time. The main protagonist is a time traveller whose mission is to save the present by looking for a solution to climate change in the future. His very mission is to exploit that contraction of time, the interval between the crisis and the end. The place he inhabits once he has reached the island is also an interval, in space – a quarantine zone –, and time – throughout the novel, he is about to enter the world of Havergey but is instead steeped into the island's past through the Archive. The chapter titles foreground the narrator's status as inhabiting an interval. They alternate John's own comments, logged in the 'Pilot's notebook', and the Archive, with its 'Scholar's book', 'autobiography of John the Gardener' and Chloë's narrative. Interpolated between those narratives are short pieces under the title 'quarantine', which act as a constant reminder that the whole narrative, the title of which is 'Havergey', is situated in an interval, a period borrowed from time and necessarily temporary, but opening up the possibility for a future, a (hypothetical) moment at the end of the quarantine for which one is to get ready by mastering the narratives of the past.

It is noteworthy that the *Plague Times* trilogy also includes quarantine, and that the plot of *The Sunlight Pilgrims* focuses on a small, isolated community in the Scottish Highlands, therefore insisting on the necessity for stories to be located not just after the end of the world but, in order to restore time and the possibility for a future, in an interval that is set aside, between the catastrophe and the end. As John the Pilot says when required to tell Ben a story about himself, '[t]hat's the thing about the life to come: it turns up in the most unlikely places, when you least expect it' (Burnside, 2017, p. 122). But the message is one of cautious optimism, as the passage from presentism to messianic time is just an opportunity to question recent history, in particular our political, economic and ecological footprint.

The ghosts from the future convey the persistence of traces of the past whose imprint on the present cannot be eradicated, as Crisp Man puts it in *The Sunlight Pilgrims,* but also Leonard in *Glister,* and the various figures whose texts constitute the archive from the future in *Havergey* contend. Consequently, if, as Engélibert (2020, p. 250) explains, closing the present by placing it under the dominance of the apocalypse is a way of using its immanence to open up the possibility of the future, the question that remains is how to use the benefit of hindsight offered by the futuristic postulate to change the present? This question is a programmatic statement, made more or less clearly in all the post-apocalytic novels under consideration in this chapter. It is represented metaphorically by the time capsule, called 'Tardis B', which conveys the pilot to Havergey, while the challenge, clearly expressed in the narrative, consists in conveying what he has learned from the future back to the present.[2]

So now, what?

Faced with the destruction of 'the Land', the damage we have caused ourselves and to our environment, and with the challenge which the carrying of information from the future represents, the task set by the narrator in *Havergey* (Burnside, 2017, p. 63) is clear:

> We needed a time of unlearning; we got a time of forgetting. Now, having forgotten so much, we have to go back and reiterate the obvious.

It is to exploit circularity and use the time that remains to start over.

No New Jerusalem, new nomadism

With the emphasis on the restoration of time, in order for the ghosts of the future to attempt to travel back to the present, it follows that the apocalypse which is presented in the six novels is an apocalypse without a New Jerusalem. The biblical safe place is parodied in *Death is a Welcome Guest*. The 'elect' are a motley crew that includes two self-proclaimed 'priests', two escaped convicts and an innocent girl named Belle, who appears again in *No Dominion* as the leader of a gang of robbers and child abductors, and the grand finale stages the public execution of father Jacob Powe's presumed murderer and the (attempted) mass poisoning of all who attend. In *Glister,* the Innertown is hardly a model of a safe haven in spite of its seclusion, while Havergey, like Orkney, plays on the idea of the remote Scottish island to suggest a sort of Paradise Lost rather than a New Jerusalem, a place in which violence in various forms catches up with the characters.

In the absence of a New Jerusalem, the characters in all the novels are turned into wanderers, introducing the figure of the nomad. In *The Sunlight Pilgrims,* in which the catastrophe is under way, the nomad is the conventionally stigmatized figure:

- – Those of you living nomadically will be particularly vulnerable.
- – Where's the nomads, like?
- – We mean the caravan community of course – you all know that's what I meant.
- – We urnay nomadic, pal, our caravans are static

(Fagan, 2016, pp. 105–106).

But post-catastrophe, the figure is implicitly or explicitly valued. It is after all as political and historical nomads that Stevie and Magnus travel through a post-apocalyptic Scotland in *No Dominion,* and the biblical association with the novel's title, the quote from Romans 6:9 which claims that 'the dead dieth no more' seems to programme their wandering positively. The figure of the nomad is even posited as the agent of the new beginning in *Havergey,* as Ben tells the traveller about his 'uncle, who was the one of the first nomads to venture north after the last great plague was finally over' (Burnside, 2017, p. 15), making nomadism the one dynamic symbol that can end the stagnation of time contained in the apocalypse. At the end of *Glister,* Leonard imagines a group of revolutionary nomads, moving from place to place and trying to live a new kind of life, and he has a sort of epiphany in which he claims that he is going to 'drive off, be a nomad, get away from here' (Burnside, 2009, pp. 192–193). Nomadism is therefore an important answer to the question raised by the ghosts from the future, or the scavengers of memories. Nomadism is both spatial and temporal, not just because the characters have been placed in the future, but because they have been strategically used by the narratives to be metaphors for the restoration of historicity by turning the referential present into the past.

Writing about Burnside's poetry in the critical volume edited by Ben Davies, Monika Szuba insists on the importance of the Heideggerian concept of dwelling, which she paraphrases as 'to be situated, to maintain a relationship with the world' (Szuba, 2020, p. 40). In *Havergey* (Burnside, 2017, p. 26), John the Pilot reverses the usual postulate of a place that belongs to someone, recognizing that 'Now I belong to Havergey', and by effectively dwelling on the island. In *The Sunlight Pilgrims* (Fagan, 2016, p. 265), this translates into the figure of the old man in the caravan park making no distinction between human and non-human, and claiming that the sky is 'his wife' (Fagan, 2016, p. 290). The nomadic figures who travel in time, relentlessly seeking to ascertain their connection to the world in this catastrophic era, have to realize that, contrary to the vision provided by the topos of the New Jerusalem, our place in the world is as provisional as the world itself, as Burnside puts it in a poem published in *The Light Trap.* The 'glimpse of something' (Burnside, 2002, p. 62) which characterizes our place in the world is, in fact, a very good description of *Havergey*, and because of the post-apocalyptic stance, the writing from the future postulate, this reading of *Havergey* in the light of Burnside's poetry enables us to think about our future world as a possibility, maybe a future to be desired even if, as Ben reminds the reader in an echo of the poem's last line, 'balance is always temporary. Provisional' (Burnside, 2017, p. 96). Therefore, in order to imagine a future, one has to fill the gap, the 30 years left out by the novel, in order to make the vision of *Havergey* a reality rather than a ghostly appearance, an island situated in some unchartered future. Our task, as readers of the novel, is to make sure we can fill in that blank, that void created in history by the futuristic stratagem, and fill it with the necessary actions to make Havergey happen. It is a political imperative steeped in deep ecology.

The ecopolitics of wandering

For Burnside, the ecopolitical message is clear: what is needed is a change of perspective on the very notion of history, a way to decentre ourselves, to steer clear of the anthropomorphic vision of the universe, to admit our creaturely status. In *Havergey*, the decentring is made obvious:

> To step off the boat at the island of Havergey is to come to a place that is, as the cliché goes, steeped in history, but it is not the history that we learned in school. […] Here, history is concealed in the land. […] Havergey has more to do with the natural world, with what you might call natural history, than the human, and when the human intrudes, it feels like something from an Arthurian romance, which isn't officially history.
>
> (Burnside, 2017, p. 134)

With the idea that history is concealed in the land, an idea which is also present at the beginning of *No Dominion*, comes a shift in perspective, the very shift that Christian Chelebourg sees at work in ecofiction:

> Ecofiction is not a literary or cinematographic genre; it is a way to resonate with the imagination of a period fascinated with its power and terrified by a future in which it can only read promises of decline.
>
> (2012, p. 229, my translation)

In this respect, all of the novels under consideration are ecofictional, in the sense that they foreground the decline of our world and the perspective of decline embodied in the various versions both of our future and of our past. Emily Horton (2014) reads *Glister* as using the Gothic sublime in an attempt to prompt ecological awareness. Fagan also stresses the urgency of this awareness when she claims that 'we're living on a planet, and our lives are very short' (Evans, 2016). This reading goes back to the time that remains and the messianic vision of time that is presented in apocalyptic works, and which finds a resonance in deep ecology. The necessity to preserve the earth as a means of survival is also put very forcefully in *The Sunlight Pilgrims*:

> The earth strikes back! … It's had enough of our bullshit, we're broken. All the way down to the bone. If human bones were rock, that's what it would say right through the middle – broke as-fuck-idiots-cunts-exterminate-exterminate.
>
> (Fagan, 2016, p. 17)

Havergey, like *The Sunlight Pilgrims,* has a culprit: the present generation, the generation that wreaks the most damage on the earth thanks to their exclusive reliance on science and their ignorance of the Land. *Havergey* has a name for them/us: the Machine People. John the Gardener's father, also named John,[3] 'used to say that he could see fairies. Scholars describe those fairies and selkies and kelpies, the spirit of the place, the genius loci' (Burnside, 2017, pp. 132–133). What *Havergey* is doing is to stress the necessity to go back to basics, the kelpies and selkies of Scottish folklore here, to 'reiterate the obvious' after a time of forgetting symbolized by the time capsule; in the case of *Havergey,* a return to the magic of place. In *No Dominion,* reiterating the obvious takes the shape of a new 'reading' of the world, quite literally:

> In the end they had agreed to burn down the capital of the island, Kirkwall. They had given themselves two weeks to strip the place of useful goods. Stevie had assigned herself to a team clearing the library. They had loaded the books willy-nilly onto vans, not bothering to distinguish by title. Who could say what would prove useful? A detective novel might spark a thought process that inspired the invention of a new form of fuel; a cookery book might spawn a cure for bronchitis.
>
> (Welsh, 2017, p. 35)

So, the ghosts from the future can be seen, not just as spectres criss-crossing the time that remains but also more positively as nomads in time, seeking to reintroduce a dynamic value to historiography.

Nomadism in time: the renegotiation of historiography

What emerges of the new method of using books salvaged from destruction in *No Dominion* is the idea, expressed by Engélibert (2013, p. 179), that the restoration of order in post-apocalyptic fiction rests on the implementation of a new kind of order. In the case of the six novels, it is a kind of order that would reassess our place in nature. In the Archive, the documents of history *par excellence*, there's no order, either chronological or order of prevalence. There is no hierarchy. The diary of John the Gardener and Chloë's 'charming attempts at a topographical description' – a patronizing description which signals its secondary status as archive material – turn out to be the most important texts, those that both explain the past and trace a path for the future. What is given pride of place in the Archive is not the Head of State, the despotic aristocrat, not even the Scholar, but the gardener, and maybe beyond the gardener, the element that the novel repeatedly goes back to – the land. Memory and history in this case disrupt the usual clichés on belonging, identity and, ultimately, political existence. They lead us back to ourselves, in the here and now, with a message from the future, from Tardis/(*plus) tard*, that history is ultimately not a power game, but that it is the history of the elements, of nature, and that man's place in it is not one of pre-eminence.4 Instead, what is suggested is a kind of community that emphasizes the *historical* continuity between the human and the non-human. 'Here, history is concealed in the land' (Burnside, 2017, p. 135), Chloë claims, while Stella in *The Sunlight Pilgrims* speaks of the earth's insurance policy in the face of the Anthropocene:

- So if winter has come to us now from millions of years ago, then time-travel is really possible. If the world has 15 million years of frozen geology there and it can enter the present and melt and bring forth another Ice Age, then it's like the planet has kept them as an insurance system.
- Insurance against what?
- Humans.

(Fagan, 2016, p. 299)

What the ghosts from the future, or the survivors, or the gardeners and pilots of this world are telling us is that in order to escape from the presentist dead end, we need to focus on discourse, more precisely on ordering the facts of the past into a narrative. Historical method is to be replaced by historiography, because historiography can move backwards; it can start from the future and work its new way towards the present. In the interview already quoted, Burnside speaks of art as a renegotiation of historiography, when he claims that it is 'a model of order, a world view [that] proposes an alternative to the disinformation and lies that permeate the atmosphere we grow up in' (McCarthy, 2011, p. 33), an alternative to what he calls the 'Authorised Version' which Ruth Cain paraphrases as 'a Bible of disappointment and lowered expectations, composed of restrictive class and gender mythologies, social and ecological violences, and convenient (often religious, but also cultural and political) lies' (Cain, 2020, p. 68). This vision goes back to Chloë's description of history as an exercise in power. The new discourse of historiography would include the land (Burnside), a reordering of the facts and stories compiled in books (Welsh) and stories based on different, more inclusive discourses for Fagan (2016, p. 105): 'My name is Constance. I would like to see texts in the library addressing issues of intolerance, hate-based crimes, and ignorance of anything different'.

The stakes are indeed high, as is indicated by the name given to the people who have found refuge on Orkney in *No Dominion* ('the survivors'), by the emphasis on survivalism in *The Sunlight Pilgrims* and by the breathless race against death presented in the pandemic trilogy: it is a question of survival.

The new community

The goal of the quarantine period in *Havergey* is twofold: it affords time for the visitor from the past to acquaint himself with the history of Havergey, the disparate, piecemeal basis of which is reminiscent of the way history is reinvented in *No Dominion*, and it gives the pilot time to assess whether he is ready to enter the community. According to Angharad, 'we must think of community first. You may be part of that community, but I don't know, yet, if that's the case' (Burnside, 2017, p. 149). The type of community which she has in mind is by necessity altered by the experience of the apocalypse (as the Orkney people too discover for themselves). It is what philosopher Jean-Luc Nancy calls an 'inoperative community'. Nancy published his essay *La communauté désoeuvrée* in 1986, in the wake of the collapse of the communist regimes of the world. He wrote it in order to rethink the meaning of the word 'community' in the face of the paradigmatic changes that were occurring and that were emptying the word of its meaning. Nancy rejects two philosophical avenues: the first one, the total fusion of individuals in the collective – chosen by fascism – the second, that of identity, which indicates that the individual is self-sufficient. Instead, he opts for a 'communauté désoeuvrée', or 'inoperative community' in the 1991 translation, to refer, not to a community that would be dysfunctional or failing, but rather 'a spontaneous, or 'unworked' inclination to come together that has no object or purpose other than itself' (Oxford reference, np). The community is a coming together motivated by a passion for sharing, 'a passion of and for community' (Nancy, 1991, p. 34). Borrowing from Bataille and Blanchot, Nancy adds that what links a community of living beings together and prompts them to open up to the other is the prospect of death.

Burnside's (2017, p. 17) own definition of community occurs early on in Havergey:

> A community is strengthened when its people deal with hardship together. … we are reminded once again how much we need one another.

In addition, *Havergey*'s third governing principle is a spiritual principle called 'interanimation' (Burnside, 2017, p. 50), meaning the mutual animation of all species, weather, atmosphere, rock and stone and tree, a principle according to which 'everything is not so much connected as continuous' (2017, p. 51) – an inoperative community. The pilot's insistence on death defines the community, as does the symbolism of locking up a character until he is ready to enter a different world, a world that, though it cannot be found on any maps as is indicated by the author's note placed as an epigraph to the novel, is much more real than the ghostly 'Scotland' buried in the vague memory of a man trying to recapture pre-apocalyptic times. It is the new world, or rather the new paradigm that Burnside is trying to conjure up in this novel, the new community, in Nancy's sense of the term, which is an outgoing, a sharing of nature, between people who know that they are mortal, by people at the other end of the spectrum from the seemingly indestructible 'Machine People' of yore, that is of our present times. What is required by Burnside in *Havergey* is no less than a change of paradigm, because the world has once again shifted since the watershed historical moment examined by Nancy. It is a shift just as significant and as global as the fall of the communist regimes: the Anthropocene.

As a result, for Burnside, the answer to the devastation brought about by history can be provided by Utopia, but Utopia of a very special kind – a state of mind based on the idea of community, with each individual symbolically being filtered through to a place where, having been quarantined, set aside to ponder about the history of the community they're about to enter, and having reflected upon the errors of their ways, can decide freely to enter the new, utopian-inspired community of like-minded people. Yet, the fundamental question raised by the book is, can John the Pilot bring the method back to the past? Can the future imprint the past, and can history be a movement back from the future?

Angharad tells the pilot that they can't let him go back now, and then, in an elliptical speech, she creates a gap in the past that he crossed in his machine, and reveals that it is a void, filled with death and destruction. She does that in a discursive way, by means of using past tenses that indicate that the people he wants to go back to are no longer there. The apocalypse that John escaped through travelling in time did happen; yet, it is only made real to him in her words:

> 'Well, all those people,' she said. 'The fact that everyone you know…' …
> 'They would have loved. They would have had children. How did it feel, to die, and not be able to explain to your children that it didn't matter? Or rather that it wouldn't matter if those children could love their own lives – full lives, lives rich in memory and forgetting…'
>
> (Burnside, 2017, p. 150)

So, balance *is* provisional in the end; the catastrophe, placed in an ellipsis throughout the book resurfaces at the end of the novel as the one survivor, the pilot, is about to have to decide whether he wants to enter Havergey. He cannot go back, only forward. The past, which is our present, has deprived him of options (a message that Burnside insists on, again and again). And in order to enter the inoperative community, he must be prepared to 'think like a gardener' (Burnside, 2017, p. 151), because 'What matters to us now, and to you, is that Havergey is a garden' (Burnside, 2017, p. 151). This signals the necessity to move beyond Utopia at this point. As Angharad points out, 'For us, Utopia is neither here nor there' (Burnside, 2017, p. 151). It is time to make the no-place into an actual place, with an emphasis on soil and the organic (garden), time to re-establish political priorities: the tyrant has rightly been replaced by a gardener. In the same way in Louise Welsh's novels, feudal lords, sectarian leaders, contemporary ruffian politicians who invite comparison with very recent political leaders are defeated and left behind by ordinary heroes, a TV presenter and a comedian. In *Havergey,* this turning of utopian space into actual place is made clear – retrospectively – by the initial author's note (2017, p. 7) which claims that '[t]hough it does not feature on any maps that have yet been drawn up, Havergey is, nonetheless, as real a place as any, and a good deal more real than some'. And it looks back to our own era, the era the pilot comes from, operating the connection between the past and the future, placing the present as we know it in a position to be history:

> 'There was a time, back in your era.' She considered a moment. 'He said that the catastrophe that threatens a degrading society is not its punishment, but its remedy.'
>
> (Burnside, 2017, p. 151)

Conclusion

The ending of *Death is a Welcome Guest* pictures Magnus going north, with hope; at the end of *The Sunlight Pilgrims,* the three protagonists huddle together, having successfully managed to create and extend the community. As to *Havergey:*

> Havergey is a wonderful place, and we have a wonderful community here. It's not like the old days, when community was just a political word. We really do have something here? Everything is shared. We don't own property individually, other than a few mementoes? What we do have is our bodies, and our ability to be well, sometimes in harsh conditions.
>
> (Burnside, 2017, p. 41)

This is a very good equivalent of Nancy's definition of community as made up of separate but interconnected beings. So, the hope that the nomadic ghosts have successfully brought back from the future is a hope in a present/ future of interconnection – a juncture –, abolishing the old/present political and social hierarchies in favour of a new inoperative community. In creating various versions of the ghost from the future, the three novels manage to use time to their advantage, as they manage to re-channel history and its attendant description of identity, opening up possibilities of being. Catastrophe is indeed a remedy which, by reversing the working of memory, can be seen as a tool that reconciles the future with the present, and reconfigure our sense of our present identity. After a time of forgetting, it is indeed high time we should, with John Burnside, Jenni Fagan and Louise Welsh, reiterate a not so obvious.

Notes

* Marie-Odile Pittin-Hédon, Aix Marseille Univ, LERMA, Aix-en-Provence, France.

1 On the topic of Scottish ghost stories as well as their rewriting in modern and contemporary fiction, see Monica Germanà (2009).
2 The very name of the time capsule, which contains the French word for 'late', 'tard', however seems to suggest that it might be too late already, while the reference to *Dr Who* places it firmly within a science fiction context, therefore also questioning its actuality in the real world.
3 Both characters and the author share the first name, suggesting a collapse of the various identities into one, a sort of universal representation of humanity.

References

Agamben, G. (2005) *The Time That Remains: A Commentary on the Letter to the Romans.* Translated by P. Dailey. Stanford, CA: Stanford University Press.

Burnside, J. (2002) *The Light Trap.* London: Jonathan Cape.

Burnside, J. (2009) *Glister.* London: Vintage. [First published 2008].

Burnside, J. (2017) *Havergey.* Beaminster: Little Toller Books.

Cain, R. (2020) '"This Learned Set of Limits and Blames": Masculinity, Law and Authority in the Work of John Burnside' in Davies, B. (ed.) *John Burnside, Contemporary Critical Perspectives.* London: Bloomsbury.

Chelebourg, C. (2012) *Les Écofictions: mythologies de la fin du monde.* Bruxelles: Les Impressions Nouvelles, pp. 67–80.

Davies, B. (ed.) (2020) *John Burnside, Contemporary Critical Perspectives.* London: Bloomsbury.

del Pilar Blanco, M. and Peeren, E. (eds.) (2013) *Spectralities Reader: Ghosts and Haunting in Contemporary Cultural Theory.* London: Bloomsbury.

Derrida, J. (1994) *Spectres of Marx: The State of the Debt, the Work of Mourning, and the New International.* Translated by P. Kamuf. London and New York: Routledge.

Engélibert, J.-P. (2013) *Apocalypses sans Royaume: Politique des fictions de la fin du monde, XXe-XXe siècles.* Paris: Classiques Garnier.

Engélibert, J.-P. (2020) 'La littérature contemporaine devant la catastrophe. Messianisme et apocalypse immanente chez Margaret Atwood, Don DeLillo, Antonio Saramengo et Antoine Volodine' in Machinal, H., Michlin, M. and Regnaud, A. (eds.) *Apocalypse.* Paris: Kimé, pp. 243–262.

Evans, K. (2016) 'Looking for Light in Darkness: A Q&A with Jenni Fagan' in *Brooklyn* [online]. Available at: http://www.bkmag.com/2016/10/12/looking-light-darkness-qa-jenni-fagan-sunlight-pilgrims-the-panopticon/ (Accessed: 5 February 2022).

Fagan, J. (2016) *The Sunlight Pilgrims.* London: William Heinemann.

Fœssel, M. (2012) *Après la fin du monde: Critique de la raison apocalyptique.* Paris: Seuil.

Germanà, M. (2009) 'Embodying the Spectral Self: The Ghost Motif in Scottish Women's Writing', *The Bottle Imp*, 6 [online]. Available at: https://www.thebottleimp.org.uk/2009/11/embodying-the-spectral-self-the-ghost-motif-in-scottish-womens-writing/ (Accessed: 21 December 2021).

Germanà, M. and Mousoutzanis, A. (2014) *Apocalyptic Discourse in Contemporary Culture.* New York: Routledge.

Hall, J.R. (2009) *Apocalypse: From Antiquity to the Empire of Modernity?* Malden, MA: Polity Press.

Hartog, F. (2012) *Régimes d'historicité : présentisme et expériences du temps.* Paris: Seuil. [First published 2003].

Horton, E. (2014) 'The Postapocalyptic Sublime: A Gothic Response to Contemporary Environmental Crisis in John Burnside's Glister (2008)' in Germanà, M. and Mousoutzanis, A. (eds.) *Apocalyptic Discourse in Contemporary Culture*. New York: Routledge, pp. 71–86.

Kermode, F. (2000) *The Sense of an Ending: Studies in the Theories of Fiction*. Oxford: Oxford University Press. [First published 1967].

McCarthy, P. (2011, Spring/Summer) 'Interview with John Burnside', *Agenda: Dwelling Places. An Appreciation of John Burnside*, 45(4)/46(1), pp. 22–38.

Nancy, J.-L. (1986) *La communauté désœuvrée*. Paris: Christian Bourgois.

Nancy, J.-L. (1991) *The Inoperative Community*. Translated by P. Connor, L. Garbus, M. Holland and S. Sawhney. Minneapolis: University of Minnesota Press.

Robertson, J. (1996) *Scottish Ghost Stories*. London: Warner.

Szuba, M. (2020) '"A Temporary, Sometimes Fleeting Thing": Home and Dwelling in John Burnside's Poetry' in Davies, B. (ed.) *John Burnside, Contemporary Critical Perspectives*. London: Bloomsbury, pp. 39–52.

Welsh, L. (2014) *A Lovely Way to Burn*. London: John Murray.

Welsh, L. (2015) *Death Is a Welcome Guest*. London: John Murray.

Welsh, L. (2017) *No Dominion*. London: John Murray.

Part II
Multi-layered identities

5 Ghosting the Victorians in A.S. Byatt, Kate Atkinson and Michèle Roberts's neo-Victorian fiction

Armelle Parey

The literary form, Katy Shaw reminds us in *Hauntology*, is 'necessarily inter-textual and haunted, a site of potential spectral agency' (2018, p. 16). Inde-pendently from the intertextual and thus multi-layered nature of all texts, contemporary fiction is particularly haunted by the past: one may note the rise of biofiction that revisits the lives of figures of the past, the resurgence of the historical novel under new forms, contemporary rewritings and expan-sions of novels considered as Victorian classics and, in a more general way, writers' awareness that they are surrounded by literary and critical ghosts: 'writers are also acutely aware of the aesthetic and stylistic forms in which they operate, as well as their relationship to a series of literary and criti-cal heritages against which they locate their own literary practice' (Bentley, Hubble and Wilson, 2015, p. 13). The past, be it literary, historical or cul-tural, relentlessly pervades and shapes contemporary fiction which tries to understand it and learn from it in its fictional representations while showing the process by which it does so.

The spectral presence of the past is particularly remarkable in neo-Victorian fiction i.e., generally speaking, contemporary novels that draw on Victorian facts, characters, themes and/or form. As early as 2008, Marie-Luise Kohlke (2008, p. 9) points to 'a recurrent spiritualist trope that acts as both metaphor and analogy for our attempted dialogue with the dead and for the lingering traces of the past within the present'. The notion of haunt-ing has often been used to refer to the relationship between past and present at the heart of neo-Victorian fiction, revealing that the ghosts of the past are transformed as they pervade the present. Indeed, in the representations it offers of the past, neo-Victorian fiction partakes of the construction of pub-lic and private memory (see Kohlke, 2008, p. 9): we are shaped by the stories we tell about the past just as our stories shape the past. In Rosario Arias and Patricia Pulham's words,

> What is at stake here is the way in which the Victorian past and the con-temporary age establish a dialogue, a two-way process, a dual relation-ship by means of which the Victorians come to life in neo-Victorianism,

DOI: 10.4324/9781003178040-8

and contemporary revisions of the Victorian past offer productive and nuanced ways of unlocking occluded secrets, silences and mysteries which return and reappear in a series of spectral/textual traces.

(2009, p. xx)

Bearing in mind 'how desire makes the spectres dance to our tune' (Kohlke, 2008, p. 14), this chapter proposes to examine how neo-Victorian fiction engages with the process of representation and narrativization of the past through the ghost, as metaphor or as character, to comment on both past and present and bring the invisible into focus, whether in terms of sensation or of silenced figures. My title uses the word 'ghosting' in the same double sense as Ann Heilmann and Mark Llewellyn (2010, p. 30): 'the endurance of the past in the present and the attempt to somehow represent spectral experience of that past in the way of a late Victorian séance'.[1] Because neo-Victorian fiction makes the past and the dead speak, this chapter will first discuss the metaphor of the ghost in neo-Victorian fiction before offering case studies of ways this haunting of the past both activates and contributes to cultural identity and memory. On the one hand, a form of immersion in the past based on the senses can be observed in A.S. Byatt's neo-Victorian fiction and, on the other hand, the foregrounding of a double temporality and the representation of ghosts, in Kate Atkinson's play *Abandonment* (2000) and Michèle Roberts' novel *The Walworth Beauty* (2017).

Metaphors of the ghost in neo-Victorian fiction

'Hauntology is "a science of ghosts, a science of what returns"' (Macherey, 1995, cited in Shaw, 2018, p. 2). Shaw, drawing on Jacques Derrida's work, examines how and why the spectral is used in English literature 'to represent interconnections between the past, present and future' (Shaw, 2018, p. 3). In fact, '[r]epresenting, addressing and engaging a dialogue with the specter' (Shaw, 2018, p. 10) is precisely what novels, including neo-Victorian ones, do when representing the past.

In Christian Gutleben's words (2011, p. 66): '[g]iving a voice to the absent or departed, prosopopoeia represents an absent presence, precisely the ambiguous ontology of the Victorians in contemporary fiction'). Neo-Victorian fiction as a whole can indeed be read as a long prosopopeia as it stages absent, dead figures and gives them a voice mostly through the representation of characters in a Victorian setting (as in Byatt's fiction) but also through the representation of Victorian ghosts in a contemporary environment (such as the murdered governess in Atkinson's *Abandonment*).

The notion of the ghost is not necessarily embodied. Indeed, the idea of the ghost or spectre also pertains to the process of literary creation, from Harold Bloom's notion of necessary distortion, 'misreading' or 'misprision' (Bloom, 1973, p. 14) of the works of earlier authors to neo-Victorian fiction's deliberate wish to appropriate the past and to make the ghosts speak. The image of the palimpsest can be called upon to evoke the ghostly presence of past texts in neo-Victorian fiction that is necessarily layered. Indeed, diffuse clichés about the Victorian era or precise source texts or characters underlie our contemporary representations of the past. Obvious examples can be found in rewritings and novel expansions, for instance, respectively, Peter Carey's *Jack Maggs* (1997) that re-imagines Magwitch, the character of the convict in Charles Dickens's *Great Expectations* and Jo Baker's *Longbourn* (2013) that expands the lives of the servants in Jane Austen's *Pride and Prejudice*.[2]

Be it embodied as a character or used as a metaphor, the idea of the ghost is plural. While it signifies the past, the ghost both calls for a reflection on the very presence of the past in the present and offers a comment on the present. Indeed, as noted by Arias and Pulham (2009, p. xxv), the ghost is 'a powerful metaphor for the dynamic relationship maintained between Victorianism and neo-Victorianism'. Neo-Victorian fiction is undoubtedly concerned with representing the Victorian past as well as with the way this representation is achieved. Fiction affects our understanding and our memory of the past, and it is noteworthy that, in turn, this understanding is affected by contemporary concerns. Because they have an 'investment in re-membering the past', i.e. assembling elements of the past into a whole, Kate Mitchell (2010, p. 32) calls neo-Victorian novels 'memory texts', i.e. 'constructed accounts of the past that emerge from and participate in contemporary memorial practices'. These novels are also turned towards the present on which they indirectly make a comment.

As Mitchell (2010, p. 35) puts it, 'the ghost signals rather the uncanny repetition of the past in the present'. Moreover, the ghost is the past *made* present. In Shaw's words (2018, p. 11): '[a]lthough it is related to something past, the specter is always current, its motivations and intervention are aimed at the present moment, and aim to highlight the precarious nature of that moment'. In so doing, in being made present, the past is affected by the present and its beliefs, views, or ideology, which means that the past and its representation fluctuate according to a changing present: 'Memory is inextricably bound to the very fabric of the present as the means by which present and past make and remake each other' (Mitchell, 2010, p. 35). For example, John Fowles' picture of the Victorian era in *The French Lieutenant's Woman* (1969), penned down at in the late 1960s, is clearly dated (see Duncker, 2014, p. 257) and influenced by its time of production and contemporary modes of thought.[3] Fowles describes a repressive Victorian era while Byatt later nuances this view, hinting at hidden liberties,[4] but both are products of their times and should be read as such. Indeed, as noted by Kohlke (2008, p. 13), 'neo-Victorian texts will one day be read for the insights they afford into 20th- and 21st-century cultural history and socio-political concerns'.[5]

The ghostly presence of the past can be intimated formally. For instance, with its 835 pages, Michael Faber's *The Crimson Petal and the White* (2002) evokes a Victorian three-decker and Patricia Duncker uses an omniscient narration reminiscent of Georges Eliot's novels in *Sophie and the Sybil* (2015). The past can also be called forth thematically in the sense that neo-Victorian fiction offers the opportunity to discuss forgotten or marginal figures, i.e. ghosts such as servants in Margaret Atwood's *Alias Grace* (1996), Jane Harris' *The Observations* (2006), Valerie Martin's *Mary Reilly* (1990) and Jo Baker's *Longbourn*, a convict in *Jack Maggs*, or female artists considered as minor in *Possession*. Looking at neo-Victorian fiction by women writers in particular, Kathleen Renk (2020, p. 5) observes that the novelists 'address the fact that androcentric history, which is "gender-skewed," renders ordinary women invisible, with the exception of women deemed great and powerful'. In fact, neo-Victorian fiction often attempts to make past invisible lives visible and as such it acts as prosopopoeia and ties in with the notion of the past as a spectre which literature can make somewhat accessible, sometimes literally through a ghost as character, since the spectre represents, in Derrida's words, 'the visibility of the invisible' (Derrida, 1994, p. 100 cited in Shaw, 2018, p. 6).

According to Kohlke (2008, p. 9):

> Haunting itself, of course, can be read as indicative of personal and cultural trauma: in Freudian terms, as the compulsion to repeat the past that has not, as yet, been adequately processed and integrated into consciousness. As such, spectrality links to the neo-Victorian's preoccupation with liberating lost voices and repressed histories of minorities left out of the public record.

In this respect, spectrality opens the way to a revision of the past as it is founded on 'a desire to look beneath and to search for alternatives to received histories, wisdoms and narratives of what has gone before' (Shaw, 2018, p. 107). As Jerome de Groot (2016, p. 108) explains, drawing on Derrida's work: 'The revenant is valuable, as it suggests the interruption of a kind of history that seeks linearity and linear temporality'. The revenant or ghost thus invites alternatives or rewritings as it disrupts the possibility of a simple or simplified tale of the past. Shaw (2018, p. 8) states: 'Like deconstruction, the specter rejects any solidification of the past'. It thus makes way for alternative versions of the past, to be found in neo-Victorian fiction that lays emphasis on the hitherto invisible figures. At the same time, 'the specter calls into question any opposition between past and present, instead suggesting that these apparently can never be neatly separated' (Shaw, 2018, p. 8). Past, present (and future) are coterminous. Shaw's idea (2018, p. 8) that '[the notion of the spectral haunt] gives voice to the hard-to-hear ... represents the formerly unrepresentable and makes visible that which was previously ignored' perfectly depicts the neo-Victorian project. Indeed, as we shall see later, the women writers under study in this chapter all seem to use neo-Victorian fiction and the ghost of the past to question the female condition and its evolution and changes in the treatment of women.

Overall, the notion of the ghost means disruption in one form or another and we shall see how this is managed or renegotiated in neo-Victorian fiction that re-plays a time (wrongly) perceived as a unified and homogeneous era and is associated with what is perceived as the traditional novel. In terms of narrative mode and approach, the spectral presence of the past can also be rendered and interpreted differently. Neo-Victorian fiction may be perceived with Heilmann and Llewellyn as a contemporary take on the past or a self-conscious reconstruction of memory: 'texts (literary, filmic, audio/visual) must in some respect *be self-consciously engaged with the act of (re)interpretation, (re)discovery and (re)vision concerning the Victorians*' (Heilmann and Llewellyn, 2010, p. 4, emphasis in the original) as opposed to stereotypical, nostalgic and unnuanced renderings of the Victorian period. The ghosting at work is thus acknowledged and questioned. On the other hand, Nadine Boehm-Schnitker and Suzanne Gruss (2014, p. 3) point to immersion as a trend in neo-Victorianism when the ghosting is seamless.[6] The two scholars thus plead for '"soft" definitions that make space for works that are "immersive, affective or nostalgic in their engagement with the nineteenth century' as they appeal to 'the emotions, the senses, or a desire to re-inhabit the past'. This is similar to Kohlke's 'new (meta) realist fiction [that] remains absolutely silent on its own fictionality' (Kohlke, 2004, p. 156), which can also be viewed in harsher words: 'the most recent generation of neo-Victorian writers have decided on a recent credo: don't innovate, imitate' (Duncker, 2014, p. 271).[7] Mitchell's notion of 'memory text' aims at going beyond this binary view of the historical text as either self-conscious or blindly nostalgic (seemingly) drawn by Linda Hutcheon in *A Poetics of Postmodernism* (see Mitchell, 2010, p. 27). Since the spectral dimension of neo-Victorian fiction indeed contributes to transforming and structuring our memory – what Mitchell (2010, p. 31) calls our 'historical imaginary' – it is important to consider various means and ways in which the spectres of the past are dealt with and put to use.

Ghosting the past through the senses in A.S. Byatt's neo-Victorian fiction

A.S. Byatt's *Possession, a Romance* was highly influential in the emergence of neo-Victorian fiction. Byatt's 1990 Booker-Prize winning novel observes the Victorians from the point of view of the twentieth century but also includes chapters when the ghosts of the past take over as the reader is directly immersed into the nineteenth century through characters' diaries and letters and through a chapter and a 'postscript' set in the past. Byatt's other texts in which she summons Victorian ghosts are 'Precipice-Encurled' (a short story published in the collection *Sugar and Other Stories* in 1987) and the two novellas 'Morpho Eugenia' and 'The Conjugial Angel' in *Angels and Insects* (1992).

Byatt's overall reliance on the senses (especially sight) in descriptions of characters, food and places has already been pointed out.[8] But this section considers this in relation to neo-Victorianism and emphasizes how Byatt's idiosyncratic ghosting of the Victorians rests precisely on sensory aspects by which we apprehend a form of materiality of the past. Indeed, she seems to make Joseph Conrad's credo her own: 'My task which I am trying to achieve is, by the power of the written word, to make you hear, to make you feel – it is, before all, to make you see' (preface to *The Nigger of the Narcissus*, cited in Ryan, 1999, p. 117).

Before we pursue this, examining the uses made of the senses in Byatt's depiction of neo-Victorian characters also reveals how the novelist addresses the common gendered distinction between thought and body, often by rejecting the dichotomy and/or by refusing to reduce each gender either to senses or to the life of the mind. In an essay in which she discusses and quotes Alfred Tennyson and Arthur Hallam in relation to her writing of 'The Conjugial Angel', Byatt points to a Victorian assumption, which she contradicts in her neo-Victorian fiction: 'the connection of woman with flesh and matter and of man with mind ... as though both men and women were not both body and spirit or mind, related in complicated ways' (Byatt 2001, p. 111). 'Morpho Eugenia' in *Angels and Insects* is a case in point of this revisionary ghosting. The novel opens in a ballroom with William Adamson as the focalizer. The ballroom is thus depicted through his sensations. Here and throughout most of the novella, William, who is otherwise introduced as a man of science, is overwhelmed by his senses. William is 'a scientist and an observer' (Byatt, 1992, p. 6), an 'ant-watcher' (Byatt, 1992, p. 10). His vision normally leads his intellect to classify objects and people, but William is overwhelmed by his senses when he first sees Eugenia Alabaster, one of the daughters of the house. Partly aware of the unusual force of this sight, he copies out in a notebook part of a poem by Ben Jonson, 'The Triumph of Charis' that relies heavily on the senses (Byatt, 1992, p. 12) and suits his vision of Eugenia. As John Berger (1990, p. 8) puts it, '[t]he way we see things is affected by what we know or what we believe'. William is at first literally blinded by Eugenia's combination of whiteness (and all he associates with it)[9] and bright coloured clothes and neither sees nor understands what is happening around him.[10] In 'Morpho Eugenia', Byatt reverses stereotypes; first, because it is the male character who is misled by his senses and second, because senses and science are shown to be linked. Matty Crompton thus seems at first a plain secondary Jane Eyre-like character. However, she shows a more acute vision that acts as a counterweight to William's impaired vision of the household. It also translates into 'incisive, careful drawings' of ants (Byatt, 1992, p. 77), as well as an ability to assess and use William's worth, manipulate him into action: 'The book I should like to see you write' (Byatt, 1992, p. 93) and, last but not least, to write stories, one of which bears a title that alludes to the ability to go beyond the visual surface of things: 'Things are not what they seem' (Byatt, 1992, p. 119). With this character, Byatt goes against the traditional reduction of woman to emotions and to the sum of her senses. As pointed out by Lena Steveker (2009, p. 65): 'Byatt's novels describe work as an essential element of female identity, affording women autonomy and independence'. In 'Morpho Eugenia', Byatt reconciles the bodily senses with the life of the mind: watching, for Matty, is an intellectual activity that leads her to write imaginative tales as she and William conduct their scientific study. Byatt's ghosts may thus modify the general public's cultural memory or apprehension of genders in terms of senses.

Second, Byatt's ghosting of the past operates through an emphasis on the senses, be they those of the characters or of the reader, in order to make us, readers, experience the past. What Arias (2016, p. 18) says of neo-sensation fiction applies here: it 'evokes the past and mobilises our own sensory perceptions, thus inviting the contemporary reader to conjure up the past through bodily memory'. Sensory descriptions in Byatt's fiction invite readers to interpret the appeal to their senses into an idea that serves to represent the past to himself or herself. And, in Silvana Colella's words: 'Access to the past – however illusory – depends on perception rather than cognition. The senses define a liminal area between past and present where connections become possible' (Colella, 2009, p. 88). Colella's remark on olfactive modality seems valid for all the senses in Byatt's fiction: 'The Victorian past is made to appear concrete, contingent and almost tangible' (Colella, 2009, p. 86). In other words, this appeal to the readers' senses could be seen as a way of immersing the reader in the text. The past is made more material and tangible to the reader, who is thus somewhat enabled to imaginatively experience the past.

Byatt gives a detailed description of what her Victorian characters wear and of their surroundings, but this does not mean that the past is equated 'with superficial detail; an accumulation of references to clothing, furniture, décor and the like, that produces the past in terms of its objects' (Mitchell, 2010, p. 3). Byatt actually imitates the habit of nineteenth-century writers such as Balzac and Dickens who describe their characters carefully in order to define them socially and psychologically. For Byatt, the details, be they in clothes or setting, are not meant to circumscribe the readers' mental representation but to feed it: 'Writers rely on the endlessly varying visual images of individual readers and on the constructive visualising work those readers do' (Byatt, 2002, p. 2). Furthermore, in the detailed descriptions of characters and their clothing, adjectives appeal to the readers' senses so that he or she can build a (visual) representation as, for example, in the following introduction of Lilias: "Lilias Papagay, a few steps ahead, wore wine-dark silk with a flounced train and a hat heavy with darkly gleaming plumage, jet-black, emerald-shot, iridescent dragonfly blue on ultramarine, plum shoulders of headless wings with jaunty tail-feathers" (Byatt, 1992, pp. 163–164).

Conversely, narrative imagination is shown to play on the senses and influence them. Thus, Mrs Papagay's imagination in 'The Conjugial Angel' is highly susceptible and closely linked to sensory reactions: on 'hearing the details' of Captain Jesse's rescues, 'she saw it all, she lived it all' (Byatt, 1992, p. 165). The words she hears bring about images that are given credence because they are treated as if brought about by her sense of sight. The result for Mrs Papagay is immersion. The episode has a metafictional dimension since the reader is like Mrs Papagay, carried into the past through a combination of sensory reaction and imagination.

The appeal to the senses does not however systematically end in immersion.[11] For instance, the scene depicted as the setting for the encounter in the 'postscript' in *Possession* appeals to the reader's senses of sight, touch and sound:

> Blue cornflowers, scarlet poppies, gold buttercups, a veil of speedwells, an intricate carpet of daisies where the grass was shorter, scabious, yellow snap-dragons… The larks sang, and the thrushes, and the blackbirds, sweet and clear, and there were butterflies everywhere.
>
> (Byatt, 1991, p. 508)

Yet, this image is far from realistic as it evokes flowers 'improbably flowering at the same time, whereas they should have in fact flowered sequentially' (Noakes, 2004, p. 20) and the description also brings to mind a visual representation by impressionist Renoir and pre-Raphaelite Millais paintings.

'Real' ghosts in Kate Atkinson *Abandonment* and Michèle Roberts's *The Walworth Beauty*

Like A.S. Byatt's, Michèle Roberts's fiction has been noted for its 'sensuous appreciation of the material world' (Rennison, 2004, p. 125). This chapter examines her latest novel to date – *The Walworth Beauty* (2017) – in terms of its narrative structure and actual use of ghosts. Indeed, this section will focus on Roberts's novel and Kate Atkinson's play *Abandonment* (2000) that both offer two instances of two interwoven narratives with a double temporality – of the type which Duncker (2014, p. 266) describes as 'two narratives on a collision course' – that establish or invite a dialogue between past and present.[12] These two texts actually feature a ghost as a literary device to signify the pervasive presence of the Victorian past. This section will consider how the spectral past is made manifest and to what end, in relation to the present: to put it simply, what is the role of the ghost in Atkinson's play *Abandonment* and Roberts's *The Walworth Beauty*? In particular, how does it contribute to forming and changing cultural memory?

Atkinson's play *Abandonment* features Elizabeth, a divorced historian who has conflictual relationships with her family. In the course of the play, she is yet again disappointed as her new boyfriend Alex leaves her. At the beginning of the play, Elizabeth moves into her newly bought flat, part of an old house in Edinburgh that is haunted by Agnes, a Victorian governess seduced and abandoned by her employer, Alec Merric, and murdered by his wife. Formally, the play juxtaposes or interweaves scenes set in the contemporary period and in the nineteenth century. Yet, for Benjamin Poore (2011, p. 157), '[m]inus the appearances of the ghost of Agnes, the play is a straightforward family drama, in which each female character is revealed to have been abandoned in some way'. The presence of the ghost and the repetitive motifs are however of paramount importance here as they both make the play a neo-Victorian one and bring on the notions attached to spectrality/the revenant.

Agnes's ghost remains unseen by the modern characters in the play but her presence-absence – as well as that of other unknown people – is materialized in the photographs that feature largely in the play:[13] they are part of the set in Act I, Scene 1 and attention is drawn to them as the sign of a loss –'All these people, lost to time' (Atkinson, 2000, p. 7)– and we later understand that they were probably taken by Alec Merric, the head of the Victorian household and a photography enthusiast, and that some of them may represent Agnes. Photographs participate in embodying the spectral of which they are a trace. Indeed, in Arias's words, 'Both the spectre and photography stage a paradoxical relationship with the past because both invoke presence and absence, life and death, present and past' (Arias, 2014, p. 118).

This presence-absence of the ghost and what it represents induces a form of co-temporality linked to 'the idea of the spectral as a virtual embodiment of that coexistence between living and dead' (Heilmann and Llewellyn, 2010, p. 167). This co-temporality means that the revenant signifies and brings about disruption. In *Abandonment*, linear temporality is literally upset by the ghost of the Victorian governess haunting the present as the contemporary narrative of Alex about to take a picture of Elizabeth is interrupted by a similar scene set a century earlier between Alec Merric and Agnes (Act I, Scene 6). The disruption suspends narrative progress and introduces the notion of repetition as the two stories unfold along similar lines. Past and present are brought together on the stage as the characters are shown to share the same concerns across the centuries. Thus, the male characters, played by the same actor, declare 'you should live in the moment' and 'we must live in the moment' while both female characters think about the future as they evoke prospective children (Atkinson, 2000, pp. 76–77). However, there is no diegetical encounter between the dead and the living until Agnes's bones are found at the very end. It is significant that the parallel situations are there for the audience's benefit, rather than for the characters (as in Byatt's *Possession* where the reader witnesses the twentieth-century characters' discoveries – and what they miss). Through the impalpability of the ghost, Atkinson's play thus points to our inability to learn from the past – 'neo-Victorian spectrality can be seen as a reflection of our inability to capture the Victorians' (Heilmann and Llewellyn, 2010, pp. 144–145) – while making us aware of this inability.

Returning to the idea that the very presence of the ghost disrupts the possibility of a simple perception or narrative of the past, the character of the ghost participates in the rather severe portrait of Victorian times often made in neo-Victorian fiction: 'Uplifting tendencies are brutally sabotaged by patterns of Othering, repetition and return, which short-circuit the teleological impetus of much Victorian fiction that conveyed an unspoken belief in notions of historical progress and self and societal development' (Kohlke, 2015, p. 66). Significantly, the ghost in *Abandonment* is one of the subalterns. In life, Agnes is a governess, partly denied visibility. Nothing in the play suggests that her murder has brought disruption to the family. On the contrary, it is suggested that all goes on as normal for the daughters of the family, confirming Agnes's social invisibility since she disappears without a trace. By the end of the play, Agnes's existence is acknowledged, if not her precise identity, as one of the characters notes: 'I think she must have been a servant in the Chalmers' family. It's easier for the lower orders to disappear' (Atkinson, Act II, Scene 13). The very last stage directions indicate 'AGNES appears in the doorway carrying a candle. She blows the candle out' (Atkinson, 2000, p. 107). Agnes's ghost seems to fade away, as if the ghost had been laid to rest by the discovery of its physical remains and its existence somehow acknowledged through Elizabeth's uncanny choice to call her daughter Agnes. Closure is achieved[14] because some form of justice has been carried out in the indirect acknowledgment of Agnes's sad end.

At first, there is no direct representation of a particular ghost in *The Walworth Beauty*. Yet, Roberts's novel is a ghost story (as noted by reviewers) in the sense that it is a tale that features several moments when a ghost seems to be present. Besides, the idea of ghosts is openly discussed and the novel culminates in a double spectral encounter.

The novel interweaves two third-person narratives in alternate chapters. It starts with Joseph Benson's story, which is set in 1851 and develops over a week. Joseph is one of the men employed by Henry Mayhew who is engaged in what will become *London Labour and the London Poor*[15] and his mission is to collect facts about prostitutes. While doing so, he meets Mrs Dulcimer, a black woman, whom he mistakenly assumes to be making a living of prostitutes in her house in Apricot Place. On the other hand, Madeleine's story, set in the twenty-first century, develops over several months. Madeleine is a 60-year-old English lecturer who has just been made redundant. As she finds herself in reduced circumstances and with time on her hands, she spends a lot of it walking about in and around her new neighbourhood. Despite being over a century apart, both characters are at times aware of some ghostly presence and walk through the same areas.

The two stories seem at first completely at odds, yet a form of symmetry gradually appears as both characters literally cover the same ground, frequenting the same locations since Madeleine moves into a semi-basement flat in Apricot Place, converted from the place where Mrs Dulcimer had her 'shelter' in the previous century. The interweaving of the two narratives maintained throughout the novel accelerates in the later chapters as the temporal frame contracts and Chapter 19 to the end are all set on the same evening. Their worlds eventually temporarily collide on Halloween.[16] The notion of symmetry gives way to the idea of geographical and temporal superposition when Mrs Dulcimer is assaulted by twenty-first century Emm, Madeleine's stalker, while Madeleine encounters Joseph whom she perceives as 'someone en route to a Hallowe'en fancy-dress party. Got up in Dickensian costume: tall hat, an overcoat with flapping skirts. Big beaky nose' (Roberts, 2018, p. 373), the scenes unfolding on the nineteenth-century Walworth Common and on its twenty-first-century incarnation as the Elephant and Castle roundabout (p. 369). These spectral encounters are literal representations of how ghosts disrupt the linearity of history.

The image of the palimpsest seems to dominate the novel: layers can be guessed at below the visible top layer as Madeleine walks the streets of London. The ghost of the past lies in the layer beneath the present and occasionally becomes visible through objects (such as Mrs Dulcimer's earring and Nelly's teapot) and apparitions. What is unusual or uncommon in Roberts' novel is the representation of a two-way movement between past and present. Indeed, if Madeleine is aware of ghosts from the past, she also herself appears to Joseph occasionally. Besides, in the participatory play set in a Victorian 'home of sinners' that Madeleine takes part in, 'Madeleine and all the others are ghosts, avatars, from the twenty-first century' (Roberts, 2018, p. 210). So is Emm, the character who parades as a vicar, when he assaults Mrs Dulcimer. Either way, the result is to establish the similarity and permeability between the two time periods as latent but undisputable.

Indeed, the strategy of double narrative at work in *The Walworth Beauty* is very different from those used in other neo-Victorian novels with a similar structure such as A.S. Byatt's *Possession* or Graham Swift's *Ever After* (1992) in which the past is the object of a quest and a retrieval. In Roberts's fiction, Madeleine has a marked interest in the past, reading Volume Four of Mayhew's *London Labour and the London Poor* (Roberts, 2018, p. 28) and raising questions such as 'So who would she and Toby have been, say, a hundred and fifty years back?' (Roberts, 2018, p. 26) or 'What did people who lived here before her eat for supper?' (Roberts, 2018, p. 216). Nonetheless, she is not actively looking to reconstruct the past: she retraces Joseph's steps unknowingly as she moves into a flat that used to be part of Mrs Dulcimer's house or catches a glimpse of Joseph's household (Roberts, 2018, p. 193). The unmotivated juxtaposition of the two narratives points to the ongoing ghostly presence-absence of the past, both there and not there.

Victorian and neo-Victorian fiction thrive on plot (Duncker, 2014, p. 271) and Roberts picks up on the double narrative of the type that was frequent in Victorian novels, as pointed out by Duncker (2014, p. 267). However, *The Walworth Beauty* does not mimic the Victorian novel, be it in terms of plot, style or language: if Fowles and Byatt occasionally echo Georges Eliot or Thomas Hardy (Sanders, 2006, p. 123), Roberts's novel does not.

A description of Henry Mayhew and his project attributed to Joseph introduces him as a controlling force that is linked to a narrative mode:

> Mayhew floated like a back-suited angel above the city. Mayhew cherished each of those individual black-dot lives, wanted each person's story, like some master novelist giving expression to all human beings. You could only do that by getting this high up, taking this distant perspective. Surveyed from this lofty eyrie, your material calmed, became manageable.
>
> (Roberts, 2018, pp. 159–160)

Conversely, Roberts opts for a narrative mode closer to the modernists. For instance, in Chapter 3 set in the evening (Roberts, 2018, p. 45), the narrative intersperses Joseph's current situation (undressing for his bath, having dinner with his family) with his reminiscences on earlier episodes of the day and of his life.

As neo-Victorian fiction conjures up the past, what does it say about it? Madeleine complains to Toby 'I've no idea how it felt like to be a London woman in those days' (Roberts, 2018, p. 197) which reads as an indictment on the lack of documentation or writing on the topic. However, the nineteenth-century narrative does not correct nor fulfil this gap but shows how it came into being. Indeed, it focuses on the viewpoint of one of Mayhew's men. Initially full of the prejudices of his time regarding women and prostitutes, Joseph Benson later gets to see beyond them but when he explains it to Mayhew, the latter fires him: Joseph's version (which is more favourable to women) is thus shown to be silenced by Mayhew who wants to tell another story.[17] Here is an illustration of Guillaume Le Blanc's link between social invisibility and the inability to make a meaningful contribution to society ("faire œuvre"): in fact, for one's contribution to society to exist, it must be acknowledged by the rest of society (See Le Blanc, 2009). Both *Abandonment* and *The Walworth Beauty* show the silencing of minor voices. In *The Walworth Beauty*, just as Joseph's point is excluded from the record, black Mrs Dulcimer's existence and shelter to girls with or without their babies goes unrecorded. Ghosts like Betsy and her child as well as Madeleine are socially invisible, Betsy as an unmarried mother and Madeleine as a redundant and ageing woman. Their representation as ghosts suggests both some form of resistance (they have not fully been erased) and desire to redress the record.

The emphasis in both Atkinson and Roberts's works is laid on the issue of sex and unmarried women becoming pregnant. Both feature female characters whose pregnancies meet different outcomes depending on the century. In *Abandonment*, Agnes is murdered while Elizabeth, herself an orphan and abandoned by her lover like Agnes was, keeps the child. In *The Walworth Beauty*, Mrs Dulcimer leaves her baby in a Victorian institution (later a museum visited by Madeleine), Betsy, victim of unwanted attentions, kills her baby whereas twenty-first-century Rose chooses to keep it and still continues her studies. While Madeleine hears the ghosts of Betsy and her baby, Elizabeth remains insensitive to Agnes's presence until she reveals the name she has chosen to give her baby. The ghosts signify the intangible but no less intrinsic presence of the past as well as point to a female genealogy.

Conclusion

As one reviewer of *The Walworth Beauty* puts it, 'Roberts imagines lives lost to history, implausible only because they don't show up in the data; people waiting for another century to get their due' (Feay, 2017). Neo-Victorian fiction acts as a prosopopeia. As it liberates lost or silenced voices directly represented as ghosts or not, it builds up a new picture of the past and contributes to modifying cultural memory: Byatt reconstructs the Victorian past by playing on sensory aspects while challenging the nineteenth century gendered dichotomy between the senses and the life of the mind; Atkinson and Roberts both add physical ghosts to complement their rendition of a past that interrogates the female condition and what we know about it.

The question of nostalgia is often considered in relation to neo-Victorian novels and their depiction of the past (see Arias and Pulham, 2009, p. xiv) but the disturbing presence created by the notion of the ghost and spectrality prevents the representation of any stable past to yearn for. This instability ensures that the past is never laid to rest and forgotten.

Notes

1 The verb has already been used with respect to A.S. Byatt. For Schor (2000, p. 237), Byatt 'ghostwrites' Victorian fiction in the sense that she borrows from the Victorians and she speaks with the dead.

2 Although Austen is not a Victorian author, contemporary revisions of her works tend to be included in the neo-Victorian whose temporal subject is rather extended: as Andrea Kirchknopf already noted in 2008, 'the so-called *Victorian* referents of twentieth-century rewritings range from Jane Austen through Thomas Hardy and as far as Virginia Woolf' (p. 55). Kucich and Sadoff's (2000) *Victorian Afterlife* also include a chapter on revisitations of Jane Austen's work. Similarly, Sadoff's (2009) *Victorian Vogue: British Novels on Screen* discusses adaptations of Austen's novels.

3 To go further on the issue of presentism in relation to neo-Victorianism, see Kohlke (2018).

4 See Hadley (2011) for a study of how the endings of these two novels offer different opportunities to women.

5 This is already the case with Fowles and even Byatt. As Duncker (2014, p. 257) puts it, 'Both Fowles's and Byatt's novels already seem to be part of a past present, a past reading of the Victorians that no longer exists'.

6 The process of immersion when reading evokes the following situation: 'When readers are caught up in a story, they turn the pages without paying too much attention to the letter of the text: what they want is to find out what happened next in the fictional world' (Ryan, 1999, p. 118).

7 Patricia Duncker is evidently close to Heilmann and Llewellyn: for her, neo-Victorian 'calls attention to its own artifice' (2014, p. 271).

8 As noticed by Silvana Colella (2009, p. 87) 'In Byatt's *Possession* (1990) [...] the visual modality predominates'. See also Alfer and Edwards de Campos (2010, pp. 97–98) and Boccardi's study of Byatt's collection of stories *Elementals* (2013, pp. 110–117).

9 Margaret Pearce (1999, p. 401) explains that '[t]he whiteness of Bredely Hall symbolizes virginity, unattainability, and power'.

10 The fact that his sense of sight (to the near exclusion of other senses) dominates his perception of Eugenia also announces that he has only a superficial apprehension of the character.

11 Silvana Colella's study of *The Crimson Petal and the White* shows that the emphasis on smell may startle the reader out of what is at times a comfortable realist narrative. The situation seems similarly complex in Byatt's work as senses may serve immersion, as seen above, but also point to self-reflexivity.

12 This is the view also held by Julie Sanders (2006, p. 123) who points out that the best-known recreations of the Victorian novel are self-conscious and entail critique and re-evaluation.

13 Indeed, for Susan Sontag (1971, p. 16), a picture is 'a pseudo-presence and a token of absence'.

14 Benjamin Poore (2011, p. 158) sees an 'extremely neat closure' at the end of *Abandonment* but the situation seems more complex than this: Elizabeth's final words may be 'No thanks, I've got everything I need' but the stage directions somewhat contradict or challenge this with 'Flash, capturing them *in disarray*, followed by darkness' (Atkinson, 2000, p. 107, italics mine).

15 *London Labour and the London Poor* is a four-volume study conducted by journalist Henry Mayhew on the basis of interviews. Volume 4 includes prostitutes as objects of studies. For a study of the representation of Henry Mayhew in contemporary fiction, including in *The Walworth Beauty*, see Louttit (2019).

16 We recognize here the situation described by Patricia Duncker in some neo-Victorian novels with a double narrative that 'set two narratives on collision course, so that the tension is generated by the dramatic structural conflict of the two tales and the possible climax can be seen approaching from afar, like a train crash' (Duncker, 2014, p. 266).

17 Indeed, Roberts explained in an interview that 'it was the gaps in what Mayhew published that really intrigued [her]' (García-Sánchez, 2019, p. 209).

References

Alfer, A. and Edwards de Campos, A.J. (2010) *A.S. Byatt, Critical Storytelling*. Manchester: MUP.

Arias, R. (2014) 'Traces and Vestiges of the Victorian Past in Contemporary Fiction' in Boehm-Schnitker, N. and Gruss, S. (eds.) *Neo-Victorian Literature and Culture: Immersions and Revisitations*. London: Routledge, pp. 111–122.

Arias, R. (2016) 'Neo-Sensation Fiction, or "Appealing to the Nerves": Sensation and Perception in Neo-Victorian Fiction', *RSV, Rivista di Studi Vittoriani*, 40, pp. 13–30.

Arias, R. and Pulham, P. (2009) *Haunting and Spectrality in Neo-Victorian Fiction: Possessing the Past*. London: Palgrave Macmillan.

Atkinson, K. (2000) *Abandonment*. London: Nick Hern Books.

Atwood, M. (1996) *Alias Grace*. London: Bloomsbury.

Baker, J. (2013) *Longbourn*. New York: Doubleday.

Bentley, N., Hubble, N. and Wilson, L. (eds.) (2015) *The 2000s, a Decade of Contemporary British Fiction*. London: Bloomsbury, pp. 1–26.

Berger, J. (1990) *Ways of Seeing*. London: Penguin. [First published 1972].

Bloom, H. (1973) *The Anxiety of Influence*. Oxford: Oxford University Press.

Boccardi, M. (2013) *A.S. Byatt*. London: Palgrave Macmillan.

Boehm-Schnitker, N. and Gruss, S. (eds.) (2014) *Neo-Victorian Literature and Culture: Immersions and Revisitations*. London: Routledge.

Byatt, A.S. (1987) *Sugar and Other Stories*. London: Chatto and Windus.

Byatt, A.S. (1991) *Possession: A Romance*. London: Vintage. [First published 1990].

Byatt, A.S. (1992) *Angels and Insects*. London: Chatto & Windus.

Byatt, A.S. (2000) *On Histories and Stories*. London: Chatto & Windus.

Byatt, A.S. (2002) *Portraits in Fiction*. London: Vintage. [First published 2001].

Carey, P. (1997) *Jack Maggs*. London: Faber and Faber.

Colella, S. (2009) 'Olfactory Ghosts: Michael Faber's *The Crimson Petal and the White*' in Arias, R. and Pulham, P. (eds.) *Haunting and Spectrality in Neo-Victorian Fiction: Possessing the Past*. Basingstoke: Palgrave Macmillan, pp. 85–110.

De Groot, J. (2016) *Remaking History, The Past in Contemporary Historical Fictions*. London: Routledge.

Derrida, J. (1994) *Spectres of Marx: The State of the Debt, the Work of Mourning, and the New International*. Translated by P. Kamuf. London and New York: Routledge.

Dickens, C. (1861) *Great Expectations*. London: Chapman and Hall.

Duncker, P. (2014) 'On Writing Neo-Victorian Fiction', *English: Journal of the English Association*, 63(243), pp. 253–274.

Faber, M. (2002) *The Crimson Petal and the White*. Edinburgh: Canongate.

Feay, S. (2017) 'London Across the Centuries', Review of *The Walworth Beauty* by M. Roberts. *The Guardian*, 21 April [online]. Available at: https://www.theguardian.com/books/2017/apr/21/the-walworth-beauty-by-michele-roberts-review (Accessed: 24 March 2021).

Fowles, J. (1969) *The French Lieutenant's Woman*. London: Jonathan Cape.

García-Sánchez, R. (2019) 'Exploring Michèle Roberts' Imagined Voices in *The Walworth Beauty*', *Women: A Cultural Review*, 30(2), pp. 206–218.

Gutleben, C. (2011) 'Hybridity as an Oxymoron: An Interpretation of the Dual Nature of Neo-Victorian Fiction' in Guignery, V. et al. (eds.) *Hybridity: Forms and Figures in Literature and the Visual Arts*. Newcastle: Cambridge Scholars Publishing, pp. 59–70.

Hadley, L. (2011) 'Feminine Endings: Neo-Victorian Transformations of the Victorian' in Tredennick, B. (ed.) *Victorian Transformations*. Farnham: Ashgate, pp. 181–194.

Harris, J. (2006) *The Observations*. London: Faber and Faber.

Heilmann, A. and Llewellyn, M. (2010) *Neo-Victorianism, The Victorians in the Twenty-First Century, 1999–2009*. Basingstoke: Palgrave.

Kirchknopf, A. (2008) '(Re)workings of Nineteenth-Century Fiction: Definitions, Terminology, Contexts', *Neo-Victorian Studies*, 1(1), pp. 53–80.

Kohlke, M.-L. (2004) 'Into History through the Back Door: The "Past Historic" in *Nights at the Circus* and *Affinity*', *Women: A Cultural Review*, 15(2), pp. 153–166.

Kohlke, M.-L. (2008) 'Introduction: Speculations in and on the Neo-Victorian Encounter', *Neo-Victorian Studies*, 1(1), pp. 1–18.

Kohlke, M.-L. (2015) 'Gothicising History: Traumatic Alterity, Repetition, and Return in Recent British Neo-Victorian Fiction' in Leggett, B. and Venezia T. (eds.) *Twenty-First-Century British Fiction, Critical Essays*. Canterbury: Gylphi, pp. 61–82.

Kohlke, M.-L. (2018) 'The Lures of Neo-Victorianism Presentism (with a Feminist Case Study of *Penny Dreadful*)', *Literature Compass*, Special issue: Neo-Victorian Considerations, 15(7), pp. 1–14.

Kucich, J. and Sadoff, D.F. (eds.) (2000) *Victorian Afterlife, Postmodern Culture Rewrites the Nineteenth Century*. Minneapolis: University of Minnesota Press.

Le Blanc, G. (2009) *L'invisibilité sociale*. Paris: Presses universitaires de France.

Louttit, C. (2019) 'Henry Mayhew as Character in Neo-Victorian Fiction and Drama', in *Writers in Neo-Victorian Fiction* [online]. Available at: https://www.canal-u.tv/video/la_forge_numerique/victorian_journalist_of_genius_henry_mayhew_as_character_in_neo_victorian_fiction_and_drama.53227 (Accessed: 17 September 2021).

Martin, V. (1990) *Mary Reilly*. New York: Doubleday.

Mitchell, K. (2010) *Victorian Afterimages, History and Cultural Memory in Neo-Victorian Fiction*. London: Palgrave Macmillan.

Noakes, J. (2004) 'Interview with A. S. Byatt' in Reynolds, M. and Noakes, J. (eds.) *A. S. Byatt: The Essential Guide*. London: Vintage, pp. 11–32.

Pearce, M. (1999) 'Problems with the Male Gaze', *Critique*, 40(4), pp. 399–411.

Poore, B. (2011) *Heritage, Nostalgia and Modern British Theatre: Staging the Victorians*. London: Palgrave Macmillan.

Renk, K. (2020) *Women Writing the Neo-Victorian Novel: Erotic 'Victorians'*. London: Palgrave Macmillan.

Rennison, N. (2004) *Contemporary British Novelists*. London: Routledge.

Roberts, M. (2017) *The Walworth Beauty*. London: Bloomsbury.

Ryan, M.-L. (1999) 'Immersion vs. Interactivity: Virtual Reality and Literary Theory', *SubStance*, 28(2), pp. 110–137.

Sadoff, D.F. (2009) *Victorian Vogue: British Novels on Screen*. Minneapolis: University of Minnesota Press.

Sanders, J. (2006) *Adaptation and Appropriation*. London: Routledge.

Schor, H.M. (2000) 'Sorting, Morphing and Mourning: A.S. Byatt Ghostwrites Victorian Fiction' in Kucich, J. and Sadoff, D.F. (eds.) *Victorian Afterlife: Postmodern Culture Rewrites the Nineteenth Century*. Minneapolis: University of Minnesota Press, pp. 234–251.

Shaw, K. (2018) *Hauntology: The Presence of the Past in Twenty-First Century English Literature*. London: Palgrave Macmillan.

Sontag, S. (1971) *On Photography*. Harmondsworth: Penguin Books.

Steveker, L. (2009) *Identity and Cultural Memory in the Fiction of A.S. Byatt, Knitting the Net of Culture*. London: Palgrave Macmillan.

6 Whose past is it before us? The shaping of identity in Scotland's 2014 referendum on independence

Philip Rycroft

On the 23rd and 24th of June 1314, an English army under the command of King Edward II was roundly defeated and put to rout by the supposedly inferior forces of the Scottish King, Robert the Bruce. Just over 700 years later, in 2014, the leader of the Scottish National Party (SNP), Alex Salmond, noted 'the surge of the great crowd' which had come to celebrate the anniversary of the battle and whose reaction to him was 'both unanimous and hugely favourable' (Salmond, 2015, p. 77).

On that same day, the Prime Minister of the United Kingdom, David Cameron, was in the town of Stirling, close to the Bannockburn battlefield, to celebrate Armed Forces Day, a 'spectacular national event ... enabling the local community to lead the nation in honouring UK Armed Forces personnel past and present' (UK Government, 2013d). This was an occasion, in the words of David Cameron, to celebrate 'what Scotland brings to the UK's armed forces and what being part of a bigger entity brings for Scotland as well' (BBC News, 2014b).

Two versions of Scotland's past were juxtaposed in the vicinity of a small town in the middle of the country. As a long and bitterly fought referendum campaign on Scottish independence drew to its climax, Alex Salmond sought to remind the people of Scotland of their proud history as an independent nation, committed to their own freedom, while David Cameron tapped into the emotional resonance of the British armed forces, in which Scots had fought alongside their compatriots from across the United Kingdom for over three centuries. Both sides appealed to different aspects of the multi-layered identities of the people of Scotland and both sides co-opted the ghosts of the past to make their case for the future of Scotland.

Scotland voted on 18 September 2014 on the question: 'Should Scotland be an independent country?'. The answer was 'no'. But with 1.6 million people voting 'yes', 44.7% of those who cast a ballot, the result was a lot closer than anyone had predicted when the campaign got underway back in 2012.

How decisive was the conjuring of the ghosts of the past in determining views about Scotland's future in 2014? On the face of it, the arguments for and against independence that dominated the debate were about the practical outcomes of self-governance in Scotland. Simply put, would people in

DOI: 10.4324/9781003178040-9

Scotland be better or worse off? This political focus was buttressed by what polling revealed about attitudes to independence. A poll conducted in 2013 examined how they varied if it meant that people would be on average £500 better or worse off. The result was striking: 52% said they would support independence if it would leave them £500 better off, but only 15% if it would leave them £500 worse off (Curtice, 2014a).

Such an unsentimental view of future prospects would seem to leave little scope for an appeal to the emotional bonds of the past. Indeed, the political discourse throughout the referendum campaign was dominated by arguments about the economy, about what currency an independent Scotland would have, about the fiscal deficit it would carry and its share of the UK national debt, about whether an independent Scotland would be welcomed as a member of the European Union, about its security and place in the wider family of nations, and all the other manifestations of statehood.

But a struggle for independence cannot be contained by appeal to material benefits alone (Rose, 1982, p. 215). Self-government is about differentiation, founded on a sense of unique identity. However, they sought to pitch the argument, those leading the debate for and against independence could not abstract their case from the tug of deeper loyalties, to a Union that had persisted for over 300 years or to a sense of Scottish nationhood with deeper roots. The ghosts of the past flitted in and out of view through the campaign and helped to determine the ultimate outcome.

This chapter will examine how narratives from the past informed and shaped the referendum campaign on Scottish independence in 2014 and how the emotional charge of that campaign was rooted in different stories of Scotland's and Britain's pasts.

The case for independence

The case for independence was set out in the document published by the Scottish government on 26 November 2013, *Scotland's Future* (Scottish Government, 2013). At 670 pages, it endeavoured to cover every aspect of the national life of an independent Scotland. Alex Salmond claimed that it was 'the most comprehensive blueprint for an independent country ever published, not just for Scotland but for any prospective independent nation' (BBC News, 2013).

The document focused determinedly on the material benefits that independence would bring to Scotland. In a key passage, the document asserted:

> Independence is not an end in itself. The Scottish Government wants us to have the powers of independence so that people who live here can build a different and better Scotland, where the many benefits of our rich and vibrant society are cherished and shared and where we work together to advance our nation as a whole.
>
> (Scottish Government, 2013, p. 3)

The document interwove the theoretical possibilities that would arise from independence, when Scotland would be able to make its own decisions, with hard-edged policy proposals which would be implemented by the incoming government of an independent Scotland, if led by the SNP. This allowed the SNP to target unpopular policies of the then Coalition government at Westminster, such as the so-called 'bedroom tax' (a restriction on benefits for those whose state-supported rental accommodation included a spare room), and to commit to popular policies such as reductions in corporation tax for businesses and an increase in the minimum wage. This was a progressive agenda, but one that sought at the same time to present itself as friendly to businesses and economic growth.

Thus, the main appeal of the document was grounded in the present, the lived experience of people in Scotland, and the promise of a more prosperous and more equitable future. This document set the tone for the wider campaign. In his major set piece speeches, Alex Salmond sustained the assault on the Coalition government and constantly emphasized the promise of better times to come for Scotland, which was, he claimed, 'the 8th wealthiest country in the league table of the world's most developed nations' (Salmond, 2013). Voting for independence was presented, not as the risky option, but the best way to secure future prosperity.

In the two debates he held with the leader of the pro-Union *Better Together* campaign, Alistair Darling, Salmond's focus again was on what Scotland *could* be, not on what Scotland had once been. The main bone of contention in both debates was the currency an independent Scotland would use. Darling won the first debate, according to the snap polls that followed it (Curtice, 2014b), and Salmond himself later recorded:

> My own questions to Darling should have been on issues that directly matter to people, like jobs and health, rather than more political debating points. I am really annoyed with myself about that, since the concentration on issues that really matter is exactly what I've been advocating at campaign meetings for the last few meetings.
>
> (Salmond, 2015, p. 139)

The case for the Union

The campaign to persuade the people of Scotland to stay in the Union responded in like coin. Led on the ground by a cross-party alliance, *Better Together*, it was left to the UK government to set out the detailed case for the Union in a series of documents published between February 2013 and June 2014 under the heading *Scotland Analysis*. Fifteen papers in all, the series covered all the main policy areas that were deemed important to demonstrate the benefits of the United Kingdom, from currency through pensions and welfare to security and defence (UK Government, 2013a). Tellingly, this was the first time any UK government had attempted to analyse in detail why the Union of the United Kingdom was still relevant and valuable to all its parts.

The key argument in the first document, *Devolution and the implications of Scottish independence*, was that devolution 'offers people in Scotland the best of both worlds' (UK Government, 2013b, p. 6). While grounded in a brief reference to the history of Scotland in the Union, the appeal was very much to the present. It stated that devolution 'has resulted in more than a decade of laws being made and policy decisions being taken in Scotland, aimed at meeting the specific needs and circumstances of people in Scotland' (UK Government, 2013b, p. 22) while at the same time Scotland continued to benefit from the collective weight of the United Kingdom in terms of macro-economic policy, security, and voice in the world.

The other aim of the document was to set out the process by which Scotland would become independent, if that was what people voted for in the referendum. This was not intended to make the process look straightforward. At its core was the contention that the United Kingdom would be the so-called 'continuator state' and would 'automatically ... exercise the same rights, obligations and powers under international law as the predecessor state' (p. 33). The practical implication of this was that Scotland, as a new state, would have to undertake a wide range of negotiations to establish itself in the international order. Critically, the paper claimed:

> There is no prospect that an independent Scottish state would automatically become a new member of the EU upon independence because there is no explicit provision for this process in the EU's own membership rules. Neither would an independent Scotland automatically 'inherit' the UK's opt-outs.
>
> (p. 45)

That not-too-subtle subtext beneath the legal argument was that the process of independence would be uncertain and potentially destabilizing. The emphasis was on the risks for the future, not an emotional appeal to the past.

This set the tone for the wider campaign against independence. One climatic moment came on 13 February 2014 when the Chancellor of the Exchequer in the UK government, George Osborne, visited Edinburgh to announce that there would be no currency union if Scotland became independent. As he put it bluntly: 'If Scotland walks away from the UK, it walks away from the pound' (BBC News, 2014a). He did so with the vocal support of his Liberal Democrat colleague in the Coalition government, Chief Secretary at the Treasury, Danny Alexander, but also of Ed Balls, then Shadow Chancellor in the Labour opposition.

This argument was couched in terms of the benefits that Scotland derived from the arrangements then pertaining in the United Kingdom. As another

Scotland Analysis paper, *Currency and monetary policy*, published in April 2013, put it:

> Scotland and the rest of the UK are economically well placed in the current UK arrangements. The status of the UK as a full fiscal and political union has played an important role in this conclusion.
>
> (UK Government, 2013c, p. 27)

As with the wider approach of the UK government and the *Better Together* campaign, this was meant to reinforce the value to Scotland of being part of the United Kingdom. Inevitably, however, what many people saw was the threat; that if Scotland became independent, the government of 'remainder' United Kingdom would not make life easy for the new State. Accentuating the negative had been informally dubbed 'Project Fear' within the *Better Together* campaign. When one of the members of the team let the words slip to a journalist, the 'Yes' campaign seized on it to point up the negativity of those campaigning against independence. (Pike, 2015, pp. 31–32) Henceforth, the accusation that sheer negativity was driving the pro-Union side was used relentlessly by the campaign for independence, *Yes Scotland*, as counterpoint to the heady optimism with which they sought to infuse the drive for independence.

This hard-edged focus on the present and the risks or benefits to the well-being of the people of Scotland of either outcome to the referendum dominated the campaign to the end. Mindful of that polling on how a gain or loss of £500 influenced opinion, the concluding paper in the Scotland Analysis series sought to boil down the argument to one number, the so-called 'UK Dividend' (UK Government, 2014, p. 27). By dint of adding together higher public expenditure in Scotland, the costs of independence and a number of other factors, the Treasury calculated that the 'dividend' was worth £1,400 per person in Scotland.

Not to be outdone, the 'Yes' campaign late in the day played the emotive card of the National Health Service, arguing that privatization of health care in England would adversely impact funding for Scotland and so threaten the provision of free healthcare. It was a tenuous argument: health policy was devolved to the Scottish Parliament and decisions on expenditure on health were made in Scotland. But it was effective (Pike, 2015, p. 128). It had Alistair Darling on the ropes in the second TV debate with Alex Salmond, held on 25 August 2014 in the Kelvingrove Museum, Glasgow (Pike, 2015, p. 108; Salmond, 2015, p. 169).

That both sides sought to base their main arguments on the risks or benefits to the practical well-being of the people of Scotland is a clear reflection of what they believed would most influence voters, in particular swing voters. As then Prime Minister David Cameron recalled in his autobiography: 'those who needed persuading weren't going to be convinced by abstract ideas of history, or an emotional appeal to unity or identity, but rather by practicality' (2019, p. 549).

This was based on the polling done for the 'No' campaign that identified 30% of the voting population, or about one million people, as swing voters, who could vote either way. This 'middle million' did not share a strong sense of common identity with the rest of the United Kingdom. In other words, their hearts inclined them towards independence, but their heads might turn them to the Union if they felt that their material prospects were at risk. Both sides feared that an undue emphasis on identity would deter this crucial middle million (Mullen, 2015, p. 21).

Summoning the ghosts of Scotland's past

Was, then, an event like the celebration of the anniversary of the battle of Bannockburn an outlier in a campaign otherwise dominated by 'practicality' and the eschewing of the 'abstract ideas of history'? This was, after all, a referendum about restoring independence to an ancient Scottish polity over 300 years after the 1707 Act of Union with England. Both sides had centuries of history to draw on, a history which could not be divorced from people's sense of identity as Scottish or British or both.

The ghosts of the past might not have had much to say about what currency an independent Scotland might use or whether an independent Scotland would be able to re-join the European Union. But they tugged at the emotions and percolated through the arguments about whether the people of Scotland would be better or worse off depending on the outcome of the referendum. Far from eschewing an appeal to the past, both sides drew on a narrative about Scotland's past to influence the decisions of voters on Scotland's future.

For the pro-Union side, this took the form of a straightforward appeal to the common endeavour that had marked the 300-year-old Union. The tone in official UK government publications was decidedly utilitarian. As the first in the series of Scotland Analysis papers put it:

> In these three centuries of partnership Scotland has seized the benefits of being part of a larger family of nations. Scotland has always been an outward-facing nation and within the UK has projected a global reach in economics and commerce, law, philosophy, the arts and sport and much else besides, punching far above its weight.
>
> (UK Government, 2013b, p. 6)

By the time the final document in the series was published, in June 2014, the UK government was emboldened to add a splash of emotion, quoting words from a David Cameron speech given in May 2014:

> Together, we created world class institutions like the NHS and the BBC. When Europe faced its darkest hour, we stood together as a beacon of hope. We pull together in this United Kingdom. When one of us needs

help, we are there for each other... We want Scotland to stay... Together we are a United Kingdom with a united future.

(UK Government, 2014, p. 5)

This paragraph encapsulated the emotional case for the Union. With England, Wales, and Northern Ireland, Scotland had stood firm against tyranny in the Second World War, had built a welfare state and founded a National Health Service. It was this case that David Cameron made in a speech to an audience in London at the Olympic Park velodrome on 7 February 2014, when he appealed to people in England, Wales and Northern Ireland to persuade their friends and relatives in Scotland to vote to stay in the Union. He claimed that:

Our Parliament, our laws, our way of life – so often, down the centuries, the UK has given people hope. We've shown that democracy and prosperity can go hand in hand; that resolution is found not through the bullet, but the ballot box. Our values are of value to the world.

(Cameron, 2014)

But the politician who most passionately advocated the case for the Union on the basis of a shared past was the former Labour Prime Minister, Gordon Brown. In a book he published in June 2014, he wrote:

There is ... a golden thread that runs through British history of the individual standing firm against tyranny and the arbitrary use of power ... But the British story is not one that focuses on political rights and civil liberties alone – for from the Liberal social reforms at the beginning of the last century through the building of the welfare state in its middle, the British people also pioneered new ways of thinking about social and economic rights.

(2014a, p. 197)

This was a theme he repeated in a series of barnstorming speeches as the campaign drew to its close in the autumn of 2014. This culminated in an emotional speech on the eve of the referendum, on Wednesday 17 September 2014, at Maryhill's Community Central Hall in Glasgow. Speaking without notes in front of an enthusiastic and noisy audience of 'No' supporters, he summoned directly the ghosts of the soldiers of conflicts past:

We fought two world wars together. And there is not a cemetery in Europe that does not have Scots, English, Welsh, and Irish lying side-by-side. And when young men were injured in these wars, they didn't look to each other and ask whether you were Scots or English, they came to each other's aid because we were part of a common cause.

(Brown, 2014b, p. i)

He went on to link this memory of shared conflict with the shared endeavour of building a welfare state:

> We not only won these wars together, built the peace together, built the welfare state together, we will build the future together. And what we have built together by sacrificing and sharing let no narrow nationalism split asunder, ever.
>
> (p. ii)

Gordon Brown had pretty much the last word of the 'No' campaign and when it came to the end, all the arguments about Scotland's currency, about pensions and jobs, about security and membership of the European Union fell away in a passionate speech that focused squarely on the emotional pull of a shared history.

The appeal to the past for the nationalist side of the argument was, perhaps surprisingly, more nuanced than that unambiguous clarion call from Gordon Brown. For sure, it was never far from the surface but in a more understated way that sought to draw the audience, in particular those already leaning towards supporting independence, into an assumed framing of Scottishness. The formulation at the beginning of Alex Salmond's foreword to *Scotland's Future* captures this flavour well:

> Scotland is an ancient nation, renowned for the ingenuity and creativity of our people, the breathtaking beauty of our land and the brilliance of our scholars. Our national story has been shaped down the generations by values of compassion, equality, an unrivalled commitment to the empowerment of education, and a passion and curiosity for invention that has helped to shape the world around us. Scots have been at the forefront of the great moral, political and economic debates of our times as humanity has searched for progress in the modern age.
>
> (Scottish Government, 2013, p. viii)

He returned to the theme in a speech he gave on 7 April 2014 to mark the opening of Glasgow Caledonian University's new campus in New York. Speaking mainly to an American audience, he allowed himself to celebrate Scotland's past, through an emphasis on Scotland's contribution 'to the rest of humanity; to the wellbeing of all, the common weal'.

He referenced two totemic elements of Scottish history in laying claim to this contribution. One was 'the sealing in 1320 of the Declaration of Arbroath – a document whose principles of elective governance are seen as having influenced the US Declaration of Independence' (Salmond, 2014b). The Declaration of Arbroath was a letter written by the barons of Scotland to the Pope in defence of the independence of Scotland from English conquest. It ends with the ringing declaration: 'For we fight not for glory, nor riches, nor honours, but for freedom alone, which no good man gives up except with his life' (Jackson, 2020, p. 132).

The second was the tradition of Scottish education which, Salmond said, was: 'one of our first inventions … [and] the most important of all – we were the first society anywhere in the world to introduce free universal education, from the 16th century' (2014b). He continued with a hubristic flourish: 'And because we had more people who had the ability to invent than anywhere else, we reached the stage where, in Arthur Herman's phrase, it sometimes seems as though Scotland has indeed invented the modern world' (2014b).

Not many of Salmond's speeches dwelt so extensively on Scotland's past, but here he set out with great clarity the foundation for the claim to progressive nationalism that was so much the hallmark of the case he made throughout the campaign (McAnulla and Crines, 2017). He used the theme in a speech given to the *New Statesmen* on 5 March 2014: an independent Scotland 'would exert a powerful and positive influence through example – the beacon of progressive opinion' (Salmond, 2014a).

This was not about a narrowly defined view of Scottishness. In a speech to the College of Europe in Bruges on 28 April 2014, he made this clear:

> We're comfortable with the idea of overlapping identities – we know that you can be Scottish and British, Scottish and European, Scottish and Polish or Scottish and Pakistani. Tartan is the distinctive national cloth of Scotland. It's made up of patterned threads of different colours. I like to think that Scottish identity is like the tartan. There are many colours, many threads, many strands to the Scottish tartan of identity.
>
> (Salmond, 2014d)

The spirit he sought to evoke was summed up in other speeches in one word: community. That, he said, was 'what the campaign for Scottish independence is about. Our human community' (Salmond, 2014c). And, somewhat poignantly, it was the word he would have used again in the speech he never gave, his victory speech had the 'Yes' side won the referendum: 'We are a nation reborn. The community of this realm has spoken' (BBC News, 2015).

Appealing to national myths

So, two versions of the past were deployed. Both laid claim to a democratic and progressive influence on the world, and both laid claim to a tradition of liberalism and solidarity. Neither appealed to a narrowly conceived ethnic nationalism. But the well-springs they drew on were quite different.

It was those defending the status quo on the Unionist side of the argument who had the harder work to do to find emotional resonance in the campaign. As the scramble to produce the *Scotland Analysis* series of documents demonstrated, there was no pre-existing articulation of the benefits of the Union of the United Kingdom. Successive UK governments had seen no particular need to evangelize on behalf of the Union. The threat of secession seemed remote. Support for independence before 2012 had rarely risen above 30% (Curtice, 2017, p. 2). Even after devolution, the structures of the central British state barely adjusted to take account of the new territorial politics (Kenny, Rycroft and Sheldon, 2021). This was the 'unthinking Union', marked by the indifference of politicians at the centre of the British state, 'not because they dislike the Union but because they do not think about it' (Rose, 1982, p. 214). It was almost as though the effort to devolve substantial powers to Scotland and Wales in 1998 and subsequently had exhausted the capacity of the British state to think deeply about what made the Union cohere.

Nor was there a great upwelling of concern in England about the prospect of Scottish independence. Prime Minister Cameron's appeal to those south of the border to act to persuade their northern neighbours to stay in the UK fell largely on deaf ears. Although only one in three supported Scottish independence, English voters polled in 2014 were largely unsympathetic to Scottish concerns, whether Scotland voted 'yes' to independence or 'no'. By a margin of over two to one, English voters rejected the proposition that an independent Scotland should be able to keep the pound. By more than four to one, they agreed that levels of public spending in Scotland should be reduced to the UK average in the event of a 'no' vote (Centre on Constitutional Change, 2014).

It is this unpromising backdrop that explains the wariness of Prime Minister Cameron to deploy the 'abstract ideas of history' and the remorseless focus of the *Better Together* campaign on head rather than heart (Pike, 2015, p. 59). Gordon Brown endeavoured to turn the tide of emotion that had swept up the 'Yes' campaign, but he was running against a powerful counter-narrative that drew deep on the mythologies of Scottish history through which the ghosts of Scotland's past wove their way.

Those myths took a distinct form. Scotland is not part of the United Kingdom by dint of coercion or military conquest; the Union of Parliaments in 1707 was, albeit disputed by some, a voluntary affair. Scotland prospered through much of the long history of the Union and many Scots were enthusiastic participants in the British imperial project. Scottish institutions, in particular Scots law, education, and church governance, were preserved by the Union. There was no great ethnic or, with the exception of the Gaelic-speaking fringes, linguistic division from England to drive nationalism. It was only late in the twentieth century that this 'banal unionism' (Kidd, 2008, p. 31) was seriously challenged by a new strain of separatist Scottish nationalism.

This nationalism drew its inspiration not so much from a long-standing threat to a national cultural identity as from the more proximate challenge of the British state to a social democratic order that was seen to be rooted in Scottish traditions (Jackson, 2020, pp. 2–3). This was civic or progressive nationalism, mobilized in the 1960s and 1970s by a perception that the

British state was failing and given further momentum by the accusation that the government of Prime Minister Thatcher had visited on Scotland a cataclysm of neo-liberal policy for which it had no mandate.

Hence, the emphasis in the Scottish government's blueprint for independence, *Scotland's Future*, on building a better future, rather than extolling a glorious past. But this had to be more than a debate about the political direction of travel of the United Kingdom, of which Scotland was part. It had to become a question of why Scotland was distinct enough from the rest of the United Kingdom to warrant a separate path into the future.

This is where the ghosts of the past slipped into the political discourse. Some of those ghosts wore ahistorical woad, as in the highly romanticized version of Scottish defiance of the English in Mel Gibson's film *Braveheart*. They hovered in the imagination of those marking the anniversary of the battle of Bannockburn. But for the most part they wore more sober guise, as the architects and advocates of a social and communal bearing in Scotland that could be contrasted with a more individualistic England.

In constitutional terms, this strain of nationalism thinking traced its origins to the brave barons who had penned the Declaration of Arbroath back in 1320. This was translated into a claim that sovereignty in Scotland had long been vested in the people, not, as in the English tradition, in Parliament (Jackson, 2020, p. 136). Co-opted too to this cause was the 1953 case *MacCormick v. Lord Advocate*, in which the Nationalist John MacCormick attempted to prove that Queen Elizabeth could not be the second of Scotland, since the first had only ruled in England and Wales. He lost the case, but generated a striking opinion from the presiding judge, Lord Cooper, to the effect that: 'The principle of the unlimited sovereignty of parliament is a distinctively English principle which has no counterpart in Scottish constitutional law' (Kidd, 2008, p. 116).

Woven into this story of popular sovereignty was the celebration of a tradition of Scottish education that stretched back to the Reformation and to the form of church governance propounded by the great Reformer John Knox and given shape by the Scottish presbytery. Knox believed that education was to prepare children for 'the business of life and the purpose of eternity' and drove a long-lasting policy to ensure that there was a school in every parish or burgh. Long before anything similar was contemplated in England, Scotland could claim a rough approximation to universal education – though for boys only (Smout, 1969, p. 422).

This was the fabric from which the sense of the Scottish 'community' was cut. Alex Salmond knew that, however tendentious the historical origins, many of the voters he was appealing to believed that Scotland had more of a communitarian tradition and was more progressive than its southern neighbour. Scotland was different and sustaining that difference meant cutting Scotland loose from a United Kingdom in thrall again to neo-liberal doctrine under the tutelage of another Conservative-led government, now led by David Cameron, committed to imposing austerity on unwilling Scots.

The practical demonstration of this difference was taken to be the rejection of the Conservatives in Scotland: 22 Conservative MPs were elected to the Westminster parliament in 1979, in the 1997 election none were, and only one was returned at successive elections between 2001 and 2015. Scotland voted centre-left and there have been plenty of commentators to ascribe that to a marked difference in Scottish social attitudes (Revest, 2016).

This perception has been well tested in social attitudes polling. There is some substance to it: analysis of the data from the Scottish and British Social Attitudes surveys in 2011 concluded that: 'Scotland is more social democratic in outlook than England' but noted that 'the differences are modest at best' (Curtice and Ormston, 2011). An analysis of the 2020 surveys also concluded that 'Scotland may have a tendency to more socially democratic politics', which shows consistency over time, although the differences were subtle (Yarde and Wishart, 2020).

'Modest difference' might be a slender reed on which to rest the case for independence. But modest differences can be made to count. What mattered was the perception of difference; that's what Alex Salmond sought to conjure when he appealed to the Scottish sense of 'community'.

How did the ghosts of the past influence the outcome?

How important were the appeals to the past in the way that people actually voted in the referendum? Distilling the emotional resonance of imagined pasts from more quotidian concerns in people's voting decisions is no simple task, not least for those who only made up their mind in the last few weeks, as was the case for around 40% of 'Yes' voters and 19% of 'no' voters (Ashcroft, 2014). But there are indications in the data that the emotional appeal to the past was an important factor in determining how many voters cast their vote.

The economic consequences of independence were undoubtedly uppermost for many. Voting intentions recorded by the Scottish Social Attitudes survey in 2014 showed a marked correlation between intention to vote 'yes' and a belief that independence would make Scotland better off (Curtice, 2014c). The main post-referendum study, conducted under the auspices of the Economic and Social Research Council, confirmed the salience of the issue of the currency, with over 95% of those believing that an independent Scotland would be very unlikely or unlikely to keep the pound voting 'no' and over 90% of those believing Scotland would be very likely to keep the pound voting 'yes'. Likewise, a large majority who believed that staying in the Union was very likely to lead to spending cuts voted 'yes' (87.8%) as did those who believed that it was very likely that the wealth gap would increase if Scotland stayed in the Union (over 90%) (Henderson and Mitchell, 2015).

The future of the economy may, then, have been the 'question of paramount importance in the minds of the electorate as the decision was made whether or not to leave the UK' (Devine, 2017, p. 250). But it was far from the only factor influencing the way that people voted. Indeed, the ESRC study found that the top three reasons for voting 'yes' were all expressed in non-economic terms: 'so that Scotland always gets the government it votes for' was the first, 'because the whole Westminster system is rotten' second; and 'because independence is the natural state of nations like Scotland' third. It was only with the fourth highest rank reason that the economy came into it: 'because it would have made Scotland economically better off'. Similarly, the most cited reason for voting 'no' was not economic: it was 'because I feel British and believe in the Union'. The second most cited reason may have been economic in origin – 'too many unanswered questions' – and the third most certainly was – 'Scotland would have been worse off' (Henderson and Mitchell, 2015).

Their sense of identity was undoubtedly one of the main drivers in the way that people voted. The ESRC study found that over 80% of those describing themselves as Scottish/not British voted 'yes' and 90% of those describing themselves as British/not Scottish voted 'no'. Those more Scottish than British voted 60% for 'yes' and those more British than Scottish over 87% for 'no' (Henderson and Mitchell, 2015).

At the very least, the evoking of images of Scotland's past gave emotional legitimacy to committed voters on both sides. Nationalism, however civic and progressive in its promises, needs to be grounded in a particular past (Jackson, 2020, p. 3). The subtle evoking of that sense of Scottish 'community' by Alex Salmond and others in the campaign told a story of that past. Likewise, a Union with no emotional appeal would rest on shaky foundations. Gordon Brown, in particular, gave people a reason to feel good – and patriotically Scottish – about voting 'no'.

In a referendum campaign in which both sides focused determinedly on the risks and opportunities of Scotland's future, as an independent nation or as part of the United Kingdom, appeals to imagined pasts were never going to be at the forefront of campaign rhetoric. But the ghosts of the past were not to be denied. They slipped quietly into the debate and helped determine which of their identities – Scottish or British – would predominate as people placed their cross on the ballot paper. One side evoked the shades of soldiers slaughtered in shared conflict and of the visionaries who had created a common welfare state and a National Health Service. The other reached back deeper into history to summon the spirits of medieval Scots who had resisted the English crown, of Protestant reformers who had engendered the Scottish tradition of communal education, and of the inventors and thinkers who had 'invented the modern world' (Salmond, 2014b).

These ghosts tugged at the heart strings. They were the guardians for those whose sense of Scottishness or Britishness was the primary motive for how they voted. They provided emotional reassurance for those whose decision was taken mainly on economic grounds. For others, they nipped at the conscience where head had overruled heart. Whatever their meaning for individual Scots, they could not be ignored.

The outcome of the 2014 referendum was closer than anticipated, with 55% voting to stay in the United Kingdom and 45% to leave. It was meant to be decisive, but in the turmoil of the post-Brexit United Kingdom, the question of Scottish independence is being asked again, with increased insistency. The ghosts of the old soldiers who linger round the sad war memorials that stand in every town and village in Scotland must wonder if they will be co-opted to battle again and who, next time, will prevail.

References

Ashcroft, M. (2014) 'Post Referendum Scotland Poll, 18–19 September 2014', *Lord Ashcroft Polls* [online]. Available at: https://lordashcroftpolls.com/wp-content/uploads/2014/09/Lord-Ashcroft-Polls-Referendum-day-poll-summary-1409191.pdf (Accessed: 28 April 2021).

BBC News (2013) 'Scottish Independence: Referendum White Paper Unveiled', *BBC Website*, 26 November [online]. Available at: https://www.bbc.co.uk/news/uk-scotland-scotland-politics-25088251 (Accessed: 27 April 2021).

BBC News (2014a) 'Scottish Independence: 'Yes' Vote Means Leaving Pound, Says Osborne', *BBC Website*, 13 February [online]. Available at: https://www.bbc.co.uk/news/uk-scotland-scotland-politics-26166794 (Accessed: 27 April 2021).

BBC News (2014b) 'Armed Forces Day Celebrations Take Place across UK', *BBC Website*, 28 June [online]. Available at: https://www.bbc.co.uk/news/uk-scotland-tayside-central-28062712 (Accessed: 27 April 2021).

BBC News (2015) 'The Referendum Victory Speech Alex Salmond Never Gave', *BBC Website*, 16 September [online]. Available at: https://www.bbc.co.uk/news/uk-scotland-scotland-politics-34267778 (Accessed: 28 April 2021).

Brown, G. (2014a) *My Scotland, Our Britain: A Future Worth Sharing*. London: Simon & Schuster.

Brown, G. (2014b) *Final Referendum Speech*, Glasgow, 17 September [online]. Available at: https://www.theguardian.com/politics/2014/sep/17/gordon-brown-appeals-to-labour-voters-vote-no (Accessed: 10 February 2022).

Cameron, D. (2014) 'The Importance of Scotland to the UK', *GOV.UK*, 7 February [online]. Available at: https://www.gov.uk/government/speeches/the-importance-of-scotland-to-the-uk-david-camerons-speech (Accessed: 28 April 2021).

Cameron, D. (2019) *For the Record*. London: William Collins.

Centre on Constitutional Change (2014) 'The English Favour a Hard Line with Scotland', *Centre on Constitutional Change*, 19 August [online]. Available at: https://www.centreonconstitutionalchange.ac.uk/news_opinion/english-favour-hard-line-scotland-whatever-result-independence-referendum (Accessed: 28 April 2021).

Curtice, J. (2014a) 'The Score at Half Time: Trends in Support for Independence', *Scot Cen Social Research* [online]. Available at: https://www.scotcen.org.uk/media/270726/SSA-13-The-Score-At-Half-Time.pdf (Accessed: 27 April 2021).

Curtice, J. (2014b) 'Who Won the Leaders' Debate: ICM's Instant Poll', *What Scotland Thinks* [online]. Available at: https://whatscotlandthinks.org/2014/08/who-won-the-leaders-debate-icms-instant-poll/ (Accessed: 27 April 2021).

Curtice, J. (2014c) 'Has the Referendum Campaign Made a Difference?', *Scot Cen Social Research* [online]. Available at: http://scotcen-what-scotland-thinks-chart-images.s3.amazonaws.com/files/62d0afd9-d75b-46ba-887c-a384017007b7/ssa-2014-launch-jc-briefing-final-2pdf (Accessed: 28 April 2021).

Curtice, J. (2017) 'From Indyref1 to Indyref2? The State of Nationalism in Scotland', *Scottish Social Attitudes* [online]. Available at: https://www.ssa.natcen.ac.uk/media/38917/ssa-2016-state-of-nationalism.pdf (Accessed: 28 April 2021).

Curtice, J. and Ormston, R. (2011) 'Is Scotland More Left Wing than England?', *British Social Attitudes 28*, 42(5 December) [online]. Available at: https://www.nuffieldfoundation.org/sites/default/files/files/scotcen-ssa-report.pdf (Accessed: 28 April 2021).

Devine, T. (2017) *Independence or Union: Scotland's Past and Scotland's Present.* London: Penguin Books.

Henderson, A. and Mitchell, J. (2015) 'The Scottish Question, Six Months On – Transatlantic Seminar Series, 27 March', *School of Social and Political Science and School of Law, University of Edinburgh* [online]. Available at: https://blogs.sps.ed.ac.uk/scottishreferendumstudy/files/2015/03/Scottish-Referendum-Study-27-March-2015.pdf (Accessed: 28 April 2021).

Jackson, B. (2020) *The Case for Scottish Independence: A History of Nationalist Political Thought in Modern Scotland.* Cambridge: Cambridge University Press.

Kenny, M., Rycroft, P. and Sheldon, J. (2021) 'Union at the Crossroads: Can the British State Handle the Challenges of Devolution', *Constitution Society* [online]. Available at: https://consoc.org.uk/wp-content/uploads/2021/04/Union-at-the-Crossroads-FINAL.pdf (Accessed: 26 April 2021).

Kidd, C. (2008) *Union and Unionisms: Political Thought in Scotland, 1500–2000.* Cambridge: Cambridge University Press.

McAnulla, S.D. and Crines, A. (2017) 'The Rhetoric of Alex Salmond and the 2014 Scottish Independence Referendum', *British Politics*, 12(4), pp. 473–491 [online]. Available at: http://eprints.whiterose.ac.uk/112690/ (Accessed: 28 April 2021).

Mullen, T. (2015) 'Introduction' in McHarg, A. et al. (eds.) *The Scottish Independence Referendum: Constitutional and Political Implications.* Oxford: Oxford University Press, pp. 3–28.

Pike, J. (2015) *Project Fear: How an Unlikely Alliance Left a Kingdom United but a Country Divided.* London: Biteback Publishing.

Revest, D. (2016) 'Are the Commitment to Scottish Independence and the Scottish National Party Evidence of a Clash of Values between Scotland and England?', *Observatoire de la société britannique*, 18, pp. 37–75 [online]. Available at: https://journals.openedition.org/osb/1807 (Accessed: 28 April 2021).

Rose, R. (1982) *The Territorial Dimension in Government; Understanding the United Kingdom.* Chatham: Chatham House Publishers.

Salmond, A. (2013) '2013 Speech to SNP Spring Conference', *UKPOL – Political Speech Archive* [online]. Available at: http://www.ukpol.co.uk/alex-salmond-2013-speech-to-snp-conference/ (Accessed: 27 April 2021).

Salmond, A. (2014a) 'Alex Salmond's New Statesman Lecture: Full Text', *New Statesman*, 5 March [online]. Available at: https://www.newstatesman.com/politics/2014/03/alex-salmonds-new-statesman-lecture-full-text (Accessed: 28 April 2021).

Salmond, A. (2014b) '"A Good Global Citizen": Alex Salmond's Speech on Scotland's Role in the World (Glasgow Caledonian University, New York, 7 April)', *Open Democracy* [online]. Available at: https://www.opendemocracy.net/en/opendemocracyuk/good-global-citizen-alex-salmonds-speech-on-scotlands-role-in-world/ (Accessed: 8 February 2022).

Salmond, A. (2014c) '2014 Speech to SNP Conference (Aberdeen, 12 April)', *UKPOL – Political Speech Archive* [online]. Available at: http://www.ukpol.co.uk/alex-salmond-2014-speech-to-snp-conference/ (Accessed: 27 April 2021).

Salmond, A. (2014d) *Scotland's Place in Europe.* Speech to College of Bruges, Brugge, 28 April [online]. Available at: https://www.reddit.com/r/Scotland/comments/247czy/full_text_of_alex_salmond_speech_to_college_of/ (Accessed: 10 February 2022).

Salmond, A. (2015) *The Dream Shall Never Die.* London: William Collins.

Scottish Government (2013) *Scotland's Future: Your Guide to an Independent Scotland.* Edinburgh: Scottish Government [online]. Available at: https://www.gov.scot/publications/scotlands-future/ (Accessed: 27 April 2021).

Smout, T.C. (1969) *A History of the Scottish People, 1560–1830.* London: Fontana Press.

UK Government (2013a) *Scotland Analysis Collection,* London: HMSO [online]. Available at: https://www.gov.uk/government/collections/scotland-analysis (Accessed: 27 April 2021).

UK Government (2013b) *Scotland Analysis: Devolution and the implications of Scottish Independence.* London: HMSO [online]. Available at: https://www.gov.uk/government/publications/scotland-analysis-devolution-and-the-implications-of-scottish-independence (Accessed: 27 April 2021).

UK Government (2013c) *Scotland Analysis: Currency and Monetary Policy.* London: HMSO [online]. Available at: https://www.gov.uk/government/publications/scotland-analysis-currency-and-monetary-policy (Accessed: 28 April 2021).

UK Government (2013d) 'News Story: Stirling to Host Armed Forces Day', *GOV.UK,* 27 August [online]. Available at: https://www.gov.uk/government/news/stirling-to-host-armed-forces-day-2014#:~:text=The%20city%20of%20Stirling%20in,next%20year's%20Armed%20Forces%20Day.&text=Plans%20will%20soon%20be%20underway, Forces%20personnel%20past%20and%20present (Accessed: 28 April 2021).

UK Government (2014) *Scotland Analysis: United Kingdom, United Future: Conclusions of the Scotland Analysis Programme.* London: HMSO [online]. Available at: https://www.gov.uk/government/publications/united-kingdom-united-future-conclusions-of-the-scotland-analysis-programme (Accessed: 28 April 2021).

Yarde, J. and Wishart, R. (2020) 'An Unequal Union? Attitudes towards Social Inequality in England and Scotland', *British Social Attitudes 37* [online]. Available at: https://www.bsa.natcen.ac.uk/media/39400/bsa37_social-inequality-in-england-and-scotland.pdf (Accessed: 28 April 2021).

7 Haunted by the lessons of 'the good war'

Post-Cold War contestation of World War II narratives

Marjorie Galelli, Michael Stricof*

June 6, 1944. Rain poured down onto Normandy as thousands of American and allied soldiers stormed its beaches in the largest amphibious landing in history to defeat Hitler's Nazi regime. Once victory was achieved, those lucky enough to survive were welcomed home as heroes and went back to their hometowns to live the American Dream and enjoy peace and prosperity. Or so the story goes. Over the decades following the end of World War II, the war and the men who fought in it have been canonized as 'the greatest generation': the standard to which all following generations should rise. While this mythologizing could have remained innocuous, by the end of the twentieth century, the glorification of World War II as 'the good war' that ended in total victory helped the United States' government sell questionable foreign and domestic policy decisions to the American public.

The memorialization of World War II took place throughout the second half of the twentieth century, but it culminated in the 1990s when a true World War II 'memory boom', played out in consumer media, shaped popular understanding of the war for the rest of the decade and into the 2000s (Huyssen, 1995). The general trend in late-1990s public memory was toward heroic representations rooted in the idea of the 'the good war'. In movies like *Pearl Harbor*, *Saving Private Ryan*, or the TV show *Band of Brothers*, World War II was depicted as a crowning achievement, a truly just war where the morally righteous capitalist democracy defeated evil fascists bent on destruction and genocide (Ramsay, 2015; Owen, 2002; Zinn, 2001). The concept of 'the good war' found its way into the simplified version of history textbooks (Crawford and Foster, 2008, p. 126), and even appeared in award-winning publications like the Pulitzer Prize winning oral history collection by Studs Terkel (1985). Triumphalism also dominated the National World War II Memorial dedicated in 2004, itself a response to a perceived cultural need to remember 'the good war' and 'the greatest generation' who fought it (Doss, 2008; Hass, 2013). As Debra Ramsay argues, the notion of 'the good war' has become one of the 'three central components' of World War II memory in the United States, along with the 'citizen-soldier' and 'the war as a visual construct' (2015, p. 10–11).

DOI: 10.4324/9781003178040-10

This chapter does not address the overall cultural representations of the war, which have been studied extensively. Instead, it focuses on two cases in which US policy was significantly influenced by the memory of World War II and how the debates that ensued included voices that dissented from the mainstream, glorified view of the conflict that was solidifying in the American mind, thereby revealing multiple layers in the war's memorialization. In the early 1990s, perhaps surprisingly, Secretary of Defence Dick Cheney tried to frame the post-World War II moment not as triumphant victory, but as the beginning of a pattern of foolish retreat and failure. He sought to protect defence budgets and military preparedness in the face of post-Cold War calls for a peace dividend by offering a sceptical view that challenged the total victory narrative. A decade later, during the lead up to the 2003 invasion of Iraq, President George W. Bush and Cheney, now vice-president, sought to bolster support for the impending Iraq War by using parallels to World War II not only to entice Americans into a new righteous war but also to scare them with the ghost of appeasement. Historians and anti-war commentators took on the mantle of the critic and tried to straighten the record by correcting the picture of World War II enshrined in America's memory and nuancing the narrative of 'the good war' that had become so dominant.

Questions of memory and identity have often been dealt with at the cultural level. Yet the underlying arguments are fundamentally social and political—cultural artefacts teach us about the dominant societal views at a given time and reflect the societal perceptions that guide specific behaviours and policies. This chapter explicitly focuses on the political use of the memory of World War II, recognizing that although the war was often used as a simple corrective to the Vietnam Syndrome, there were also some politicians, historians and journalists advocating for a much more complex vision of World War II.[1] It is these more nuanced depictions of 'the good war', and the degree of success encountered by individuals challenging an identity-defining memory, that are at the heart of our study. Then Secretary of Defence Dick Cheney's construction of a less victorious narrative of World War II to justify his plans for a post-Cold War military force and the debates around the Iraq War in 2002–2003 demonstrate that policymakers repeatedly relied on World War II analogies, often using different layers of the war's memory as a scare tactic to promote their own agendas.

World War II and the Post-Cold War Era

By the 1990s, World War II exerted a particularly powerful and optimistic pull on American memory. It combined 'giant scale, moral clarity, American unity and total American victory' (Sherry, 1995, p. 449). This last element, *total American victory*, is what some policymakers in the George H.W. Bush administration contested. The end of World War II, brought about by the nuclear bombing of Hiroshima and Nagasaki, created a victory that was much less comfortable than popular memory would later suggest. Uncertainty about atomic weapons and growing mistrust with the Soviet Union clouded the American victory. However, by the time the Cold War had ended, this moment of uncertainty had largely faded from memory, especially in comparison with the more recent, nationally damaging memory of Vietnam. It nevertheless haunted policymakers who sought to avoid what they perceived as the mistakes of past victories.

The Cold War is over, now what?

After framing foreign policy for nearly five decades, the end of the Cold War left American policymakers without a sense of direction, leading them to take a deeper look at the past and eventually sparking a debate among themselves and with the public about the lessons of 'the good war'. The early 1990s were defined by both optimistic assessments of lasting peace and an uncomfortable feeling of uncertainty. The new millennium promised either the 'end of history' (Fukuyama, 1989) or a new 'clash of civilizations' (Huntington, 1993a), casting doubt on America's foreign policy leadership. The post-Cold War period lacked a defining overall goal or ideal which could be reduced to a catchy name like 'containment', the umbrella term for Cold War grand strategy. As several historians demonstrated, finding the right label for the country's foreign policy was a priority for George H.W. Bush and Bill Clinton, yet both struggled to explain American international relations in this new era. Bush's solution, the 'New World Order', was evocative, but lacked substance.[2] Clinton's 'Democratic Enlargement' never caught on and was retired by the end of his first term (Chollet and Goldgeier, 2008, pp. 18, 27, 64-47; Brands, 2008, pp. 4–5, 79–85, 108–110).[3]

Just before the end of the Cold War, one of the top Soviet experts on the United States and advisor to the Kremlin, Georgi Arbatov, commented: 'We are going to do something terrible to you, you will no longer have an enemy' (*Telegraph*, 2010). Indeed, in this overall atmosphere of uncertainty, the loss of America's Cold War enemy deprived the nation of a key element of its recent identity—that of the good guys battling towards victory against an 'evil empire' (Reagan, 1983). At the start of the decade the memory of the Vietnam War was still dominant. Military strategy, and specifically the 'overwhelming force' required by the 'Powell Doctrine' was a direct response to the supposed lessons of Vietnam (LaFeber, 2009, pp. 72–74).[4] When this new set of guidelines yielded victory in the First Gulf War, military intervention was once again presented as the solution, freeing the nation from the ghost of its greatest failure. As George H.W. Bush claimed: 'By God, we've kicked the Vietnam Syndrome once and for all' (1991). Such statements helped make way for the 1990s 'memory boom'. However, before World War II memory came to play a prominent part in bolstering support for foreign crusades against evil enemies, policymakers first used it as a cautionary tale.

Concerns about unlocking savings from defence through the 'economic conversion' of defence industries and military bases to commercial or public goods were a natural reaction to the end of the Cold War. The post-World War II period was commonly understood as a moment of unprecedented American prosperity due in part to post-war reconversion. The congressional Office of Technology Assessment (1992) included an in-depth analysis of post-World War II reconversion as a framework for understanding opportunities in the 1990s. The political press seemed to share a general understanding that the end of the Cold War could lead to real demobilization and economic benefits like those achieved in the 1940s. Reporters persistently badgered President Bush about a possible 'peace dividend'.[5] An early example of this occurred on 4 December 1989, at a news conference in Brussels when journalists raised questions regarding the United States' continued commitment to NATO. One journalist in particular challenged Bush by speculating about America's role in Europe considering the reduced tensions on the continent and asking: 'will there now be more money for the poor, the homeless, public housing—the nation's really badly in need of repair infrastructure?' (Bush, 1989).

The narrative of economic parallels between 1945 and 1989 was matched by a debate about defence policy that also relied on the memory of the post-War moment. Prominent intellectuals, like Harvard's Samuel Huntington, recognized the early 1990s as a new phase for American defence policy. Writing for *Joint Force Quarterly*, a Pentagon publication, he argued that the last transformative moment had occurred in 1946 when the World Wars' force structure gave way to the Cold War's 'defence establishment' (1993b, p. 38). The same issue of *Joint Force Quarterly* included an essay on Guadalcanal, one of the first major US battles of World War II, which served to demonstrate how the seemingly new post-Cold War focus on joint operations fit into a historical narrative dating back to World War II (Willmott, 1993). The nation's top military advisor, Chairman of the Joint Chiefs of Staff Colin Powell, also saw the 1990s as a moment of historical weight equivalent to World War II. Borrowing language from Franklin Delano Roosevelt, Powell labelled it 'a fourth rendezvous with destiny' (1992a, p. 44). The previous three had been the Revolutionary War, the Civil War, and World War II (including its Cold War aftermath). With these and other parallels to the 1940s, the defence policy debates of the 1990s were clearly entangled with contesting lessons of World War II and its immediate consequences.

'If history is any guide, we will blow it'

In response to economic calls for defence cuts and a sense that history was waiting for another dramatic transition, the Bush administration found itself arguing against the mainstream view that America's victory in World War II had been total. Secretary of Defence Dick Cheney directly responded to congressional pressure to cut the defence budget by using the example of

US demobilization after World War II as a cautionary tale. Cheney wanted Congress and the public to fear the looming ghost of too extensive reductions in US military power.

Cheney was sceptical of what Tom Engelhardt later labelled 'victory culture' (2007)—an underlying current in American identity that believes that the United States is simultaneously innocent and warlike, always the initial victim in armed conflict but also the ultimate winner—which had helped justify expansion and conquest from the colonial period through World War II. Cheney recognized that victory culture had always been hollow since the US became the world's premier power, and he argued that the myth of an indestructible America was foolish and empty. The country had paid dearly for believing in its own power in the past and it would be inappropriate to disengage from world leadership. In Cheney's view, preparation and mobilization were necessary to protect US interests, but achieving them required overcoming resistance in the American public by contesting the memory of World War II victory.

The Secretary of Defence was particularly concerned with maintaining sufficient forces for future challenges. Although Cheney accepted a 25% reduction in military forces as part of an overall budget deal in 1990, he was very conscious that cuts would go further unless he could provide a compelling counter-narrative to teach the public and Congress about their danger. As Cheney later explained:

> I was probably more concerned about having a story to tell and a rationale for why we need to preserve some significant capability rather than I was with what the absolute levels were. … 'Peace dividend, peace dividend', we heard that over and over and over again. We kept trying to make the argument that this is not about a peace dividend. This is about making sure we have enough force to deal with what is a very uncertain situation out there.
>
> (2000, p. 91)

Cheney frequently used historical references, especially to the start of the Cold War, when building his narrative of uncertainty. The Secretary of Defence's 1991 *Annual Report* claimed that the massive defence cuts after World War II were a mistake, blaming them, at least in part, for creating the opportunity for subsequent Soviet expansion. The report proclaimed, 'Today we have an opportunity to avoid a similar cycle of mistakes and crises', before concluding, 'The keystone of our strength remains the commitment of the American people to their defence', and 'Friends and adversaries alike can have no doubt about America's ability and will to carry out our responsibilities as a powerful force for freedom in the world' (Cheney, 1991, p. x). Overzealous cuts had to be avoided to ensure America's commitment to defence remained a priority. Other key military strategy documents from the time opened with warnings that the new post-Cold War world was potentially just as dangerous and more uncertain than before the fall of the

Soviet Union. The 1992 *National Military Strategy* repeated this sentiment: 'The real threat we now face is the threat of the unknown, the uncertain' (Powell, 1992b, p. 4).

It was not only the Secretary of Defence that relied on World War II to influence policy in the post-Cold War era. Richard Nixon joined the fray as a foreign policy commentator, using this contested version of the end of World War II to argue for continued American military engagement. In his last book, *Beyond Peace* (1994), Nixon referenced World War II in the traditional sense of righteous American victory, while using the post-war peace as a reminder of the shortcomings of American withdrawal. Despite the hopes of long-lasting peace, Nixon argued, 'in 1946, less than a year after the end of World War II and the founding of the United Nations, the Soviet Union launched the Cold War' (p.167), which was a direct consequence of America's foolish belief that a new era of peace had been achieved. This argument made it clear that Nixon thought that beliefs in peace at the start of the 1990s were equally foolish and bound to have a similar outcome, if the past offered any lesson for the present.

Nixon and Cheney were joined by foreign policy specialists, such as structural realists John J. Mearsheimer and Kenneth M. Waltz, in invoking the ghost of the World Wars. Mearsheimer's widely-read article in *The Atlantic Monthly*, 'Why We Will Soon Miss the Cold War'' (1990a), argued that the end of Cold War bipolarization would lead to greater anarchy, conflict, and likely war in Europe. Beyond his Hobbesian theory, Mearsheimer tried to rely on historical examples, using both World Wars to debunk various emerging theories of international peace. He believed that World War II demonstrated how misguided people were to believe that after a long period of conflict, future wars would be unlikely. Mearsheimer's less widely cited article in *International Security* from the same summer drew on the World War II parallel even more explicitly. Entitled 'Back to the Future: Instability in Europe after the Cold War' (1990b), it claimed that the end of Cold War polarization would likely lead to fractures within Europe like those that occurred before 1947. For Mearsheimer and other structural realists (Waltz, 1993), the best prediction of the future would be found looking back at the past, and the past they saw was full of unpredictable conflicts.

Cheney was consistently sceptical of the United States' ability to predict the future and correctly plan for the next, in his view inevitable, conflict. The 1992 *Defense Planning Guidance* claimed, 'As a nation we have never before succeeded in pacing reductions without endangering our interests' (Cheney, 1992a, p. 3). At a hearing before the House of Representatives Committee on the Budget, Cheney (1992b, p. 2) was even more blunt in assessing the defence drawdown: 'If history is any guide, we will blow it. Every single time in this century ... we have gotten it wrong'. The consequences were significant. 'The vacuum that the United States left was filled' by new adversaries and ultimately the country had to go to war, at higher cost in blood and treasure than if the nation had stayed engaged and prepared. For Cheney

(1992a, p. 5; 1993, p. 6), the only responsible solution was to maintain US power capable of 'Shaping the Future Security Environment'. To this end, he felt he had to haunt Congress and the American public with the ghost of his version of post-war history in which a failed peace led to bloody and costly conflict. This was a very different narrative of the World War II victory than the triumphalism that was predominant in mainstream consciousness. It was also a very different narrative than that which would initially be used by the next Bush administration.

The early post-Cold War period contained a mix of optimistic belief that defence cuts could lead to greater wealth, counterbalanced by uncertainty rooted in the new chaotic international environment and a significant economic recession. Ultimately, defence policymakers were successful in limiting the defence drawdown but, despite Cheney's attempt to scare Americans with memories of the challenges of 1945, the unease of the post-Cold War seems to have reinforced the public's desire to understand the end of World War II through the lens of total victory through unconditional surrender and the period of economic prosperity that followed as the very opposite of the morally unclear and economically challenged early 1990s. This period was followed immediately by a 'memory boom' in which World War II was revisited and simplified greatly.

World War II and the Run-Up to the Iraq War

On 11 September 2001, terrorists struck at the heart of the United States, destroying symbols of American might in New York and Washington and striking a blow to the country's image as an untouchable superpower. In the wake of these attacks, the new George W. Bush administration adopted a foreign policy approach that would later be known as the 'Bush doctrine'. It posited that ensuring the United States' security did not simply require that the country be capable of defending itself in the wake of attacks on US soil, but rather, that it should conduct pre-emptive strikes in order to prevent such attacks. Based on this reasoning, the administration decided to attack Iraq and Saddam Hussein's dictatorial regime.

In addition to the overall preventive war framework, the Bush administration used many rhetorical devices in order to convince the American people of the righteousness of the war to come, none more forceful than its repetitive evocations of World War II. The simplified, glorified memory of World War II that permeated the previous decade offered the administration the tool it needed to present the invasion of Iraq as the twenty-first century's version of a crusade against evil, with the Baathists cast in the role of the Nazis and Saddam as Hitler. Talking about Iraq, along with Iran and North Korea, in his 2002 State of the Union Address, President Bush stated: 'States like these, and their terrorist allies, constitute an axis of evil, arming to threaten the peace of the world'. The label 'axis' he used here directly evoked the collective memory of the Axis powers defeated by the Allies in

1945. At the same time, people pushing back against the administration's decision to invade Iraq also summoned the ghost of World War II to bolster their argument. In short, in the months surrounding the invasion of Iraq in March 2003, World War II became a prism through which both proponents and opponents of the war cast their competing views of the present.

The administration's case to the American public: World War II glorified

When the administration started to make its case to the American public in early 2002, the message was simple: Iraq and its dictator represented an imminent threat to national security and therefore needed to be stopped, by any means necessary. After all, nobody wanted 'the smoking gun to be a mushroom cloud', as National Security Advisor Condoleezza Rice famously stated during an interview on CNN (CNN, 2002). This warning played into one of the 'lessons' that the administration suggested the American people draw from World War II on the dangers of appeasement. The use of World War II by the administration was twofold: first, drawing parallels between Saddam and Hitler helped demonize the Iraqi dictator in terms familiar to the American people, thus justifying the need for intervention. Second, the failure of appeasement gave urgency to the situation, as the ghost of Munich was brandished to caution the public about the consequences of waiting too long to address the situation.

Building on the 'axis of evil' line of the January 2002 State of the Union speech, Bush and his advisors were quick to associate Saddam's regime with that of Hitler's and to foreshow their intervention in Iraq as a new righteous crusade against a monstrous enemy in order to defend humanity. One such reference occurred a few days before the beginning of Operation Iraqi Freedom. In his 17 March 2003 'Address to the Nation on Iraq', Bush (2003a) stated: 'One reason the U.N. was founded after World War II was to confront aggressive dictators, actively and early, before they can attack the innocent and destroy the peace'. Later in the same speech he added: 'In the 20th century, some chose to appease murderous dictators, whose threats were allowed to grow into genocide and global war'. Both instances clearly established a parallel between the former Nazi Führer and the President of Iraq.

With this rhetoric, Bush was using World War II as a cautionary tale and advocating against repeating the error committed by European powers in Munich in 1938, when British Prime Minister Neville Chamberlain and his French counterpart Edouard Daladier opted for appeasement instead of confronting Hitler following his annexation of the *Sudetenland* in Czechoslovakia. Starting in 2002, 'the ghost of Munich' became a prominent piece of the debate (Logevall and Osgood, 2010). This infamous episode was referred to frequently by the Bush administration and its supporters. For instance, during the same CNN Late Edition that saw Rice make her comment about not wanting 'the smoking gun to be a mushroom cloud', Wolf Blitzer interviewed Republican Senator Richard Shelby, then Vice Chairman of the Senate Intelligence Committee, who stated:

> Look back in history, Wolf. 1936, look what Hitler did. He went into the Rhineland, nothing happened. 1938, he annexed Austria, nothing happened. And then ... we didn't, but England and France helped him dismember Czechoslovakia in 1938, and then he seized the rest of it, and then war began September the 1st, 1939.
>
> (CNN, 2002)

Although these examples were taken out of their larger historical context, the simple evocation of Munich played into American fears by conjuring the darkest of prospects for the future—a repetition of the atrocities perpetrated by the Nazi regime.

Challenging the narrative

As soon as the Bush administration began to use World War II as a justification for the war in Iraq, voices started to express dissent in the media. They also often chose to rely on parallels with World War II to make their case, by explaining to the American public why the situation in Iraq was widely different from that which preceded World War II, and why, even if some parallels were apt, invading Iraq would not bode well for the United States.

First, articles pointed out that one would be hard pressed to establish a direct parallel between pre-World War II Germany and present-day Iraq. Military historian Gerhard Weinberg (2002), for instance, argued that 'those who talk of Munich ... do little justice either to the dilemma of those who negotiated with Adolf Hitler then or to those who must weigh the need for military action today'. In terms of the balance of power in particular, the United States were in a significantly more powerful position in 2002 than that of Britain and France in 1938. This imbalance, according to Weinberg, made it all the more difficult to use the Munich analogy in order to present a war in Iraq as a necessity and not an act of aggression. One critic even went as far as reversing roles in his interpretation of the parallel to World War II. In an article published in the *New York Times*, journalist David E. Sanger (2002) likened the possibility of a pre-emptive strike against Iraq to the Japanese attack on Pearl Harbor in 1941. In other words, if the United States were to go ahead with its plan to intervene in Iraq, it would likely be the aggressor in the eyes of the rest of the world, which would tarnish the country's reputation and significantly hinder international support for the Global War on Terror.

Subsequently, historians challenged the notion that occupying Iraq in the early 2000s would lead to a success-story akin to that of Germany and Japan following their occupation in the second half of the twentieth century.

In September 2002, former Secretary of the Navy James Webb sought to leverage history in order to prevent the war and cautioned against the invasion of Iraq in the light of the occupation that would follow. He detailed the differences between Iraq, a multi-ethnic country with no unifying figure, and post-World War II Japan, a homogenous nation still unified by the emperor, in order to show 'how inapt the comparison is'. 'The issue before us', Webb stated, 'is not simply whether the United States should end the regime of Saddam Hussein, but whether we as a nation are prepared to physically occupy territory in the Middle East for the next 30 to 50 years' (Webb, 2002).

In the fall of 2002, others expressed similar concerns about the eventual cost of the occupation that would follow the war. They used data from the US occupations of Germany and Japan post-World War II to show what the situation was truly likely to require in Iraq when switching to what the military calls 'Phase IV', post-conflict operations. Journalist Vernon Loeb raised specific questions about the cost of the post-war reconstruction of Iraq. Citing a study by the Army's Center of Military History, Loeb warned his readers that 'the U.S. military would have to commit ... 100,000 [peacekeeping troops] in Iraq if it were to occupy and reconstruct [this nation] on the scale that occurred in Japan and Germany after World War II' (2002). Michael O'Hanlon (2002) also brought up similar financial issues in a *New York Times* article entitled 'The Price of Stability', in which he stated that the costs of occupying Iraq 'will be substantially higher than anything publicly acknowledged by the administration so far'.[6]

It was not only opponents to the war who criticized the way that analogies to World War II were being used. In the fall of 2002, *The Washington Post* published a column by Richard Cohen in which he too questioned the accuracy of parallels between World War II and a potential invasion of Iraq by highlighting the flaws in the administration's narrative. Arguing against Condoleezza Rice's claim that the United States liberated the German people, Cohen wrote, 'The problem is that Germany was not liberated. Instead, Germans fought on behalf of a criminal regime until the bitter end'. He concluded, 'Iraq will have to be "liberated" the usual way— by a bitter war and a protracted occupation'. This particular example is striking, as it shows that critics of the analogy were not necessarily critics of the war itself, as Cohen affirmed that he would support the overthrow of Saddam's regime. His main concern was that hasty comparisons with World War II were misleading, as the actual war had little to do with the myth engrained in American memory. Despite historians' efforts, the more complex version of World War II described in well-researched scholarship never resonated with the American public, even though it was widely broadcast in the media. The Bush administration had made its case and, at least in part thanks to its use of World War II imagery, by the beginning of 2003, more than half of the US population favoured a military intervention in Iraq, and, in the days following the invasion, that support rose to 70% (Gallup, Inc., 2003).

Change of tone in the administration

After the initial success of the invasion, which prompted President Bush to stand on the deck of the *USS Abraham Lincoln* in front of a banner that read 'Mission Accomplished' in May 2003, the situation rapidly deteriorated. As Iraq sank deeper and deeper into chaos, both the administration's discourse and that of the media began to adapt. Although the administration kept clinging onto its parallel to World War II, its discourse started to refer to a much more historically accurate version of the war. Most journalists shed the World War II analogy altogether and started to refer to another war instead: the Vietnam War.

Once it became obvious that getting out of Iraq might turn out to be more difficult than expected, Bush and his team started to adapt their rhetoric to try to maintain public support for the war. Instead of focusing on the triumphal outcome of the war, President Bush and his advisors started to stress the difficulties that 'the greatest generation' encountered and to remind people of all the obstacles that 1940s GIs had had to overcome. On 25 August 2003, as she was addressing Veterans of Foreign Wars in Texas, Condoleezza Rice said, 'There is an understandable tendency to look back on America's experience in post-War Germany and see only the successes. But as some of you here today surely remember, the road we travelled was very difficult'. A couple of months later, in a speech given on 6 November 2003, President Bush talked specifically about the occupation and reconstruction of Iraq in parallel to that of Germany and Japan in 1945. He stated then that:

> Some sceptics of democracy assert that the traditions of Islam are inhospitable to the representative government. This 'cultural condescension', as Ronald Reagan termed it, has a long history. After the Japanese surrender in 1945, a so-called Japan expert asserted that democracy in that former empire would 'never work'. Another observer declared the prospects for democracy in post-Hitler Germany are, and I quote, 'most uncertain at best' – he made that claim in 1957.
>
> (Bush, 2003b)

As these two examples demonstrate, rather than using the mythical story of World War II, President Bush and his advisors started to rely on a more complex version, akin to that which had been presented by journalists as early as 2002 in order to push back against the war, to reassure the American public as the occupation phase started to look more difficult.

The two layers in the Bush administration's use of World War II as an analogy for its campaign in Iraq show politicians' equal ability to exploit popular memory of historical events as well as their more accurate description by historians, depending on which best helps politicians make their case. The administration's degree of adaptability attests to its acute awareness regarding its use of historical analogies and suggests that they were not used by chance, but intentionally designed to manipulate public opinion.

It seemed for a while that the success of Operation Desert Storm in the early 1990s had put an end to the so-called 'Vietnam Syndrome', but with the rise of the insurgency in Iraq, its ghost came back with a vengeance. While in late 2002 and early 2003 there were barely a handful of articles suggesting a connection between Vietnam and Iraq, by the fall of 2003 these parallels had become commonplace. In October 2003, the *New York Times* published a piece boldly entitled 'Why Are We Back in Vietnam?' In this column, Frank Rich claimed 'you can tell that the administration itself now fears that Iraq is becoming a Vietnam'. Eventually, the military began dusting off the counterinsurgency tactics it had developed in Vietnam and tried to apply them to the Iraqi theatre.[7] Despite the Bush administration's best efforts to associate Operation Iraqi Freedom with the glorified imagery of World War II, it was not enough to prevent the ghost of the Vietnam War from coming back to haunt the nation.

Conclusion

The memory of World War II ingrained in the American mind makes it a powerful political tool. In the post-Cold War era, policymakers have repeatedly sought to co-opt its many layers to promote their own agendas, including in ways that contested traditional interpretations and often deployed the ghost of World War II as a scare tactic. In the early 1990s, Dick Cheney understood that preserving defence budgets in the face of calls for a peace dividend was as much a battle of narratives as a strategic reality. Drawing on the end of World War II and the subsequent rise of the Cold War, Cheney challenged the traditional triumphal reading of 'the good war' followed by total victory. Instead, he reframed the narrative to scare Congress and the American public into recognizing the inherent uncertainty and risk of the period. In the run-up to the 2003 invasion of Iraq, the George W. Bush administration also relied on World War II parallels, combining the frightening ghost of Munich with analogies to past dictatorial regimes to sell a new fight against 1940s evil reincarnate. Critics of the war relied on equally symbolic and chilling World War II analogies, such as comparing pre-emptive war doctrine to the attack on Pearl Harbor. As the war progressed, more complex historical comparisons used by the Bush administration to reassure the American people when the occupation gave no sign of improvement had less success. Beyond the simple, positive vision of World War II (contrasted to the quagmire of Vietnam) these examples illustrate a more complicated memory in which multiple readings of the past have competed since the Cold War to justify American policies and foreign interventions. When used as a cautionary tale haunted by an easily identifiable ghost, these readings of the past proved effective.

Notes

* Michael Stricof, Aix Marseille Univ, LERMA, Aix-en-Provence, France.
1 The 'Vietnam Syndrome' refers to the United States' supposed reluctance to employ military force abroad following the collective trauma of the Vietnam War.
2 Bush coined 'New World Order' in a speech on 11 September 1990 in the context of Iraq's invasion of Kuwait. He defined it as an objective for the post-Cold War. It remained a vague concept, as Bush described it as an era of harmony, with justice, security and freedom from terror (Bush, 1990).
3 'Democratic Enlargement' or 'Engagement and Enlargement' was a term coined by speechwriter Jeremy Rosner in response to National Security Advisor Antony Lake's desire to come up with a catchphrase for Clinton's overall foreign policy following criticism that the administration lacked direction (Brinkley, 1997). Elaborated by Lake in a speech in August 1993, 'Enlargement' represented 'Containment' in reverse: expanding democratic capitalism by 1) shoring up traditional allies, 2) supporting emerging market democracies, especially in Eastern Europe, 3) containing powers that did not have market democratic systems, and 4) providing humanitarian assistance that encouraged the development of capitalism and democratic government (Lake, 1993).
4 The 'Powell Doctrine' provided a list of conditions for foreign military interventions. Built on the previous 'Weinberger Doctrine', it stipulated that the US should only intervene when in the country's vital national interest, with popular support and using overwhelming force.
5 These questions were spread throughout his presidency, occurring: in 1989 on 29 November, 4 and 8 December; in 1990 on 12 and 19 January, 7 February, 13, 15 and 16 March, 3 April, 8 June, 6 July, 17 September and 18 December; in 1991 on 6 February, 31 July, 29 August, 27 September and 6 November; and in 1992 on 3 February, 11 March, 9 April, and 9 and 17 June. All 24 times the peace dividend was referenced by President Bush in public can be found in the Public Papers of the president, accessible online at the George H.W. Bush Presidential Library and Museum: https://bush41library.tamu.edu/archives/public-papers/.
6 This article was part of an ongoing conversation between the author, Philip H. Gordon, and Ken Adelman. The latter had famously claimed that 'demolishing Hussein's military power and liberating Iraq would be a cakewalk' (2002).
7 Lessons from the Vietnam War influenced the creation of the Army's new Counterinsurgency doctrine in 2006 (laid out in Field Manual 3-24) and led to the publication of scholarly works such as the collection of essays edited by Gardner and Blatt Young (2007).

References

Adelman, K. (2002) 'Cakewalk in Iraq', *The Washington Post*, 13 February.

Brands, H. (2008) *From Berlin to Baghdad: America's Search for Purpose in the Post-Cold War World*. Lexington: University Press of Kentucky.

Brinkley, D.G. (1997) 'Democratic Enlargement: The Clinton Doctrine', *Foreign Policy*, 106 (Spring), pp. 110–27.

Bush, G.H.W. (1989) 'The President's News Conference in Brussels. 4 December', *George Bush Presidential Library and Museum* [online]. Available at: http://bush41library.tamu.edu/archives/public-papers/1298 (Accessed: 11 February 2015).

Bush, G.H.W. (1990) 'Address before a Joint Session of Congress. 11 September', *Miller Center* [online]. Available at: https://millercenter.org/the-presidency/presidential-speeches/september-11-1990-address-joint-session-congress (Accessed: 1 August 2021).

Bush, G.H.W. (1991) 'Remarks to the American Legislative Exchange Council. Washington, DC, 1 March', *American Presidency Project* [online]. Available at: https://www.presidency.ucsb.edu/node/265226 (Accessed: 10 November 2018).

Bush, G.W. (2002) 'President Delivers State of the Union Address. 29 January', *White House Archives* [online]. Available at: https://georgewbush-whitehouse. archives.gov/news/releases/2002/01/20020129-11.html (Accessed: 13 May 2021).

Bush, G.W. (2003a) 'March 17, 2003: Address to the Nation on Iraq', *Miller Center* [online]. Available at: https://millercenter.org/the-presidency/presidential-speeches/ march-17-2003-address-nation-iraq (Accessed: 20 October 2016).

Bush, G.W. (2003b) 'November 6, 2003: Remarks on Freedom in Iraq and Middle East. *Miller Center* [online]. Available at: https://millercenter.org/the-presidency/ presidential-speeches/november-6-2003-remarks-freedom-iraq-and-middle-east (Accessed: 20 October 2016).

Cheney, R. (1991) *Annual Report to the President and the Congress.* Washington, DC: Government Printing Office.

Cheney, R. (1992a) *Defense Planning Guidance FY 1994–1999.* Washington, DC: Department of Defense. Incoming FOIAs, National Security Archive.

Cheney, R. (1992b) *102 Congress, House of Representatives, Fiscal Year 1993 Defense Budget: Hearing Before the Comm. on the Budget.* Washington, DC: Government Printing Office.

Cheney, R. (1993) *Defense Strategy for the 1990s: The Regional Defense Strategy.* Washington, DC: Department of Defense.

Cheney, R. (2000) 'Interview by Philip Zelikow, Tarek E. Masoud, Richard Betts and James H. McCall, 16–17 March, Dallas, TX', *George H.W. Bush Oral History Project*, Miller Center, University of Virginia.

Chollet, D. and Goldgeier, J. (2008) *America Between the Wars: From 11/9 to 9/11; The Misunderstood Years Between the Fall of the Berlin Wall and the Start of the War on Terror.* New York: Public Affairs.

CNN (2002) 'Late Edition with Wolf Blitzer: Interview with Condoleezza Rice; Pataki Talks about 9–11; Graham, Shelby Discuss War on Terrorism', *CNN Transcripts*, 8 September [online]. Available at: http://transcripts.cnn.com/ TRANSCRIPTS/0209/08/le.00.html (Accessed: 17 November 2018).

Cohen, R. (2002) 'Hitler and Bad History', *The Washington Post*, 24 September [online]. Available at: https://search.proquest.com/docview/2075065457/abstract/ E51A05F7B33B454DPQ/21 (Accessed: 10 September 2018).

Crawford, K.A. and Foster, S.J. (eds.) (2008) *War, Nation, Memory: International Perspectives on World War II in School History Textbooks.* Charlotte: Information Age Publishing.

Doss, E. (2008) 'War, Memory, and the Public Mediation of Affect: The National World War II Memorial and American Imperialism', *Memory Studies*, 1(2), pp. 227–250.

Engelhardt, T. (2007) *The End of Victory Culture: Cold War America and the Disillusioning of a Generation*, 2nd rev. ed. Amherst: University of Massachusetts Press.

Fukuyama, F. (1989) 'The End of History?', *The National Interest*, 16(Summer), pp. 3–18.

Gallup, Inc. (2003) 'Seventy-Two Percent of Americans Support War Against Iraq', *Gallup*, 24 March [online]. Available at: https://news.gallup.com/poll/8038/

SeventyTwo-Percent-Americans-Support-War-Against-Iraq.aspx (Accessed: 14 May 2021).

Gardner, L.C. and Blatt Young, M. (eds.) (2007) *Iraq and the Lessons of Vietnam, or, How Not to Learn from the Past*. New York: New Press/W.W. Norton.

Hass, K.A. (2013) *Sacrificing Soldiers on the National Mall*. Berkeley, Los Angeles and London: University of California Press.

Huntington, S.P. (1993a) 'The Clash of Civilizations?', *Foreign Affairs*, 72(3/Summer), pp. 22–49.

Huntington, S.P. (1993b) 'New Contingencies, Old Roles', *Joint Force Quarterly*, 2(Autumn), pp. 38–43.

Huyssen, A. (1995) *Twilight Memories: Marking Time in a Culture of Amnesia*. New York: Routledge.

LaFeber, W. (2009) 'The Rise and Fall of Colin Powell and the Powell Doctrine', *Political Science Quarterly*, 124(1/Spring), pp. 71–93.

Lake, A. (1993) 'From Containment to Enlargement', *Johns Hopkins University School of Advanced International Studies, Washington, DC*, 21 September [online]. Available at: https://babel.hathitrust.org/cgi/pt?id=mdp.39015051567645&view=1 up&seq=1 (Accessed: 1 August 2021).

Loeb, V. (2002) 'Study: New Demands Could Tax Military: Historical Precedent Suggests 100,000 Troops Would Be Needed to Rebuild Iraq', *The Washington Post*, 23 September [online]. Available at: https://search.proquest.com/docview/2074997845/abstract/465B98BB031B4738PQ/21 (Accessed: 10 September 2018).

Logevall, F. and Osgood, K. (2010) 'The Ghost of Munich: America's Appeasement Complex', *World Affairs*, 173(2), pp. 13–26.

Mearsheimer, J.J. (1990a) 'Why We Will Soon Miss the Cold War', *The Atlantic Monthly*, 266(2/August), pp. 35–50.

Mearsheimer, J.J. (1990b) 'Back to the Future: Instability in Europe after the Cold War', *International Security*, 15(1/Summer), pp. 5–56.

Nixon, R. (1994) *Beyond Peace*. New York: Random House.

Office of Technology Assessment (1992) *After the Cold War: Living with Lower Defense Spending*. Washington, DC: Government Printing Office.

O'Hanlon, M. (2002) 'The Price of Stability', *The New York Times*, 22 October [online]. Available at: https://search.proquest.com/docview/92179607/abstract/465B98BB031B4738PQ/6 (Accessed: 10 September 2018).

Owen, A.S. (2002) 'Memory, War and American Identity: *Saving Private Ryan* as Cinematic Jeremiad', *Critical Studies in Media Communication*, 19(3/September), pp. 249–282.

Powell, C.P. (1992a) 'U.S. Forces: Challenges Ahead', *Foreign Affairs*, 71(5/Winter), pp. 32–45.

Powell, C.P. (1992b) *National Military Strategy of the United States*. Washington, DC: Government Printing Office.

Ramsay, D. (2015) *American Media and the Memory of World War II*. New York: Routledge.

Reagan, R. (1983) 'Remarks at the Annual Convention of the National Association of Evangelicals in Orlando, Florida. 8 March', *American Presidency Project* [online]. Available at: https://www.presidency.ucsb.edu/node/262885 (Accessed: 10 May 2021).

Rice, C. (2003) 'National Security Advisor Condoleezza Rice Remarks to Veterans of Foreign Wars', *White House Archives*, 25 August [online]. Available at: https://georgewbush-whitehouse.archives.gov/news/releases/2003/08/text/20030825-1.html (Accessed: 3 November 2018).

Rich, F. (2003) 'Why Are We Back in Vietnam?', *The New York Times*, 26 October [online]. Available at: https://search.proquest.com/docview/92522313/abstract/E51A05F7B33B454DPQ/18 (Accessed: 10 September 2018).

Sanger, D.E. (2002) 'Beating Them to the Prewar', *The New York Times*, 28 September [online]. Available at: https://search.proquest.com/docview/92195338/abstract/E51A05F7B33B454DPQ/20 (Accessed: 10 September 2018).

Sherry, M. (1995) *In the Shadow of War: The United States Since the 1930s*. New Haven, CT: Yale University Press.

Telegraph (2010) 'Georgi Arbatov obituary', *The Telegraph*, 14 November [online]. Available at: https://www.telegraph.co.uk/news/obituaries/politics-obituaries/8132697/Georgi-Arbatov.html (Accessed: 24 June 2019).

Terkel S. (1985) *The Good War: An Oral History of World War II*. London: Hamish Hamilton.

Waltz, K.M. (1993) 'The Emerging Structure of International Politics', *International Security*, 18(2/Autumn 1993), pp. 44–79.

Webb, J. (2002) 'Heading for Trouble: Do We Really Want to Occupy Iraq for the next 30 Years?', *The Washington Post*, 4 September [online]. Available at: https://search.proquest.com/pagepdf/2075237867/fulltextPDF/465B98BB031B4738PQ/48?accountid=14556 (Accessed: 10 September 2018).

Weinberg, G.L. (2002) 'No Road from Munich to Iraq', *The Washington Post*, 3 November [online]. Available at: https://search.proquest.com/docview/2076195365/abstract/465B98BB031B4738PQ/5 (Accessed: 10 September 2018).

Willmott, H.P. (1993) 'Guadalcanal: The Naval Campaign', *Joint Force Quarterly*, 2(Autumn), pp. 98–106.

Zinn, H. (2001) 'The Greatest Generation?', *The Progressive*, October [online]. Available at: www.progressive.org/0901/zinn1001.html (Accessed: 29 March 2021).

Part III
Reclaimed identities

8 Haunting in a postcolony

Race, place and intergenerational trauma on a South African campus

Veeran Naicker and Kathy Luckett

The concept of haunting has been deployed in postcolonial studies to refer to uncanny experiences. It is 'frequently portrayed as the Freudian *unheimlich* of history and is figured as an interruptive or affective moment in the course of Western consciousness where the repressed colonial scene returns' (O'Riley, 2007, p. 1). In settler societies and with reference to the emergence of diasporic communities in post-war Europe, ex-colonists have typically used psychic defence mechanisms to disavow their 'shared' colonial history of violence and exploitation.[1] But for those working in African and Afro-American studies (Gordon, 1990; Shaw, 2018) hauntology has become an analytical tool for uncovering the traumatic memories of the middle passage and the Black Atlantic that were excluded from North American and British national discourses. Hauntology has been used to engage with the traumatic and repressed secrets lurking in the psychic crypt of the collective unconscious of the colonized. It is considered a means of healing the ghosts of the past, through reclaiming a sense of agency for one's ancestors. By interrogating subjugated knowledges, hauntologists work to unveil phantomic secrets and exorcize malicious spirits from colonial discourse, thereby hoping to heal the spectral present and reaffirm dehumanized cultures (Peterson, 2019; Oelofsen, 2020; Wale, 2020).

In this chapter, we relate the concepts 'haunting' and the 'uncanny' to a sense of place – the University of Cape Town (UCT) – an elite, historically white university in the South African postcolony. While student protests related to financial and academic exclusions are a regular occurrence at the start of each academic year on historically black South African campuses, in March 2015, for the first time since 1994, a student protest movement that became known as RhodesMustFall (RMF) erupted on an elite historically white campus, the University of Cape Town. The initial goal of RMF was to remove the statue of arch-imperialist, Cecil John Rhodes, experienced as a symbol of racism and whiteness and to draw attention to the 'black pain' suffered by black students on that campus. The protest movement soon spread to other universities and the list of student demands grew. By the end of 2015, 16 universities and 11 colleges had been shut down by protesters who physically prevented all learning activities. The protests

DOI: 10.4324/9781003178040-12

and boycott of classes continued through 2016–2017 and the #RMF protest was superseded by a broader student movement, FeesMustFall (FMF). South African students now demanded 'free decolonized education for all'; a call that was taken up more widely on campuses with colonial histories, particularly in the United Kingdom, the United States, Canada and Australia.[2] In an attempt to force students back to lectures and protect university property, university managers called in poorly trained police and private security forces. This resulted in cycles of often extreme violence and counter-violence that went on for more than two years until the beleaguered president promised free higher education to all students from poor families.

In South Africa, the protesters in these Fallist Movements are from a generation of students who have to grapple with integrating the massive contradiction between what they have been promised (freedom and equality) by the false narrative of the 'rainbow nation' and what they experience daily (ongoing poverty and misrecognition) (Wale, Gobodo-Madikizela and Prager, 2020). When they do manage to enrol at an elite historically white university, such as UCT, they find that the high academic standards including the high levels of English language proficiency required, the whiteness of institutional culture and the taken-for-granted structural privileging of white people, make it impossible for them to participate as equals in academic life.

Against this backdrop of the South African student protests (2015–2017), this chapter shows how, for black students and staff, UCT has been, and continues to be, experienced as a spectral space where they feel a sense of 'the unhomely, alienating, strange, oppressive and terrifying' (Wolfreys, 2008, p. 171). Working with the relationship between haunting, traumatic memory and place, we discuss how the Rhodes statue was a phantomic reminder for black students of centuries of oppression and exploitation at the hands of white settlers. According to Long (2021, p. 23), the majority of South Africans, but particularly the victims of apartheid and the black youth, remain unable to integrate the country's traumatic history into the national political unconscious. Following Long (2021), we argue below that the youth, the generation born after 1994, colloquially referred to as the 'born-frees', suffer intergenerational trauma. This is a generation who have been promised socio-economic transformation and political liberation, but who are subjected to structural inequality in terms of power, property and education and who, in many cases, suffer similar forms of discrimination and everyday violence as did their parents (Wale, 2020, pp. 3–4). This chapter engages with psychic explanations for the manifestations of 'senseless violence' by South Africa's youth (Long, 2021, p. 23). The focus of our analysis is the discourse produced by the RMF student activists at UCT. Of course, we recognize that similar studies are being and should be undertaken on the discourses of whiteness and other groups, but such topics are beyond the scope of this chapter.

In the first section of the chapter, we contrast Derrida's conceptualization of hauntology with Heidegger's notion of fundamental ontology. Thereafter, we motivate why, for our purposes, Derrida's work on the ghost as an ethical encounter does not go far enough for our analysis of black student protest discourse on a historically white South African campus. Instead, we turn to Abraham and Torok's (1994) psychoanalysis of intergenerational trauma and their concepts of the psychic crypt and the phantom (see below). In the second section, we delve deeper into the nature of intergenerational trauma and compare it with individual, historical and structural trauma. Our analysis demonstrates how tropes of alienation, trauma and the neurosis of victimization are reflected in black student discourses at UCT. Further, we show how haunting operates in relation to place, inculcating an uncanny feeling of alienation and exclusion, especially when spectral psychic trauma is 'shot through with material and social forces' (Wale, Gobodo-Madikizela and Prager, 2020, p. 16). In the third section, we discuss the political and psychic limitations of victimization discourses that were evident in the discourse of some student activists. In the conclusion, we argue that both material redress and psychic healing are conditions for transformation, social cohesion and a future in this haunted postcolony.

The first author is a black PhD student in Sociology at UCT and the second author is a white female academic also from UCT. The data was gathered during the protest period, 2015–2017, when the second author was Director of the Faculty of Humanities' Education Development Unit[3] at UCT. It was collected through recording one-on-one interviews with student activists and thereafter transcribed by the second author (unless permission was refused, in which case the second author took notes). Many of the student activists involved in the protests were from the Humanities Extended Degree (ED) programme and eight kindly agreed to be interviewed during or soon after the protests. A second data source was essays written by black students registered on the ED Programme about their experiences of studying at UCT. These essays were written and gathered during 2014–2017 from cohorts of about 300 students per annum.[4] The first author worked as research assistant on this project from 2014 to 2015.

Ontology, hauntology and the spectral turn

In twentieth century philosophical thought, following Heidegger's rejection of Descartes's representational subject in a metaphysical onto-theology (Dreyfus, 2003), the term ontology was deployed to interrogate 'all types of objects, and what makes it possible for them to come into being' (Hacking, 2002, p. 2). Heidegger drew attention to the fact that objects or things, our theoretical ideas, the different ways of being human and the social roles we enact, all become available to us because they emerge from our everyday practical activities in the world. The act of ordering these objects to make sense of 'what there is' becomes the study of being or 'fundamental ontology' and signifies what is present in relation to our being in the world (Hacking, 2002, p. 2). Deciphering the historical processes by which objects and different types of objects emerge in the reality that we have played a role in constituting is known as 'historical ontology'.

However, Heidegger's Western conception of history as a developmental, unilinear and universal march through time cannot elucidate the multiple experiences of trauma endured and carried from the old colonial world (Wale, Gobodo-Madikizela and Prager, 2020, p. 8). Thus, postcolonial scholars have argued that the psychic fracturing and consequent traumatized subjectivity of Indigenous habitants in settler colonies as effects of law-founding and law-preserving everyday violence cannot be accounted for by fundamental ontology (Mbembe, 2017, pp. 163–167; Veracini, 2018). Derrida (2006, p. 77) described this as 'time being out of joint', which requires a conceptual and methodological shift from historical ontology to hauntology.

In the 1990s, Derrida's 'Spectres of Marx' (2006), in which he reconceptualized the ghost as 'spectre', provided scholars with a new concept and analytical tool. For those working within the contours of deconstruction, this turn to Marx's work provided an ethical impetus that had hitherto been lacking (Spivak, 2013, p. 318). Whereas Marx had advocated the ultimate disappearance of the spectre or ghost, personified as revolutionary spirit; for Derrida, as soon as one attempts to eliminate a ghost, 'one deprives oneself of the very thing that constitutes the revolutionary movement itself, that is to say, the appeal to justice, what I call Messianicity, which is a ghostly business' (Derrida and Stiegler, 2013, p. 48). In Derrida's hauntology, the violent absences and exclusions in Western ontology are remedied by his placing of the ghost in the discursive location of the Levinisan 'other' (implying an infinite responsibility) (Davis, 2013, p. 53). That said, Derrida's concept of the 'spectre' is primarily a deconstructive trope that vacillates between 'life and death, presence and absence...it does not belong to the order of knowledge' (Davis, 2013, p. 56) which limits its therapeutic potential. Furthermore, over the years, the text has become controversial for its idiosyncratic mode of reading Marx.

In attempting to formulate a socio-diagnosis of racial subjectivity in the South African postcolony, we turn rather to the scholarship of psychoanalysts, Nicolas Abraham and Maria Torok (1994). They set out to investigate how the undisclosed trauma of earlier generations can disturb the lives of their descendants. They theorized that this hidden ancestral trauma sits in the ego of the descendant as a phantom that works to prevent past shameful secrets from coming to light. Critically, rather than returning from the dead to reveal a secret or right a wrong, they suggest that the phantom is a liar, 'its effects are designed to mislead the haunted subject and to ensure its secrets remain shrouded in mystery' (Davis, 2013, p. 54). For Abraham and Torok, if psychic knowledge is to be therapeutic, the secret of the phantom, a discursive lie about the past, must be illuminated; phantasmic dissimulations 'can and should be put into words so that the phantom and its noxious effects on the living can be exorcised' (Davis, 2013, p. 58). As we will show below, this therapeutic work on collective trauma is important for our analysis.

Intergenerational trauma and phantomic haunting at the University of Cape Town

Settler societies were founded on a violent, genocidal logic that aimed at the 'replacement or displacement' of the Indigenous or native population in question (Mamdani, 2015, p. 604; Veracini, 2018, p. 364). In most postcolonial societies, the settler system is regarded as having been defeated through the transfer of sovereignty to Indigenous national governments, usually led by ex-liberation movements. But a few settler societies remain which can be regarded as 'successful' from the settler point of view. These include the Americas, Australasia and South Africa (Mamdani, 2015, p. 596). However, the meagre settler population in South African made the total displacement of the Indigenous population untenable (Thompson, 1990, p. 37). Instead, the 'native question' was solved through imposing extreme forms of racist necropolitical governance imbued with an instinct of destruction (Mbembe, 2019, p. 88) that involved land dispossession and controlling the movement of Indigenous populations through Manichean forms of racial spatialization. Mamdani compares the South African system to that of the United States thus,

> The ethnic cleansing of the African population of South Africa began as early as 1913 when the Natives Land Act declared 87 percent of the land for whites and divided the remaining 13 percent into tribal homelands for the native population. These homelands were called reserves. I wondered why the name sounded so uncannily like the American reservation.
>
> (Mamdani, 2015, p. 608)

Steve Biko, founder of the Black Consciousness Movement, described the life of black people under apartheid thus,

> I think the black man is subjected to two forces in this country. He is first of all oppressed by an external world through institutionalised machinery, through laws that restrict them from doing certain things, through heavy conditions, through very poor pay, through very difficult living, through poor education, these are all external to him, and secondly, we consider this the most important, the black man has developed a certain state of alienation, he rejects himself, precisely because he attaches the meaning white to all that is good and he equates good with white. This arises out of his living and it arises out of his development from childhood.
>
> (Biko, 2008, pp. 110–111)

And more recently, Mbembe describes the destructive effects of the South African migrant labour system,

> Despite industrialisation's need for cheap black labour, one of the greatest fears of the apartheid government was African urbanisation and migration to the white cities. Its solution was the migrant labour system by means of which it could control and transfer labour between the rural areas (reserves, later Bantustans or 'homelands') and urban townships – a necropolitical rationality that destroyed African kinship structures.
>
> (Mbembe, 2019, p. 44)

Building on Fanon's (2001, 2017) analysis of the psychic effects of colonialism, Long (2021, p. 44) argues that the enduring consequence of land dispossession and the cultural destruction of South African Indigenous populations has been a 'crippling indignity of deprivation' leading to feelings of inferiority and shame. In this section, we explore the implications of this for the contemporary generation of black South Africans. We begin by summarising different types of trauma to explain the phenomena of intergenerational trauma. Then, by reading closely 'through' the discourse of RMF students, we hope to show how this form of trauma became manifest at UCT during the protests (2015–2017).

In order to cope with complexity – much of which escapes our comprehension – we habitually turn our lives into stories by engendering narrative structures that imbue our lives with meaning. Further, in order to forge a sense of personal identity, we must wrestle with the narratives we are born into, be they beneficial, destructive or incommensurable (Van der Merwe and Gobodo-Madikizela, 2007, pp. 1–5). In this context, individual trauma as an 'affect' concerns 'the shattering of life's narrative structure, a loss of meaning – the traumatised person has "lost the plot"' (Van der Merwe and Gobodo-Madikiela, 2007, p. 6). Therapists have conceptualized individual trauma as a violent rupture, a loss of fundamental integrity and dignity in which the self loses its autonomy – including the capacity to capture that abyssal experience in words (Van der Merwe and Gobodo-Madikizela, 2007, pp. 25–26).

Many traumatized subjects are products of historical trauma, 'an event which refers to a single huge disaster, which can be personal (for instance, a rape) or communal (like a flood)' (Van der Merwe and Gobodo-Madikizela, 2007, p. 11). But, as noted above, for black people living in townships and under white servitude during apartheid, daily life was not only a source of historical trauma but also of structural trauma, described by Biko as machine-like, 'a pattern of continual and continuing traumas' (p. 11) that 'develop daily into neurotics through a sheer inability to relate the present to the future because of a completely engulfing sense of destitution' (Biko, 2008, p. 61). Biko believed this led to an 'inferiority complex', or rather, in his gendered terms, to the emasculation of the Black Man. Long (2021, pp. 49–54) names the effect of structural trauma together with material deprivation as one of chronic feelings of shame. He describes how this leads to a craving for respect and dignity which when denied, easily erupts into violence, substance abuse and eventual self-destruction.

Against this backdrop of historical and structural trauma suffered by black people under the apartheid regime, we now focus on the experience of black students on a historically white campus, culminating in the RMF protests of the 'born-frees' at UCT (2015–2017). We argue that while, as a collective, this group of students have suffered neither historical nor structural trauma, they may well experience intergenerational trauma, which, as mentioned above, is hidden ancestral trauma that sits in the egos of the descendants as a phantom.

> The phantom is a formation of the unconscious that has never been conscious – for good reason. It passes – in a way yet to be determined – from the parent's unconscious into the child's … The presence of the phantom indicates the effects, on the descendants, of something that had inflicted narcissistic injury or even catastrophe on the parent.
>
> (Abraham and Torok, 1994, pp. 174–175)

The extracts below are taken from essays written by first-year and second-year students on the Humanities Extended Degree Programme during 2014–2017. The students were asked to write about their early experiences at UCT. Most of these students would have come from poor schools and entered the university with lower school-leaving scores than required for regular admissions. The extracts were selected to illustrate their feelings of cultural alienation and inferiority as they compared themselves to mainstream middle-class students.

> English is the medium of instruction in this University, this constant use of the English is – in a way – altering my attitude, mannerisms, and ultimately is making me feel like I'm turning into someone else.
>
> Particularly in first year, I swam in self-defeatism, self-doubt, and low self-esteem. 'Black and Stupid' were some of my everyday inferences through which I made sense of myself and my abilities.
>
> I perceived myself as both intellectually inferior and an underachiever, who neither could cope nor compete with intellectual 'normals' in mainstream; that I was neither as bright nor did I have the type of academic potentialities displayed by intellectual normals, and that I had a deficit, needing extra help, 'intervention' and 'fixing'.

However, not only does this generation of 'born-free' students (re)experience a sense of inferiority and shame on this campus, historically reserved for whites only but they also experience the place as unhomely, an uncanny place of haunting, where the symbols and representations of a largely unconscious racist system (sustained by the culturally dominant white settler society) trigger memories of intergenerational trauma (Wolfreys, 2008, p. 178). For these students, entry into an uncanny place, such as UCT, can result in 'a recollection of, or encounter with, past experiences and perceptions, making the concept of location immensely powerful as well as layered … These sites are anything but empty' (del Pilar Blanco and Peeren, 2013, p. 395).

In an interview, this student activist explained his experience of the 'white world' of UCT's campus and his fear of challenging it,

> The life of Black People is a life of (a) Nervous Condition. This is true at UCT for all Black people … It is this life of Nervous Condition that drives me and many others either to go mad or commit suicide … We were fearful of what will happen to us while we are in the White world if we were to radically disrupt White power.

The uncanny also signifies 'the return' of repressed secret memories, and those modes of thought hitherto considered banished from consciousness into the unconscious. The surfacing of repressed (past) traumas, even across generations, can fracture one's sense of self (Jervis, 2008, p. 395). It is for these reasons that Mbembe argues for the importance of symbolic access (as well as material access) to black students,

> Decolonisation of buildings and public spaces is inseparable from the democratisation of access; we need to create the conditions that will allow black students to say of the university, 'This is my home. I am not an outsider here. I do not have to beg or apologize to be here. I belong here'.
>
> (Mbembe, 2016, p. 30)

It should not have been surprising then that the statue of Cecil John Rhodes, mining magnate, Prime Minister of the Cape colony and founder of the campus, became the ultimate spectre for black students on the UCT campus. The more-than-life-size bronze statue of Rhodes was erected on a lofty plinth in the very centre of the campus vista, framed by a colonnade of steps and pillars. With Devil's Peak in the background, the statue of Rhodes looked to the East, over the rest of the campus, over the Cape Flats and beyond to the hinterlands of the Western Cape. Ironically, in many cases, the statue and what it stood for was not even recognized by apolitical white students, many of whom arrived on campus by car (Shepherd, 2020, p. 567). It was the majority of black students who arrive on campus by bus or on foot who daily had to climb the steep steps that led up to the statue of Cecil John Rhodes. For black students, the statue was an uncanny presence from the past that haunted them and reminded them of their ancestors' trauma, as expressed by this RMF activist,

> By throwing poo at the statue of Rhodes we were showing our disgust with which Rhodes mistreated our people in the past. Equally, we are showing disgust at the manner in which UCT celebrates the genocidal Cecil Rhodes. In short, the act of poo is our institutional critique of UCT.

Due to pressure from the RMF, and after much debate, the Council of UCT approved the removal of the statue on 9 April 2015, one month after the protests had begun.

Our analysis of the RMF protest discourse now turns to reflect on the implications of Abraham and Torok's (1994) conceptualization of the phantom in the 'psychic crypt' manifesting as a discursive lie or dissimulation. One activist explained the importance of forging a collective, race-based identity and politics thus:

> RMF students … rejected the vision of non-racialism as 'fake rainbow-ism'.… We used the 'politics of black pain' to give us a voice, to unite us across political affiliations, to silence whites and to authorize us to speak on behalf of all black students instead of the democratically elected SRCs (Student Representative Councils).
>
> (Chikane, 2018, p. 143)

He explained the shift from non-racial to Africanist politics thus,

> Black Consciousness ideas were consolidated in RMF – we were all reacting to white institutional racism. We used a race-based analysis and agreed not to talk about class, ('amandla awethu' was replaced with 'izwe lethu'[5]). We took the black South African lived experience as the basis for identity … so in the beginning, intersectionality was expressed under a black umbrella.

In a context of white privilege and inequality, the common sense of injury and victimhood shared by black students easily became a platform for a collective black identity and also for moral absolutism in which the good black is locked in battle with the evil white (Long, 2021, p. 92). The examples below are taken from an interview with a RMF activist in 2018,

> We wanted to get rid of the gaze of white people so that we were free to talk about race with whites out of the room. We needed to separate from whiteness to understand our self-worth – we had to learn how to love ourselves – it was a form of liberation – it was psychic recuperation.

> Together we asserted what it means to be black and powerful – this felt good, it became addictive. RMF became a form of rehab for sharing experiences of being black at UCT – it was like the AA we were all victims of whiteness – we shared some heart-breaking experiences.

While the political and psychic logic for subaltern groups to separate themselves from dominant groups has long been asserted and recognized, a number of postcolonial scholars (see Mbembe, 2001; Xaba, 2017; Long, 2021) warn of the dangers of simply inverting the same colonial discourse deployed by former colonial masters that remains based on pathological racial stereotypes. Further, the myth of racial homogeneity and identity can be linked to a paranoid and conspiratorial worldview which can lead to a politics of *ressentiment*[6] with neurotic psychic effects. Mbembe names this condition a 'neurosis of victimisation',

> As discourses of inversion, they draw their fundamental categories from the myths they claim to oppose and reproduce their dichotomies: the racial difference between black and white; the cultural confrontation between civilized peoples and savages; the religious opposition between Christians and pagans; the very conviction that race exists and is at the foundation of morality and nationality. ... A perverse operation has been taking place, the result of which has only strengthened Africans' ressentiment and their neurosis of victimization.
>
> (Mbembe, 2002, pp. 256–257)

We discuss the political and psychic limitations of discourses of *ressentiment* in more detail in the next section below.

In some activists' utterances, it is possible to detect the lie of the phantom at work, insisting on the righteousness of an innocent, black subject who stands defiantly in a relation of hatred against white privilege and evil.

> In RMF we acted out violence to attack symbols of racism and whiteness. We learnt that the best way to gain attention is to hurt whites 'where it hurts them most'.
>
> (Chikane, 2018, p. 56)

Another student interviewee, who did not want to be quoted directly, described how in the safety of the spaces they occupied (renamed Azania House), therapy was practised by the RMF collective on students who came forward to be viscerally 'purged' or 'exorcized' as they 'vomited out' the 'bad white spirits' that had possessed them. Long (2021, pp. 78–89) argues that it is because the promise of a life of dignity and freedom at the university has turned into one of shame and envy, that the students felt compelled to act out a repressed desire for revenge based on the discursive lie that everything white – including the university – is evil and must be destroyed.

He goes further to argue that the unconscious phantom most feared and hated by the black students is a form of 'destructive envy' – a hidden desire to be white and middle-class – which can lead to a violently reactive and compulsive rejection.

The victimization complex

Over time, the RMF movement became dominated by student leaders affiliated to the Pan-African Student Movement of Azania (PASMA) which required a certain Africanist or 'woke' disposition from its members. Not only were whites excluded from the movement from the outset, but gradually 'coconuts',[7] 'other Africans', and women were marginalized. As the Africanist agenda became dominant in the RMF leadership, so did feminist and LGBTQI+ members become disgruntled with the patriarchal, authoritarian style of certain male leaders.

In March 2016, a small group of transgender activists disrupted and trashed the commemoration exhibition of the founding of the RMF the previous year. They expressed their outrage at the movement for its failure to recognize and include their identities by painting slogans in red paint over the exhibits, such as

> We are done with the arrogant cis-hetero-patriarchy of black men
> The revolution will be black-led and intersectional or it will be bullshit

This was the first public display of dissension in the movement. This dramatic event marked the beginnings of the fracturing and eventual dissolution of the movement. It gradually became absorbed under a broader national campaign for free decolonized education led by the FeesMustFall movement that had been initiated at the University of the Witswatersrand the previous year. These critiques are historically important for they signal that the new generation of female activists who identify as womxn (*sic*) will no longer tolerate the imposition of a homogenous racial or gendered identity, based on an internalized inversion of colonial stereotypes, that includes domination and leadership by a strong African Man capable of the violent destruction of the enemy.

Since then, feminist activists such as Xaba (2017) and Matandela (2017) have critiqued the RMF for its failure to integrate their own and other intersectional identities under its umbrella of blackness. They attribute this to the fact that the African anti-colonial discourses on which the movement drew – Fanon and Black Consciousness[8] in particular – both conceive of women as secondary supporters in an anti-colonial struggle against black emasculation.

Feminist critics of Black Consciousness politics argue that its patriarchal perspective is based on a syncretic combination of African and Christian cultures. Psychoanalysts have shown how the Christian tradition splits the image of the woman into either Mary, the pure Virgin Mother, or Eve, the sinful temptress (Mitchell, 1990, pp. 121–135). In African culture, the ideal of the dutiful, loyal and faithful mother has been preserved in the Black Consciousness tradition (Magaziner, 2010, pp. 166–167). Feminists have pointed out how these traditions combine to deform society's psychic understanding of gender roles, endorsing a worldview in which women are regarded as objects and rape is not a crime (Meldrum, 2006, p. 211).

Once the male student leadership of the RMF became invested in an inversion of colonial racial stereotypes and patriarchal militancy (Xaba, 2017), it became clear that their attempts to produce a narrative of cleansing violence and inner healing lacked the resources to integrate personal and intergenerational trauma into the collective psyche. Nor could this discourse offer the psychic resources needed to engender a desire for reciprocal recognition of difference or any form of mutuality or human solidarity. Mbembe (1999) notes that the discourse remains trapped in a subjectivity of victimhood rather than subjecthood. He has diagnosed this condition as a 'neurosis of victimisation'. In a recent interview, Mbembe (2019) lamented the protestors' shift to locating a decolonial movement on a purely identitarian, affective model. He fell out of favour with the student movement for expressing his concern that they were basing their model of subjectivity on affect alone, namely 'I am my (black) pain' (Mbembe, 2019).

Mbembe (1999) first used the term 'victimisation complex' in contrast with the cosmopolitan affirmative ethico-poetic notion of 'Afropolitanism'. His conceptualization of the victimization complex was *ressentiment*-laden and thus Nietzschean. With reference to xenophobia, Mbeme interpreted 'indigeneity *versus* foreignness' in terms of Nietzsche's system of a good *versus* evil system of *ressentiment*-laden slave morality. In 2001, in African *Modes of Self-writing*, he confirmed that this was also a neurosis. At the time, he used the term to explain a series of violent events happening in Africa, outside of South Africa,

> During the second half of the [nineteenth] century, a form of bio-racism (autochthons versus non-natives) appeared on the continent, politically nurtured by a culture of victimisation and ressentiment ... Almost every time the victim turns against an imaginary torturer, an imaginary torturer who, coincidentally, always has had nothing to do with the original wound ... These events create an extreme power of destruction, as we have in Rwanda and elsewhere.
>
> (Mbembe, 1999, p. 28)

Like other postcolonial thinkers before him, Mbembe (2017) seeks to explain how racializing logics have 'endured and renewed themselves, despite the economic logics and political hopes' of Afro-Marxist liberation discourses that had 'promised their dissolution' (Pillay, 2015, p. 3).

Mbembe (2019) argues that this form of politics, which he now terms 'necropolitics', is widely practiced in the African postcolony and is based on 'Black reason'. He traces how the narratives and legends drawn around the Black Atlantic from the fifteenth to nineteenth centuries coalesced into a 'political rationality', which, with its attendant psychic, affective and material relations, provided the discursive formation for the first iteration of 'Black reason'. The second form of 'Black reason' appeared in the Afro-Marxist and Nativist anti-colonial and postcolonial discourses at the time of decolonization. Both these discourses 'were transformed into genuine systems of power/knowledge and institutional practices whose effects have endured until today' (Mbembe, 2002, p. 631). Mbembe's argument is that the discourse of 'Black reason' cannot provide an adequate foundation for the governance of contemporary African populations because it is based on simple moral inversions of colonial stereotypes and a victimization complex. This leads to the continued practice of racial technologies of domination in the postcolony. Mbembe's harsh conclusion is that the governmental institutionalization of the neurosis of victimization gets expressed through an instinct of destruction (Mbembe, 2019, p. 151).

Conclusion

As we contemplate a future in which healing the phantoms (intergenerational trauma and a neurosis of victimization) in the South African political unconscious becomes possible, we argue below that the material conditions that constituted these phantoms in the first place will have to be addressed. In concluding, we point to the importance of economic redress – and in particular the restoration of rights to land and property – if we are to engage honestly with healing the phantoms of victimhood and envy which erupted from the South African psychic crypt in 2015 in the historical space of the University of Cape Town.

In this chapter, we have argued that two forms of South African hauntings, or intergenerational traumas could be added to the slave trade (Mbembe, 2017, pp. 33–44) and the fratricidal phantoms established by Mbembe[9]. The first form of intergenerational trauma experienced by the majority of black South Africans is an effect of the necropolitical dispossession, forced removals and unjust partitioning of the land. The second form of haunting is based on a dialectic of *ressentiment* (Pithouse, 2016) which we have discussed in relation to the RMF protests at UCT. While we were not able to deal with the first mode of hauntology in this chapter, we acknowledged how the violent effects of land dispossession continue into the present as material inequality and exclusion – thus playing a critical role in the constitution of South Africa's haunting present. These two related forms of haunting mean that not only have intersubjective relations and the possibility of community and a common solidarity been compromised in South Africa but violence continues to be internalized in the national psyche, exhibiting itself in repe-titious, cyclical displays of 'senseless violence' (Long, 2021).

In our analysis of a politics of *ressentiment* on a historically white South African campus, we found symptoms in student protest discourse of the phantomic aspects of Pan-Africanist and Nativist discourses. Our analysis suggested that many, particularly male student activists, identified with an inversion of racial stereotypes and forms of militancy founded on a colonial 'metaphysics of difference' inherited from the apartheid era (Xaba, 2017). Our analysis further suggested that a neurotic need to crush the phantom of white envy by a black victim may explain the extreme anger, hatred and violence that erupted against whiteness, symbolized by the University of Cape Town, during the protests. We also pointed to the political and psy-chic limitations of a politics of *ressentiment*. First, because an identitarian model of the subject cannot sustain political solidarity. Second because, while unleashing the emotional pain of the phantoms of intergenerational trauma, it lacks the psychic resources to deal with the phantom's deception and dissimulations, thus offering no therapeutic capacity to move its victims beyond cycles of violence and counter-violence.

Finally, while we propose that methods of psychic healing are vital for reconstructing fractured psyches in the postcolony, we insist that these practices cannot be divorced from addressing the material inequalities that continue to produce envy and *ressentiment* in South African society. Thus, for any form of reciprocity and healing of social relations to take place in this ghostly postcolony, symbolic and psychic practices of reconstructing the subject will need to be accompanied by restructuring the racialized ownership of land and property in ways that offer material reparation for the exploitation, dehumanization and indignities suffered under past colo-nial and apartheid necropolitical governments. The heated contestations around the current move by the ANC government to change the Consti-tution to enable the expropriation of land without compensation,[10] sug-gest that this touches a 'raw nerve' in the psychic complex of the white population – many of whom will no doubt resort to violence to protect their property.

We would like to end on a more personal note. Despite our critical analy-sis of aspects of the RMF protest discourse presented above, we wish to be clear that we are not standing in judgement of the individual protestors con-cerned. Many activists showed enormous courage and paid a high personal price for their actions (such as academic failure, suspension and expulsion). That they drew (uncritically) on the only alternative political discourses known and available to them is not surprising. The one-on-one discussions we had with some of the activists, especially the women, suggest that they themselves were taken aback by the waves of rage and fury that enveloped them during protest actions, as phantoms were unleashed that hitherto had remained hidden. In closing, we believe that what is required from those in privileged positions in South African is a much better understanding of how the weight of past injustices sits like a phantom in the unconscious of the living. We should not have been surprised that the weight of intergenerational trauma, especially when compounded by ongoing structural and visible inequality, became an unbearable burden for the psyches of young black South Africans to carry. The only appropriate response is material redress together with recognition, compassion and an 'infinite responsibility' for the other (Davis, 2013, p. 56; Derrida, 2013, p. 42).

Notes

1 For Charles Mills, 'whiteness' is a deliberate structure of ignorance and historical erasure, not simply a racial category. Mills notes that 'white normativity manifests itself in a refusal to recognize the long history of structural discrimination that has left whites with differential resources' (Mills, 2007, p. 28). Whiteness mirrors what psychoanalysts term the disavowal of genocidal or foundational violence of settler societies.

2 These include *Decolonising the Mind*, *Why is my Curriculum White?*, *Liberate my Degree*, *We are the University* the *Critical Internationalisation Network* and a range of decolonizing collectives, networks and groups based in specific institutions.

3 In South Africa, Education Development Units run Extended Degree Programmes that are structured to give students more time and additional academic support to complete an undergraduate degree. They were set up by white, elite universities during the apartheid era as a means of admitting black students with lower admissions scores. Post-apartheid, the government has continued to fund these programmes as a means of redress and to equalize the student composition on historically white campuses.

4 This research project was given ethical clearance by the Research Ethics Committee of the Centre for Higher Education Development, UCT (2014–2018). In all cases, interviewees and essay writers signed consent forms for staff from the Humanities Education Development Unit to use the data for research purposes on condition of confidentiality.

5 The significance of these slogans is as follows: 'amandla awethu' (power is ours) is an ANC slogan, the ANC has traditionally held to a non-racial vision of a new South Africa that includes whites, whereas 'izwe lethu' (the country/land is ours) is a PAC slogan implying that the land belongs to and should be reclaimed by and for black people.

6 The term *ressentiment* was used in the nineteenth century by the French bourgeoisie to describe the envy of the 'have-nots'' for the haves' (Jameson, 2002, p. 189). Nietzsche (2003) appropriated the term to diagnose the history of Western metaphysics, morality and subject formation. Mbembe (2001) builds on Nietzsche's analysis, to argue that African discourses on the self have continued to operate within a Western Christian discursive framework, to the extent that racialized colonial categories continue to be used but now their values are inverted and internalized, signalling the creation of nativistic conceptions of an essentially good homogenous black subject, defined in response a hostile world of evil others, usually whites.

7 In post-apartheid South Africa, the term 'coconut' is deployed to denigrate black people who try to behave like whites. A coconut is usually someone who attended a formerly white school, lives in the suburbs and has benefited from a Western education, despite the psychic trauma of coercive assimilation (Hlongwane, 2013, pp. 18–19).

8 Black Consciousness is a philosophy first developed by Steve Biko. The goal of Black Consciousness, as a form of political psychology, is to liberate the 'Black man' from his psychological and material inferiority, a servile and dependent condition. It aims to produce a self-determining agent infused with a politically affirmative group pride (Biko, 2008, p. 74). Importantly, Black Consciousness philosophy operates according to African humanist principles and enables a subversive response to colonial and apartheid South Africa (Cloete, 2019, p. 104).

9 Mbembe (2017, pp. 116–117) argues that conspiratorial thinking is a symptom of the transgenerational neurosis of victimization. He uses the notion of fratricide (a phantom or little secret) to explain the transgenerational trauma that has haunted Africans from the time of the slave trade when African slave traders consumed European commodities in exchange for their own people. He goes on to argue that in postcolonial Africa, this phantom has been unconsciously institutionalized as a death drive which manifests in the necropolitical governance of African populations by self-serving African leaders.

10 Three decades of land reform in post-apartheid South Africa have failed to undo the racial structuring of land ownership for the poor majority. The current government has sought to rectify this through its 2019 Draft Expropriation Bill which will change the SA Constitution to allow it to enforce land expropriation without compensation (Mokoena and Sebola, 2020, p. 400).

References

Abraham, N. and Torok, M. (1994) The *Shell and the Kernel: Renewals of Psychoanalysis Volume 1*. Translated by N. Rand. Chicago, IL: The University of Chicago Press.

Biko, S. (2008) *I Write What I Like: A Selection of His Writings*. Edited by A. Stubbs. Johannesburg: Picador Africa.

Chikane, R. (2018) *Breaking a Rainbow, Building a Nation: The Politics behind #MustFall Movements*. Johannesburg: Picador Africa.

Cloete, M. (2019) 'Steve Biko: Black Consciousness and the African Other-the Struggle for the Political', *Angelaki: Theoretical Journal of the Humanities*, 24(2), pp. 104–115.

Davis, C. (2013) 'État Présent: Hauntology, Spectres and Phantoms' in del Pilar Blanco, M. and Peeren, E. (eds.) *The Spectralities Reader: Ghosts and Haunting in Contemporary Cultural Theory*. London: Bloomsbury, pp. 53–60.

del Pilar Blanco, M. and Peeren, E. (2013) 'Possessions/Spectral Places: Introduction' in del Pilar Blanco, M. and Peeren, E. (eds.) *The Spectralities Reader: Ghosts and Haunting in Contemporary Cultural Theory*. London: Bloomsbury, pp. 395–402.

Derrida, J. (2006) *Spectres of Marx: The State of Debt: The Work of Mourning and the New International*. London: Routledge.

Derrida, J. and Stiegler, B. (2013) 'Spectographies' in del Pilar Blanco, M. and Peeren, E. (eds.) *The Spectralities Reader: Ghosts and Haunting in Contemporary Cultural Theory*. London: Bloomsbury, pp. 37–52.

Dreyfus, H. (2003) 'Being and Power Revisited' in Milchman, A. and Rosenberg, A. (eds.) *Critical Encounters: Foucault and Heidegger*. Minneapolis: University of Minnesota Press, pp. 30–54.

Fanon, F. (2001) *The Wretched of the Earth*. Translated by C. Farrington. London: Penguin Books.

Fanon, F. (2017) *Black Skin, White Masks*. Translated by C.L. Markmann. New York: Pluto Books.

Gordon, A. (1990) *Ghostly Matters: Haunting and the Sociological Imagination*. Minneapolis: University of Minnesota Press.

Hacking, I. (2002) *Historical Ontology*. New York: Harvard University Press.

Hlongwane, G. (2013) '"In Every Classroom Children Are Dying", Race, Power and Nervous Conditions in Kopano Matlwa's Coconut', *Alternation*, 20(1), pp. 9–25.

Jameson, F. (2002) *The Political Unconscious: Narrative as a Socially Symbolic Act*. London: Routledge.

Jervis, J. (2008) 'Uncanny Presences' in Collins, J. and Jervis, J. (eds.) *Uncanny Modernity: Cultural Theories, Modern Anxieties*. London: Palgrave Macmillan, pp. 10–50.

Long, W. (2021) *Nation on the Couch: Inside South Africa's Mind*. Cape Town: Melinda Ferguson Books.

Magaziner, D.R. (2010) *The Law and the Prophets: Black Consciousness in South Africa, 1968–1977*. Athens: Ohio University Press.

Mamdani, M. (2015) 'Settler Colonialism: Then and Now', *Critical Inquiry*, 41(3), pp. 596–614.

Matandela, M. (2017) 'Redefining Black Consciousness and Resistance: The Intersection of Black Consciousness and Black Feminist Thought', *Agenda*, 31(3–4), pp. 10–28.

Mbembe, A. (1999) *Afropolitanism*. Translated by L. Chauvet. London: African Remix.

Mbembe, A. (2001) 'African Modes of Self-Writing', Translated by S. Rendall, *Public Culture*, 14(1), pp. 239–273.

Mbembe, A. (2002) 'On the Power of the False', Translated by J. Inggs, *Public Culture*, 14(3), pp. 629–641.

Mbembe, A. (2016) 'Decolonizing the University: New Directions', *Arts and Humanities in Higher Education*, 15(1), pp. 29–45.

Mbembe, A. (2017) *Critique of Black Reason*, Translated by L. Du Bois. Johannesburg: Wits University Press.

Mbembe, A. (2019) *Necropolitics*. Translated by S. Corcoron. Durham, NC: Duke University Press.

Meldrum, A. (2006) 'South Africa on trial', *Current History*, 105(691), pp. 209-213.

Mills, C. (2007) 'White Ignorance' in Sullivan, S. and Tuana, N. (eds.) *Race and Epistemologies of Ignorance*. New York: State University of New York Press, pp. 13–38.

Mitchell, J. (1990) *Psychoanalysis and Feminism: A Radical Reassessment of Freudian Psychoanalysis*. New York: Penguin Books.

Mokoena, B.T. and Sebola, J.P. (2020) 'A Multi-criteria Decision Urban Development Framework for Land Expropriation in South Africa: A Strategic Approach', *International Archives of the Photogrammetry, Remote Sensing and Spatial Information Sciences*, 43, pp. 399–407.

Nietzsche, F. (2003) 'The Anti-Christ' in Nietzsche, F. (ed.) *Twilight of the Idols and the Anti-Christ*, Translated by M. Tanner. New York: Penguin Classics, pp. 127–199.

Oelofsen, M. (2020) 'Listening to the Quiet Violence in the Unspoken' in Wale, K., Gobodo-Madikizela, P. and Prager, J. (eds.) *Post-Conflict Hauntings: Transforming Memories of Historical Trauma*. Belfast: Palgrave Macmillan, pp.177–202.

O'Riley, M.F. (2007) 'Postcolonial Haunting: Anxiety, Affect, and the Situated Encounter', *Postcolonial Text*, 3(4), pp. 1–15.

Peterson, B. (2019) 'Spectrality and Inter-generational Black Narratives in South Africa', *Social Dynamics*, 45(3), pp. 345–364.

Pillay, S. (2015) 'Identity, Difference, Citizenship or Why I Am No Longer a Non-racialist', *Creating African Futures in an Era of Global Transformations: Challenges and Prospects*. CODESRIA 14th General Assembly proceedings [online]. Available at: https://www.academia.edu/32893054/Why_I_am_no_longer_a_Non_Racialist_Identity_CItizenship_Difference (Accessed 11 July 2022).

Pithouse, R. (2016) *Writing the Decline: On the Struggle for South Africa's Democracy*. Johannesburg, Jacana Media (Pty) Limited.

Shaw, K. (2018) *Hauntology: The Present of the Past in Twenty-First English Literature*. London: Palgrave Macmillan.

Shepherd, N. (2020) 'After the #Fall: The Shadow of Cecil Rhodes at the University of Cape Town', *City: Analysis of Urban Change, Theory, Action*, 24(3–4), pp. 565–579.

Spivak, G.C. (2013) 'From *Ghostwriting*' in del Pilar Blanco, M. and Peeren, E. (eds.) *The Spectralities Reader: Ghosts and Haunting in Contemporary Cultural Theory*. London: Bloomsbury, pp. 317–334.

Thompson, L. (1990) A *History of South Africa*. New York: Yale University Press.

Van der Merwe, C.N. and Gobodo-Madikizela, P. (2007) *Narrating Our Healing: Perspectives on Working through Trauma*. Newcastle: Cambridge Scholars Publishing.

Veracini, L. (2018) 'Settler Collective, Founding Violence and Disavowal: The Settler Colonial Situation', *Journal of Intercultural Studies*, 29(4), pp. 363–379.

Wale, K. (2020) 'Intergenerational Nostalgic Haunting and Critical Hope' in Wale, K., Gobodo-Madikizela, P. and Prager, J. (eds.) *Post-Conflict Hauntings: Transforming Memories of Historical Trauma*. Cham: Palgrave Macmillan, pp. 203–228.

Wale, K., Gobodo-Madikizela, P. and Prager, J. (2020) 'Introduction: Post-Conflict Hauntings' in Wale, K., Gobodo-Madikizela, P. and Prager, J. (eds.) *Post-Conflict Hauntings: Transforming Memories of Historical Trauma*. Cham: Palgrave Macmillan, pp. 1–25.

Wolfreys, J. (2008) 'The Urban Uncanny: The City, the Subject, and Ghostly Modernity' in Collins, J. and Jervis, J. (eds.) *Uncanny Modernity: Cultural Theories, Modern Anxieties*. London: Palgrave Macmillan, pp. 168–180.

Xaba, W. (2017) 'Challenging Fanon: A Black Radical Feminist Perspective on Violence and the Fees Must Fall Movement', *Agenda*, 31(3–4), pp. 96–104.

9 First World War memorial ghosts and the reshaping of South African identity

Remembering the SS Mendi in Delville Wood

Gilles Teulié*

"Everyone sat up at the mention of the *Mendi*. The room was suddenly a cauldron of excited voices. 'What did he say about the *Mendi*?' 'Said he survived the *Mendi*.' 'Fucking ghost!'" (Khumalo, 2017, p. 215) This quotation from South African Zulu fiction writer Fred Khumalo underlines the long-lasting impact that the story of the *SS Mendi* had on South Africans. Through his novel *Dancing the Death Drill* (Khumalo, 2017), Khumalo pays tribute to the South African victims, all from the 5th Battalion of the South African Native Labour Corps and the crew of the ship, who drowned on their way to France on 21 February 1917, after their ship was accidently rammed into at 5 am by an allied ship off the shores of the Isle of Wight.[1] His main protagonist, Pitso Motaung, a coloured South African (of White and Basotho descent), who survived the wreck, is therefore labelled a 'Fucking Ghost' by members of another battalion a few months later in France. Khumalo's story and tribute to fellow black and coloured South Africans originates from an event that took place in a gloomy atmosphere, at sea, when a thick fog prevented the captain of the *SS Darro* from seeing the *SS Mendi* on that ill-fated night. The fog evokes ghost stories, those ghosts from the past that come to haunt the living as shown by the many publications and films about another maritime catastrophe, that of the *RMS Titanic*. Khumalo admits, in articles and in his 'author's notes' at the end of his novel, that the 'story about the sinking of the *SS Mendi* has haunted him from the time he was a child' (2017, p. 313). He adds that he didn't hear of the event through his grandparents' recollections that shaped his imagination, but through his primary school choir as '[...] we were introduced to a haunting dirge, *Amagorha eMendi*. Written in isiXhosa, the short haunting piece of music was composed by Jabeez Foley [...]' (Khumalo, 2017, p. 313). This 'haunting piece of music' explains why he was obsessed by this story, especially as little information on the topic was available for decades: 'The ancestors whispering to me and my classmates through the pages of that book were silent on why black men had enlisted in a war that was clearly not theirs in the first place' (Khumalo, 2017, p. 314). The ghosts of the *SS Mendi* are still present for him through time:

DOI: 10.4324/9781003178040-13

> Years later when I was already a journalist and novelist, I realised that the hooks of the *Mendi* story were digging deeper into my psyche. The story wouldn't leave me alone. I realised that, in order to exorcise myself of the *Mendi* demons, I simply had to write the story once and for all.
>
> (Khumalo, 2017, p. 314)

Later, he visited France and saw the South African Native Labour Contingent's graves which motivated him to write his novel: 'the story of the *Mendi* is at the heart of our nationhood, but we have yet to do justice to this narrative. This is my humble contribution towards this effort' (Khumalo, 2017, p. 315). 'Doing Justice' to the nearly forgotten ghosts of the abyss is what Khumalo aims at, underlining that few people in South Africa knew the story, as maybe it was not the proper time to revisit the event and to stop the ancestors from whispering: 'the stories had always been there – it was just that they did not make sense at the time' (Khumalo, 2017, p. 314). In a highly segregated country like South Africa, the fate of those 607 Black and Coloured men couldn't match the thousands of White South African soldiers who gave their lives on the Somme Battlefield. The latter were commemorated by the White South African governments throughout the decades following the end of the First World War. This was the case until the 1994 first multicultural elections in South Africa, which led to reshaping South African identity in terms of its Great War memorial politics. The greatest deed attributed to the South African contingent on the Western European front was the Battle of Delville Wood (*Devil Wood* for some) which took place near Longueval in the Somme and only involved White soldiers. The first South African Infantry Brigade's mission was to defend that area. For several days, from 14 to 20 July 1916, some 3,000 South African 'springboks', as they were then nicknamed, were subjected to horrendous German bombing, attacks, and counter attacks. They held their ground but lost two thirds of their forces. After the war, the resting place of many a British and South African Tommy on the outskirts of Longueval, as well as the battlefield, were given to the South African government by its French counterpart, to become a memorial sanctuary.

The notions of commemoration, collective memory, and national identity are the background to the study of the reshaping of South African identities through addition to and extension of the Delville Wood memorial site. The ghosts from the past come back to haunt the living to remind them that a rewriting of South African memory is called for. With the end of apartheid, reclaiming identity was necessary. How have such commemorations served the different South African political agendas? How have they enabled South Africans to elaborate a consensual South African memory constructed on temporal layers in a specific space in France over the course of the last century? This chapter's focus will be set within a wider framework, analysing evolving identity phenomena. These are constantly reappraised according to the power of one group or the other, as shown by Hanna Smyth's article on the topic, in which she compares the Canadian Monument at Vimy Ridge and its South African equivalent at Delville Wood as 'sites of hybridity' as 'both Canada and South Africa encompassed multiple identities' (Smyth, 2016, np). British historian Jay Winter posits that each nation develops its own commemorative language, as the dead are used as a pretext for unfolding a political message (Winter, 1995, p. 85). Within the scope of the story of the Delville Wood monument, this chapter will deconstruct the process of reshaping South African identity by performing memorial and political rituals such as the reburial of a Black soldier within the stronghold of apartheid ideology, or by opening an additional room in the museum to display the sinking of the *SS Mendi* – an event that took place in the Channel rather than at Delville Wood *per se* – inside the reduced space of the memorial, thereby establishing what Anne Hertzog calls the spatialization of war memory (Hertzog, 2003, p. 2).

Preserving memorial ghosts to build a more balanced South African memory

According to French philosopher Paul Ricœur, going through the various stages of a shared memory, for people who have lived or witnessed an event, leads to the development of a collective memory for the whole community, including those who were absent from the event, as well as to the commemorations linked to places consecrated by tradition (Ricœur, 2004, p. 149). The South African government opened its memorial site in Delville Wood in 1926 followed by the Canadians who built a monument at Vimy in 1936, while the Australians and New Zealanders inaugurated theirs at Villeneuve-Bretonneux in 1938. The Delville Wood monument itself provides an interesting example of the ideology that presided over its conception (Teulié, 2018). This is illustrated by features of the building. The avenue of tall oak trees leads to an arch flanked on either side by a semi-circular wall. On top of the arch's dome stand a horse and two men. The two men represent the Greek heroes Castor and Pollux, intended to embody Afrikaners and South African Anglophones, who were united in 1910 within a new dominion, the Union of South Africa, thereby excluding Black and Coloured South Africans: 'In the Middle is a bronze horse, with a nude youth on each side, representing the two white races to whom the destiny of South Africa is given' (*The Examiner*, 1926). The relative unity is that of South African Whites who, after clashing in the disastrous Anglo-Boer War, had accepted to shed their blood side by side in Delville Wood. The unity of the two 'peoples' was visibly marked on inauguration day by the presence of the Right Reverend Dr (Michael Bolton) Furse Anglican bishop of St Alban (and former bishop of Pretoria) for the Anglophones and a 'dominee' (pastor) Moderator of the Dutch Reformed Church, Dr Van der Merwe, for the Afrikaners. It was described as a 'solemn dedication ceremony, which touched all hearts alike by its beauty and its sadness' as the sacrifice of South African troops was 'a warning against human passion and national folly' (*Dundee Courier*, 1926). The Memorial's leaflet published in 2006 states that '[...] the Memorial now reflects the true spirit of the South African nation, a nation forged from the struggle for liberation' (Keene, 2006, np), even though one may wonder which struggle is at stake (the struggle against imperialism or apartheid), thus challenging this notion of 'unity'.

During the Second World War, South Africans once again joined with their Commonwealth allies in the fight against the Germans. Delville Wood commemorations continued, contributing to the war effort by reminding young soldiers of their fathers' deeds. Consequently, in June 1952, a new element was added to the Delville Wood monument to commemorate all the South African fallen in the Second World War as well as the War in Korea (Teulié, 2018). The ceremony was essentially attended by anglophone South African veterans. The (radical) Afrikaner government of Daniel François Malan, elected in 1948, and which officially started apartheid, was not interested in commemorating British-South African friendship. To avoid having an 'Anglophone South African' monument at Delville Wood, the apartheid government decided to mark the Afrikaner presence (and ideology). A stone 'Voortrekker' cross was erected on top of the Cross of Sacrifice to pay tribute to the Boer/Afrikaner community and their sufferings against indigenous Bantu populations during the Great Trek (1830s and 1840s) and against the British during the two Anglo-Boer Wars (1880–1881 and 1899–1902). The cross thus became a symbol of disunity. The cross, set at the heart of the pentagonal building, which was inaugurated on 11 November 1986, was meant to remind the visitors that even under siege, South Africa could resist any enemy. A parallel was to be drawn with the apartheid regime, under pressure from attacks launched by the military branch of the ANC and under an international boycott, which led P.W. Botha to declare a state of emergency. The pentagon-shaped building houses the Delville Wood Museum and is built in the star shape of its military defence fort counterpart in the Cape – the Castle of Good Hope – built by the Dutch in the seventeenth century. The Delville Wood 'fort-museum' is an extension to the memorial which is now composed of four major sections: the first one is the cemetery near the road where visitors can park, then the oak avenue (2) leading to the Castor and Pollux monument (3), through which the visitor can reach the museum and the Cross of sacrifice (4).

The historical choice of building a symbolic defensive structure to host a museum, was given an official seal of approval for it emanated from the South African government as if the apartheid regime was stating that whether in South Africa or abroad, White South Africa would always defend itself. This is what Paul Ricœur calls an 'obligated memory' when he writes: 'At this level of appearance, imposed memory is armed with a history that is itself "authorized", the official history, the history publicly learned and celebrated' (Ricœur, 2004, p. 86). This leads him to conclude: 'A history taught, a history learned, but also a history celebrated. To this forced memorization are added the customary commemorations. A formidable pact is concluded in this way between remembrance, memorization, and commemoration' (Ricœur, 2004, p. 85). The multicultural elections that saw Nelson Mandela become president brought new perspectives to the country. Memorial politics were part and parcel of the project to rehabilitate Black and Coloured South Africans. Indeed, until then, the great absentees of the commemorations were the Black South African participants in the war, who had been evicted from commemorations, arguably because they were non-combatants. Thus, during the centenary commemorations (2014–2017), South African Native Labour Corps soldiers were honoured and their courage celebrated. They had enlisted as auxiliary troops whose duty was to perform logistic work, such as unloading ships, carrying equipment, setting camps, etc. A better balance was met between commemorating White and Black participation in the Great War, when the remains of the first of these Black soldiers who died in France and were buried on French soil were unearthed and buried a second time in front of the Cross of Sacrifice inside the courtyard of the memorial's 'fort-museum', the French equivalent of the Castle of Good Hope, at the very heart of what used to be an Afrikaner stronghold – in itself another form of *laager*, the defensive camp from the Great Trek which will be translated into the apartheid laws as the new *laager*. The epitaph reads BELEZA MYENGWA, S.A. NATIVE LABOUR CORPS 27th NOV 1916. This metonymical soldier, who embodies all Black South African soldiers, has finally penetrated the White men's stronghold just as the Zulu warriors tried to penetrate the *laager* during the Great Trek. He may rest in peace as South Africa is 'his' once again. What is more, his physical presence testifies to the reality of the participation of Black people in the conflict.

Reshaping South African identity

Memory shapes identity, hence the important question of what is to be remembered by a society. Paul Ricœur underlines that presence and absence go hand in hand, and the choices made around representations of the past will give the community its own historical truth:

> The phenomenology of memory, from the time of Plato and Aristotle, has proposed one key for the interpretation of the mnemonic phenomenon, namely, the power of memory to make present an absent thing that happened previously. Presence, absence, anteriority, and representation thus form the first conceptual chain of discourse about memory. The ambition of the faithfulness of memory would thus precede that of truth by history, whose theory remains to be worked out.
>
> (Ricœur, 2004, p. 229)

Bringing back the memory of those who were forgotten was the South African government's new agenda between 2014 and 2017. The long forgetting of the participation of Black South Africans in the conflict was ended and replaced by a shared memory between the different ethnic groups. It was not meant to be a 'rewriting' of history such as had been done with the erasing of the memory of former apartheid leaders such as Hendrik Verwoerd (Marschall, 2010, p. 140), with the toppling down of their statues, or Afrikaner placenames being replaced by Black African ones. It was more like counter-balancing a one-sided (white) vision of history for instance by erecting statues to former leading opponents to segregation and apartheid such as Gandhi, Nelson Mandela or Oliver Tambo. The reshaping of South African Identity became a reality on 6 July 2014 at Delville Wood when an official reburial ceremony of Native Labour Corps soldier, Beleza Myengwa took place in the courtyard of the fort-museum with pomp and circumstance. The then deputy president of the Republic of South Africa, Cyril Ramaphosa, declared: 'This ceremony is even more symbolic and significant as it marks the beginning of the Centenary of the First World War and it also coincides with the 20th Anniversary of our freedom in South Africa' (2014, np). The speech delivered on that day at Delville Wood was conventional. It was meant to honour South African soldiers who had shed their blood for their country and also for liberty and particularly for the liberty of other people:

> As we commemorate the 98th Anniversary of the Battle of Delville Wood, we will not only commemorate the lives of South Africans who perished on foreign soil during the First World War but will also remember those South Africans who fought and died in other wars for the liberation of various countries in Africa and Europe.
>
> (Ramaphosa, 2014, np).

The speech also tied the bonds of Franco-South African friendship, but what was new was that Black people who had fought inside South Africa against a South African apartheid government were also honoured: 'We also remember those who took part in the liberation struggle of South Africa' (Ramaphosa, 2014, np). This part of the speech enabled the Deputy President to remind his audience that France also had links with the ANC and to mention the Freedom Fighters he was celebrating:

> Our inspiration is anchored by the fact that we also achieved our own liberation, 20 years ago. As with you, our freedom was won through the efforts and sacrifices of our people, reinforced by those outside our country, including many activists here in France, who shared our vision of freedom and democracy.
>
> (Ramaphosa, 2014, np)

By associating anti-apartheid activists with Delville Wood soldiers, Ramaphosa implied that the apartheid regime (associated to First World One Germans) was the enemy of a free, democratic South Africa and that its downfall was a necessity to build a modern South Africa: 'This commemoration will always remind us of our past as we progress as a nation towards building a better life for all' (Ramaphosa, 2014, np). The blood of Black South Africans (who died in France during the Great War) and that of Black Freedom Fighters in the apartheid era were associated with the blood of White South African combatants. Former and recent fights were thus intrinsically linked.

But South African authorities were not done with the reappraisal of the First World War South African memorial space. On 12 July 2016, the President of the Republic of South Africa, Jacob Zuma, went further, by unveiling the 'Memorial wall' at Delville Wood:

> The Centenary Commemoration was succeeded by the inauguration of the Memorial Wall depicting names of all South African Soldiers who paid the supreme sacrifice during the First World War irregardless of race, colour or creed. The names are engraved in alphabetical order so to ensure a natural integration.
>
> (Delville Wood, 2020)

The two walls border the pathway from the Arch of Triumph to the Museum. Each wall bears the names of 14,000 South African soldiers who died in the twentieth century, regardless of their ethnic origin. Hence, one can find African, Anglophone, and Afrikaner names such as 'Tshomolokshe P.' along with 'Tucker E. E.' or 'Mbuti J.' and 'Mbuzi M.' followed by 'Mc Lincken J. G.' and 'McAlister R. M. P.', or 'Dillon J. T.' followed by 'Dinababa F.' and 'Dingelali N.', while columns are filled with 'Dupreez', 'Dutoits', 'Mac-Intoshes', and 'Bakers'. The plaque at the entrance of the museum insists on the ethnic origin of the South African soldiers 'Honouring Black and White soldiers who paid for the supreme sacrifice in theaters of operation' during the First and the Second World Wars. In his address at the opening of the centenary of the battle ceremonies, President Jacob Zuma was even clearer than Ramaphosa had been two years earlier, when he declared: 'Today we take forward the work that the democratic government began in 1994, to reverse the negative and painful impact of colonialism, racism and apartheid in our country' (Zuma, 2016, np). Before praising the White South African soldiers who had died a century before, he reminded his audience of what was at stake for him and his government: 'We are here to honour in particular, black people who fell in this war, who were not accorded the respect and recognition they deserved, and which is equal to that of their white compatriots' (Zuma, 2016, np), thus reflecting on a very biased South African Military history.

Symbolically, the *SS Mendi* and its long-forgotten ghosts finally entered port, not in Le Havre harbour, in France, their original destination, but in the middle of the Somme area, inland, in the memorial site of Delville Wood. This site being South African property, there was a logic to the *SS*

Mendi being commemorated there as it is part of the South African political message that Europe and the world should remember, thus acknowledging the sacrifice of young South Africans for the safeguard of liberty and peace. The message was to be completed with the recognition of the sacrifice of the Native Labour Corps, as the reburial of the Black soldier at the heart of the memorial may not have been enough. A tragedy, with a vast number of Black Africans' death would add to the global picture of First World War human sacrifices. Thus, it was in the 'fort-museum' that, in 2017, a room was devoted to the wreckage and the people on board. Entitled 'Loss of the SS Mendi. We die like brothers', it displays a very modern museography. Visitors are welcomed by a huge panel representing the Steamer Ship before the disaster. To give a personal touch to the evocation, a large portrait of a Black man is displayed. He embodies the South Africans on board the *Mendi*. His role is visible as he is wearing a pastor's robe. We learn that he was Isaac Wauchope Dyobha, chaplain to the Black soldiers, a Xhosa born in Doornhoek near Uitenhage and Port Elisabeth in 1852, educated by protestant missionaries at Lovedale mission. He was among the victims of the disaster. The exhibition adds that he was 'a prominent member of a group of East Cape African intellectuals, who encouraged the population to join the Labour Corps in the hope they would benefit politically from this show of Loyalty'. Reverend Dyobha is the key character in this museum display, a sort of common thread probably because of the famous words that he is said to have uttered before death, as we shall see, but also because he was an intellectual and a spiritual guide. Although no known survivors reported the legendary words of Reverend Isaac Wauchope Dyobha, they have been recorded as part of the events. As the ship was about to sink, he is reported to have said:

> Be quiet and calm my countrymen, for what is taking place is exactly what you came to do. You are going to die... But that is what you came to do... Brothers, you are drilling the death drill. I, a Xhosa say you are my brothers, Swazis, Pondos, Basutos, and so all, so let us die like brothers. We are the sons of Africa. Raise your war cries brothers, for though they made us leave our assegais [spears] in our Kraals [village-camp], our voices are left with our bodies [...].

Whether the pastor did say these words is uncertain, but what is true is that they are now part of the display and have entered the commemorative process.

Diving into an abyssal past

The aquatic atmosphere of the *SS Mendi* room is remarkable as the turquoise blue and emerald-green colours of the walls evoke the Channel seabed. Traditional items found in war museums are displayed in that room as in the other rooms of the museum. Yet, while the previous rooms present objects retrieved from the local archaeological site of Delville Wood – that is infantry weapons and ammunition, rusty tools and helmets, belt buckles, etc. – the Mendi room, the last one in the visit, exhibits objects retrieved from the bottom of the sea in 1974 – plates, cutlery, four portholes with cracked glass, an empty gun shell, etc. – to which were added items donated by the victims' families. Among them is the photograph of Colour Sergent Robert Alexander MacTavish, a White soldier (8th Platoon, C company, 5th battalion SANLC), which is a token to the fact that the display is not just a tribute to Black and Coloured soldiers, but to all South Africans. There is a strong appeal to the visitor's emotions in an attempt to bring the visitor as close as possible to the victims so that the empathy process can work. There are excerpts from letters sent by victims just weeks or days before the disaster, such as that by R. A. MacTavish writing to 'Bert', his wife and the mother of his six children. The visitor knows that the message of hope in the letter was to be shattered a few days later and that the father's body would be buried in England, not even in South Africa. The letter of Captain Lewis Hertzler, medical officer is an ill-omen of the tragedy that is about to begin 'It was a weird experience visiting the men on watch at midnight, the ship heaving and rocking... the whole sky dark, the fog increasing the invisibility of everything, the ship's siren booing every minute making one jump'. But beyond the traditional museum displays, a modern touch was added to that commemorative room with a digital extension to the exhibition. Within the contexts of the Bristol Cultural Development Partnership and Arts Council of England, Associate Professor of Cultural Interdisciplinary Practice at the University of the West of England at Bristol, Shawn Sobers created a film project in 2014 with Rob Mitchell to pay tribute to the men of the *SS Mendi* (Sobers, 2014).

Entitled 'Inconsequential Monuments', the 23-minute film was still presented in the museum through a television viewing along with headphones in July 2017 when I visited the memorial. The film alternates informative contents, such as a map of the place where the *Mendi* sunk, with more artistic images whose objective is to renew the memorial process. This is what is indicated by the artist on his website:

> Using the *SS Mendi* tragedy as the context, the film explores different forms of remembrance in an anthropological style, building on the aesthetic of the Elmina film, [...] with the dispassionate computerised voice. The forms of remembrance explored are pilgrimage, judicial process and law, empathy, creative expression, and civic memorial.
>
> (Sobers, 2014)

These different elements are referred to as 'categories of memory'. The first of these 'categories' gives the background to the whole memorial process by once again focusing on the place where the events took place: the sea.

Entitled 'The Spirit of the Place', it shows the greenish waters at the bottom of which lay the *SS Mendi*. The female voice overstates that in popular imagination, the sea is at once both peaceful and threatening. It then explains that the *SS Mendi* is at the bottom of that sea around 40 metres below the surface. Like in a play, this first part could be seen as the setting.

Then, there is a close-up on the lips of the man who lends his voice to Judge J.G. Hay Halket in 'Category 2'. The latter was the magistrate before whom the hearings of the sinking of the *SS Mendi* took place on 8 August 1917 in London. In a very administrative and emotionless way, he reads the account of the wreckage, and the fate of the *SS Mendi* is described in detail, while a map of the area between England and France is displayed on the screen before the lips are seen reporting again. The tragedy is enhanced by the report which states (2'15) 'No attempt was made by the *SS Darro* to hail the other vessel, to lower a boat out into the water, or in any way to ascertain the damage that had been done to her or what assistance could be rendered' (2'26) nor did the captain of the *SS Darro*, responsible for the collision, react to the shouts from below like the other crew members of the Darro (2'36) 'though it does not appear to have occurred to him that these shouts might have been from people in difficulties in the water, and he took no steps to find out where they came from' (2'42). A text concludes this section with these words: 'Of the 646 men who drowned, on the *SS Mendi*, 607 of them were Black South African troops. None of the 607 received medals of recognition, unlike their European counterparts [...]' and finally (3'34): 'This was a South African Government decision'. The film underlines the contempt which Black South African troops were subjected to.

'Category 3' is entitled 'Empathy and identity as tribute'. It displays colour photographs of Black or Coloured British soldiers, fully clothed, who are swimming underwater in a swimming pool whose water is crystal clear, contrasting thus with the sea's greenish and non-transparent water. These soldiers' own voice-over expresses their thoughts and connects them, as Black soldiers to the black soldiers who died on board the *SS Mendi*. The first soldier to speak for example, Gareth 'Gas' Gray, 56 years old, 1st battalion Gloucester Regiment, states that he agreed to be part of 'this remembrance, if you like of the *SS Mendi*' (4'09–12) as many acts carried out by people of colour had not been remembered at all. He liked the idea of remembering the men of the *SS Mendi*, by having 'a photoshoot in a swimming pool' (4'35). He adds that swimming with clothes on would make you think what soldiers would feel like when they know they are going to die, something he had experienced. He also says that the bizarre thing when you are about to die is wondering about 'who remembers you' (5'55). Raymond J. Fielding, another of the soldiers who agreed to be part of the commemorative video, has so much empathy with the men onboard the *Mendi* that he includes himself as a Black soldier: '**we** fought for Queen and country' and therefore '**we** should be remembered' (7'08). The news section of the University of the West of England at Bristol's website points out that 'The interviews are very poignant as the soldiers featured in the beautiful photograph narrative have all faced death and identify with the South African troops and the horror of drowning'. The webpage adds 'This film asks: how do communities respond to personal memorial and the fate of the *SS Mendi*?' (UWE Bristol, 2015, np). Thus, this film is both a tribute to those who died but also a reflection on what it means as an educational device to remember what is to be remembered and why.

'Creative Expression as Memorial' (15'32) is 'Category 4'. It shows a Black underwater dancer in a public swimming pool, performing topless as if he himself had unwillingly fallen in the water, to a musical accompaniment of sub-marine sounds, drums, and classical music. The sequence also uses cross fading to lead the spectators from the swimming pool to the greenish waters of the early part of the film and immerse them in the sea for a moment. A poem written by Rob Mitchell (2014) can be heard, which denounces the way Black soldiers were treated and echoes the apartheid years: 'And here's he, Chief Bokleni-among the servants, farmers and labourers, miners conscripted to fetch, carry, drop, to build roads and rails and latrines. No more than servant to the white man's war machine – wondering who will remember his name'. And again: 'Come closer. Your wars are done. So, let's erase this ethnic face-off now you're simply Kaffir,[2] in the new Union of South Africa'.

'Category 5' is called 'Permanent Physical Memorials'. It is a sort of conclusion that shows the various commemorative sites throughout the world that honour the victims of the *SS Mendi*. The film's credits finally unfold on the image of the water of the Channel with the rhythmic music of a drum and the relentless surf of the sea in the background, thus associating Africa and the sea, the resting place of the South African soldiers who drowned. The webpage hosting the artist's film concludes with the idea that honouring the sacrifices made by their ancestors 'is not limited to African peoples, all nations on earth partake in such ancestor remembrance rituals, whether that be in the form of D-Day ceremonies, erecting statues, naming places after people, and other acts of civic remembrance' (Sobers, 2014). This is echoed in the following quotation which puts the fate of the Black soldiers and that of White South African soldiers on an equal footing:

> Shawn's film is part of a wider exhibition at Delville Wood titled, 'We Die Like Brothers', brought together by Graham Scott, Senior Archaeologist at Wessex Archaeology and Susan Hayward Director of the Russell-Cotes Art Gallery & Museum. The exhibition tells the wider story of the SS Mendi and South African involvement in World War One, and a formal commemoration of those who died.
>
> (UWE Bristol, 2015, np)

What is thus at stake is to find a memorial balance to come to terms with the past in a democratic country. Black soldiers, formerly excluded from the memory of the war, are now reinstated, as underlined by President Zuma:

> Care has been taken that the new murals in the Museum will depict the involvement of the South African Native Labour Corps in the Great Wars, as well as the Sinking of the *SS Mendi*. The transformation of the Delville Wood Memorial will therefore represent a powerful message of reconciliation and provide some redress that will further consolidate the diversity of our South African nation.
>
> (Zuma, 2016, np)

Conclusion

The fiction story of Pitso Motaung told by Fred Khumalo is one of many examples of the legacy of the *SS Mendi* in the lives of South Africans. The main character at the end of the novel knows he may be executed for a crime he has committed. On the day of his trial as the French judge steps into the tribunal, Pitso starts singing and dancing to everyone's great astonishment:

> I am dancing my death drill. No-one can take it away from me. This death drill is my truth. They made me leave my spear, my shield, back home those many years ago. So I am going to fight with my words, turn my words into bullets. This dance is my history, my heritage, my story that they tried to supress. This is my death drill, my dance of death, my dance of truth.
>
> Like the men on the *Mendi*, he danced, the rhythmic slamming of feet gaining momentum with each movement. Slam-slam! Slam-slam!
>
> (Khumalo, 2017, pp. 311–312)

This conclusion to the novel, which echoes Reverend Dyobha's last words on board the *SS Mendi*, illustrates how Black and Coloured South Africans were ill-treated by their White counterparts, and the different elements mentioned 'my heritage', 'my story', and my 'dance of truth' echo Ricœur's 'truth of history' as quoted earlier in this chapter. Pitso survived the *SS Mendi* disaster but had to hide in France pretending to be an Algerian, as he was afraid of being accused of starting a riot and, what is more, had been bullied and threatened by Officer Haig (a White officer), whom he saw kicking the face of Black soldiers who were trying to board his lifeboat after they all found themselves in the freezing waters of the Channel, thus sentencing most of them to death. It was only many years later, that Pitso Motaung, then a waiter at the famous Parisian restaurant *La Tour d'Argent*, served a customer whom he recognized to be Officer Haig. The latter met his doom on that day as, recognizing Pitso, he tried to kill him. Pitso was quicker. Pitso's last words in the novel suggest that although Black and Coloured South Africans served their country, there was an attempt to erase the memory of their deeds. As a tribute to his brothers who had died on that fateful day, Pitso performs his Dance drill.

The People of the Abyss, as Jack London once put it referring to the destitute London EastEnders, could be applied to the case of the South African Native Labour Force victims on board the *SS Mendi* as 'the ghosts of the abyss' who come back to haunt the living. Even though Louis Botha's White South African government paid tribute in Parliament to the Black men (and some White officers) who disappeared on that fatal day, the following years did not recognize their contribution to the South Africa war effort. They are still haunting people as Khumalo's novel was turned into a play: from Friday 29 June to Saturday 14 July 2018, Nuffield Southampton Theatres presented the world première of the play *SS Mendi, Dancing the Death Drill*, based on Khumalo's book. Many 'Mendi memorials' were erected in South Africa in Port Elizabeth, Atteridgeville (Pretoria), Avalon cemetery (Soweto), Libode (Easter Cape), Simon's Town and University of Cape Town's Campus (Cape Town). Today, the highest medal of Valour in South Africa is 'The order of the Mendi' and Armed Forces Day is annually commemorated on the anniversary of the catastrophe in South Africa.

Yet, one may wonder why the *SS Mendi* is commemorated in Delville Wood. Professor Albert Grundlingh of Stellenbosch University was quoted in an article saying that there had always been commemorations for the *SS Mendi* in South Africa but that the apartheid regime had minimized Black participation in the war and that in the 1980s Freedom Fighters could not lean on ancestors who had, according to them, collaborated with White power (Niewoudt, 2015, np). One could add there were different layers of commemoration at Delville Wood:

> Originally conceived as a monument to commemorate the fallen South African soldiers of the First World War, it also serves as a means of reflecting South African's dominant internal and competing political ideologies, through time a political motive which overshadows the former.
>
> (Battin, 2006, np)

Thus, it was only after the election of Nelson Mandela, Grundlingh contended, that 'the ANC appropriated the *SS Mendi* post-apartheid, perhaps because the organization has a weak military history. Its military wing, Umkhonto we Sizwe, was known for armed propaganda rather than armed engagement' (Battin, 2006, np), adding that it was normal for a group to have heroes to wordship. Even though the political use of the *SS Mendi* was denied by ANC authorities, this was perhaps not necessary, as all commemorations are political and the reclaiming of a more balanced South African identity a vital evolution of the memorial process at Delville Wood, in an effort to redress the wrongdoings of the past when only White soldiers were celebrated throughout the memorial site. It took a change of government in

South Africa in 1994 and the awakening of the *SS Mendi*'s ghosts to allow for a more balanced commemorative process to be launched. Memory and commemoration are sensitive issues. Fortunately, South Africans have accepted the inclusion of Black soldiers, although non-combatants, in the memorial process, furthering the will to be a united nation if not a 'rainbow nation'. This reclaimed memory and identity has reshaped South African representations of its past and given credit to all the actors of the new South Africa.

Notes

* Gilles Teulié, Aix Marseille Univ, LERMA, Aix-en-Provence, France.
1 Of the 823 men from the 5th battalion who were on board, 616 died. Six hundred and seven were Black or coloured South Africans. Thirty crew members also died.
2 One should remember that the word Kaffir (Kaffer in English and Cafre in French) from Arabic origin was a very offensive word during apartheid.

References

Battin, P. (2006) 'Commemorative Politics. The Delville Wood South African National Monument at Longueval, France', *South African Military History Journal*, 13(5) [online]. Available at: http://samilitaryhistory.org/vol135pb.html (Accessed: 21 March 2021).

Delville Wood (2020) 'The Memorial Wall'[online]. Available at: http://www.delvillewood.com/memorial_wall2.htm (Accessed: 7 August 2020).

Dundee Courier (1926) 'South Africa's War Dead', *Dundee Courier*, 11 October, p. 5 [online]. Available at: https://www.britishnewspaperarchive.co.uk/search/results/1926-10-01/1926-10-31?basicsearch=%22war%20dead%22&phrase search=war%20dead&retrievecountrycounts=false&newspapertitle=dundee%20courier&sortorder=score (Accessed: 3 January 2022).

Hertzog, A. (2003) 'Musées de la Grande Guerre et identité territoriale en Picardie: les territoires pétrifiés', 6èmes Rencontres de Théo Quant, Université de Franche-Comté [online]. Available at: http://thema.univ-fcomte.fr/theoq/pdf/2003/TQ2003%20ARTICLE%2036.pdf (Accessed: 21 July 2020).

Keene, J. (2006) *The Delville Wood Memorial & Commemorative Museum, Department of the Somme, France.* Johannesburg: Delville Wood Commemorative Museum Trust/South African National Museum of Military History.

Khumalo, F. (2017) *Dancing the Death Drill.* London: Jacarada.

Marschall, S. (2010) *Landscape of Memory: Commemorative Monuments, Memorials and Public Statuary in Post-apartheid South Africa.* Leiden-Borston: Brill.

Mitchell, R. (2014) 'Inconsequential Monument', Poem [online]. Available at: https://ssmendiproject.wordpress.com/ (Accessed: 31 Oct 2021).

Niewoudt, S. (2015) 'Fallen Soldiers of SS Mendi Dragged into Battle', *Mail & Guardian* (South Africa), 27 March [online]. Available at: https://mg.co.za/article/2015-03-27-fallen-soldiers-dragged-into-battle/ (Accessed: 26 September 2021).

Ramaphosa, C. (2014) 'SA: Cyril Ramaphosa: Address by the Deputy President of South Africa, at the 98th Commemoration of the Battle of Delville Wood,

France', *Polity*, 6 July [online]. Available at: https://www.defenceweb.co.za/joint/government-affairs/address-by-deputy-president-cyril-ramaphosa-at-the-98th-commemoration-of-the-battle-of-delville-wood/ (Accessed: 7 January 2022).

Ricœur, P. (2004) *Memory, History, Forgetting.* Translated by K. Blamey and D. Pellauer. Chicago, IL and London: The University of Chicago Press.

Smyth, H. (2016) 'Identities Set in Stone? The Delville Wood and Vimy Memorials as Sites of Hybridity', *Defence-in-Depth,* Defence Studies Department, King's College London, 10 April [online]. Available at: https://defenceindepth.co/2016/04/20/identities-set-in-stone-the-delville-wood-and-vimy-memorials-as-sites-of-hybridity/ (Accessed: 21 July 2020).

Sobers, S. (2014) 'African Kinship Series – SS Mendi', Film [online]. Available at: http://www.shawnsobers.com/african-kinship-series-part-4-ss-mendi-emotional-science-film/ (Accessed: 22 February 2021).

Teulié, G. (2018) « Un héritage sud-africain en mutation: Mémoire préservée et commémorations contextuelles de la bataille de Delville Wood (1916–2017) » in Barbier, M.-C. and Perrot, C. (eds.) *Afrique du Sud. Mémoire, héritages et ruptures.* Paris: L'Harmattan, pp. 17–38.

The Examiner (1926) 'Delville Wood – South Africa's Memorial – A Battle Scarred Ground', *The Examiner* (Launceston, Tas.), 12 October, p. 5 [online]. Available at: https://trove.nla.gov.au/newspaper/article/51368027 (Accessed: 3 January 2022).

UWE Bristol (2015) 'Moving Film by UWE Academic Commemorates Fate of SS Mendi Soldiers at Exhibition in the Somme', University of the West of England at Bristol Website, 10 July [online]. Available at: https://info.uwe.ac.uk/news/uwenews/news.aspx?id=3130 (Accessed: 28 September 2021).

Winter, J. (1995) *Sites of Memory, Sites of Mourning: The Great War in European Cultural History.* Cambridge: Cambridge University Press.

Zuma, J. (2016) 'Speech on Delville Wood Centenary', *DefenceWeb,* 13 July [online]. Available at: https://www.defenceweb.co.za/joint/government-affairs/speech-zuma-on-delville-wood-centenary/ (Accessed: 7 August 2020).

10 Blyton's ghosts
Childhood receptions in India and Britain

Tanvi Chowdhary and Sara Thornton

Blyton's popularity remains an unexplained cornerstone of children's literature. *The Famous Five* and *Secret Seven* mystery stories, the boarding school stories and the *Noddy* series have never been out of print yet Blyton's literature is home to a dubious and complicated legacy. Her stories – particularly the boarding school titles – borrow values from a Victorian tradition and an imperial past. With time, and as her readership has grown beyond the borders of Britain, subsequent editions have been expurgated to reflect modern sensibilities, and to accommodate critique of her xenophobic tendencies. For many readers, the memory of reading Blyton contains both awareness of hegemonic constraints and a potential for creativity since her imaginary scapes seem to enable reinterpretation and counter-narratives.

Two childhood responses are remembered here – one South Asian and the other British. The cultural and chronological distances of each reader from the historical conjuncture of 1940s Britain when Blyton, at the height of her output, wrote and first published the *Famous Five* stories or the boarding school narratives of *St. Clare's* and *Malory Towers* are different: the time of reading took place in one instance in the early 2000s in South Asia and in the second in the early 1970s in Britain, not so long after Blyton's death. Both receptions are responses to certain ghosts: the imperial presence in caste-divided India and a feudal class system still haunting 1970s Britain. If we are dogged by the ghosts of past times, we are not necessarily dominated by them. Edward Saïd's vision of cultural imperialism in which one narrative will block and hinder less hegemonic narratives (1993) will be overlayed with more multidimensional reading processes. An implied reader (Iser, 1978) or 'implied visitor' to a garden or a theatre performance (Bennett, 1990; Hunt, 2004) will wander through the world of Blyton as through a landscape, registering certain scenes and not others, adapting the story as they go, along with its props and its ideologies, turning these impressions towards personal needs, allowing new narratives and histories to form. If the ghosts of the past colour the present, then the present also colours the writings of the past. The two readers will look back on their own haunting of Blyton's writings, analysing their trajectories and habits of mind, while rethinking these impressions from an adult present.

DOI: 10.4324/9781003178040-14

Blyton in Lucknow and Delhi

Writer Sandip Roy has likened Blyton's influence to that of the East India company:

> In a sense, Blyton's influence over Indians is probably more outsized than her influence over British children. In England, she might have been a phenomenally successful children's writer. In India she was, as we call it nowadays, an influencer. She colonized young Indian minds far more effectively than the East India Company. And we willingly remained in the enchanted woods of Blyton long after we had expelled the British themselves.
>
> (Roy, 2019, np)

I would argue that the process of assimilating Blyton is not simply one of submission to a colonizing power nor only a matter of the empire 'writing back' (Ashcroft, Griffiths and Tiffin, 2002); it is a more minute negotiation with the food, beverages, places and picnics which confer a value onto English culture only accessible to children from a certain ethnicity and economic background. The foundation for this enquiry lies in my personal experience of reading Blyton with a certain consent and a simultaneous resistance to her fictional contract in order to find my own place within her writing.

Every bookstore in India with a children's section hosts stacks of Enid Blyton books. Some of the more recent editions feature cartoons and caricatures appealing to a new wave of readers, all accompanied by the trademark Enid Blyton signature. In 2004, Universal Bookstore of Bhootnath Market in Lucknow, Uttar Pradesh, had a hardcopy of *The Bed that Ran Away and Other Stories* that was purchased by my father long before I had any say over what I was reading – a copy that has since been lost to the libraries of my old school in the Gomti Nagar district of the town. A staple of the Indian birthday party present, Enid Blyton's books still dominate the shelves of the children's sections in the pan-India chain bookstores *Landmark* and *Crossword*. Her popularity throughout the Indian subcontinent has remained constant ever since her stories first appeared, continuing after the Indian Independence Act of 1947, and prospering today with a variety of rewritings and adaptations. Many of Blyton's stories are translated into Hindi and Bengali as well as other South Asian languages although I read Blyton, as many middle-class Indian children still do, in English – a language seen as both hegemonic and aspirational.

Blyton's stories frequently construct spaces overlaid with the rules of the adult world, becoming accessible to children through their own juvenile reclamation of space and language. Her intrepid heroines, adventurous boys and trotting dogs transgress the terrain of grown-up rules, while maintaining the 'values' of an English education. The adventures experienced by the cast of *The Famous Five, The Five Find Outers* and *The Secret Seven* feature the crossing of multiple boundaries, as the children reimagine spaces, making them exciting and expandable through the solving of mysteries. Blyton's heroes and heroines imbibe the 'English sense of honour' (Blyton, 2016, p. 82), allowing them to balance their mischief with responsibility. Values of kindness, goodness, generosity and honesty are frequently portrayed as the building blocks of 'strong characters' (Blyton, 1945, p. 30). The children maintain close ties to the foundations of English society, ones that Blyton admired; indeed, her conformity to gender roles, racial stereotypes and class relations has garnered international debate on how appropriate her writing is for children today (Smith, 2011; Roy, 2019). While the Secret Seven dress up as 'red Indians' (Blyton, 1950, p. 7), the girls at St. Clare's become strong characters so that they might better fulfil their roles as 'finest wives and mothers' for England (Blyton, 1945, p. 107).

Although Blyton's writing defers to the rules of an imperialist and patriarchal society, she also portrays heroines such as Georgina Kirrin from *The Famous Five*. 'George' blurs the gender binary, by dressing as a boy, choosing to be called George, and is described with values typically assigned to boys, such as 'bold', 'daring', 'hot-tempered' or 'loyal'. George's refusal to accept her female self and her attempt to ascribe to a male-coded *tomboy* identity is, of course, caught in the essentialism of gender roles. At the same time, she does not try to influence Anne in this direction or to question women's roles more generally (such as her mother's). As a child, I was unable to articulate such ambiguities; my awareness came from my struggle to understand more concrete customs and objects.

Mothers in kurtas, feasts of sardines and ginger ale

When I first tried to imagine what Blyton's mothers looked like, I was unable to picture what an English mother would wear. Having no reference for the same, I imagined that they would wear *kurtas* with pant trousers (*churidar* or *dhoti*). This is rooted in my own upper-caste, upper middle-class upbringing and history. However, my focus is not the distance between the postcolonial reader and Blyton's writing, but the bridging of that distance, one that requires a certain imposition of 'Indianness' onto Blyton's England. The alien symbols of the imperial power are inescapably a part of Blyton's books for she uses cultural signifiers such as food that can pose certain problems for young South Asian readers: the midnight feasts in Blyton's boarding school and the picnics of *The Famous Five* are packed with identifiers such as sardines, kippers, sausages, treacle, ginger beer, chocolate cake, jam tarts – largely unavailable foods which are alien to Indian readers. Meadows, forests and cottages are intimately associated with such emblematic foods: they are the spaces where food is shared outside of the control of the parental/adult eye. The English sense of values that Blyton instils through the representation of the countryside, school life, traditions and 'sense of honour' with the children's rituals of sharing, give the Indian child the task of reconfiguring, among other things, alien gustatory experiences and translating them into their own world.

Where language shapes the landscape that it attempts to construct, food becomes the cultural signifier that gives it value – providing a realistic and emotional bridge for the readers who have experienced the tastes and textures described. According to Zeba Vagh: 'we crave freedom and familiarity. Blyton served up both with the abundance of her picnic sandwiches' (2020, np). For Blyton, national selfhood seems to come largely from food. Keeling and Pollard explain this phenomenon: 'in the earliest texts of world literature the integral role of food as a cultural signifier, [is] not only the product of a culture but one that gives shape to the *mentalités* that structure thought and expression' (2009, p. 4). For Elizabeth Gargano, the 'rituals and customs of family life' are centred around the 'shared family meal' (2008, p. 208) which, in this case, is a meal shared by children, facilitated by the adults who are conscious of their children's dietary needs. Mothers supply secret clubs with biscuits to nibble on, pack 'tuck boxes' of food for the girls travelling to boarding schools and organize picnics outside. As Elizabeth Thiel says:

> The myth of home and family that resonated throughout the early part of the century had simultaneously been replicated through popular children's literature to create a template for a world in which father and mother, devoted to the moral and/or spiritual well-being of their offspring, were ever-present and ever-mindful of their duties.
>
> (2008, p. 5)

Within Indian readership, the ability to imagine these foods is marked by a certain class division. Middle-class Indian households have access to this language, this literature and the leisure to recreate these experiences. According to Rachel Dwyer, the old professional middle classes are challenged by the emergence of new monied, consumerist middle classes with 'non-landed wealth' and speaking English 'as one of their major languages' (2007, p. 225).

Early writing for Indian children such as R.K. Narayan's *Swami and Friends* attempts to develop, according to Superle, a 'sense of Indianness, particularly when they utilise Western forms' (2011, p. 111). While analysing contemporary Indian children's literature, Superle notes the mimicry of the English form, superimposed with signifiers that are typically 'Indian'. The form that is used to construct this imagined 'Indianness' is one that attempts to subvert colonial expectations, while recreating upper-caste Indian identity. Thus, in the Blyton-inspired story by Devika Rangachari, *When Amma Went Away* (2002), the benevolent Patti feeds the children on plates and plates of South Indian food, including *idlis, dosas* and *rasam*. As Superle has said: 'Although some references to food can seem innocuous, when viewed as an overarching trend, the use of food as a means to convey

Indianness becomes recognisably a nation-building technique' (2011, p. 117). Interestingly then, the cultural currency of the unavailable English 'ginger ale' becomes as much a part of the imaginative experience of childhood literature, as the upper-caste food in Indian literature for children. When reading Blyton, the aspiration and idealized value of these cultural signifiers create a postcolonial distance, while the rewriting of cultural signifiers in an Indian context creates a vernacular Blyton. This scope for negotiation and even opposition on the part of the readership shows that a piece of writing or a book or even a space like a garden or a theatre stage (Bennett, 1990; Hunt, 2004) is interpreted and recreated by the reader or visitor using personal experience. The meaning of a text is not an inherent or natural phenomenon, but is formed in an on-going way within the relationship between the text and the reader (Jauss, 1982). The child reader will learn to imbue the kippers with personal gustatory values and tastes or translate them into known foods.

Rabitting and meadows, summers in faraway places

Blyton's childhood places are located at the intersection between nationhood and childhood. Her stories become the point of introduction, for many children of urban middle-class households in India, to what seems at first an alien world. Yet, her stories are steeped, historically, in the work and life of a culture that has not only been the alien oppressor of India but also an essential part of its cultural make-up. Blyton's influence on national identity and selfhood for a reader who is not ethnically white, becomes a complicated negotiation between two different structures of power: one that is external and the other internalized. The *bildungsroman* was a means to showcase 'upward mobility and ambition in a bourgeois society' (Mukherjee, 2014, p. 133). Upward mobility is a feature of the fully established mercantile economy – one that allows readers to inscribe aspirational value into a life they hope to attain. It is found primarily through the institution of education: 'individuals were encouraged, through books such as *Jane Eyre* and *David Copperfield* to aspire to intellectual, social, and perhaps most importantly, ethical and moral success' (Judy, 2011, p. 22).

While the children of the *Far Away Tree* experience abstract worlds in 'distant, unusual locations' (Orestano, 2015, p. 58), the Secret Seven's obstacles are adults who treat them in a patronising manner: during their very first mystery, the postman begins by telling them, 'Don't ask silly questions and waste my time! You children – you think you're so funny, don't you?' (Blyton, 1950, p. 30). Similarly, Bets, in *The Mystery of the Burnt Cottage*, enters the world of the 'older' children when traversing the meadows with Scamper, uncovering clues (Blyton, 2014). For these children, the adult landscape is accessible through a re-creation of language and a remapping of the land through secret spaces, hidden rooms and houses. These are accessible to no one but themselves since they straddle the boundary between what is societally acceptable, and what could be considered, according to Mr. Goon, as 'snooping' (Blyton, 2014).

Within this construction of the adult world, the 'designation of special spaces of childhood' is marked by the exclusivity of spaces 'into which only children may pass' (Cecire, Field and Roy, 2015, p. 1). The adult sphere is constraining and normative while secret spheres are sought after by the children – an escape to Kirrin Island for example or the secret passages in an old farmhouse. Even transgressive childhood spaces such as Wonderland, Neverland or Narnia (Manlove, 2003; Nikolajeva, 2012; Miller, 2016), all of which are inaccessible to adults, are available only to children who are ethnically white and middle-class. Indian identity then becomes a negotiation between the white space that rejects it, and the postcolonial identity that must negotiate with the persistent effect of the imperial power.

Nothing conveys this more clearly than the boarding school stories in which middle-class codes of conduct are followed by the pupils in *Malory Towers, St Clare's* or *The Naughtiest Girl* series. The stable incomes of their fathers, who are typically doctors or lawyers, are part and parcel of a nationhood that creates good English girls. This literary construction betrays the anxiety to maintain the cultural currency of an English existence:

> The need to maintain the superiority of the British race, and 'improve' the areas in which it was feared to be deteriorating, necessarily involved considerations of class and opened up another area for the direction of imperial girlhood. If working-class girls in England's cities were thought 'uncivilised' then they could not be expected to fulfil their future function as responsible mothers.
>
> (Smith, 2011, p. 9)

The rising prevalence of convent schools in a colonial context also aspired to the English way of life but many Indian children had no access to these spaces, nor to the cultural markers and signifiers attached to them. The 'literary gymnastics' (Thiong'o, 1994, p. 8) that is involved in using an alien knowledge in imagining the Indian reality through a 'language of conceptualisation that is foreign' (Thiong'o, 1994, p. 17), is one that is fraught with the tensions of imperialism. For the Indian child, according to Coats: 'Whiteness has come to be associated with a philosophical tradition of valorizing appearances and ideals over substance and materialism; it is more interested in the Symbolic than in the Real, which threatens it' (2004, p. 128). Blyton uses traditional symbols in her stories so that her narrative 'inscribes the dominance of white power and white culture' (Hourihan, 2005, p. 57). These are symbols that Indian children often feel unable to access, and yet however, feel profoundly close to. And, as Indian identity has become a more stable category (albeit Hindu, i.e. associated with upper-caste privilege), able to juggle the pasts of colonialism with the currents of modern South Asia, Blyton's world has become more flexible and accessible.

In her analysis of Elizabeth Knox's *Dreamhunter Duet,* Ruth Feingold states that the struggle for a second or third generation immigrant is 'in relation to both the new land and a semi-remembered ancestral homeland' (2015, p. 133). The postcolonial position of having a foothold in the English world of Blyton and the Indian version of the same makes the reading of Blyton doubly complicated. Her world is both familiar and unfamiliar, a colonial burden that provides the postcolonial reader with a template to imagine it while maintaining distance. The negotiation between Blyton's England and the experience of India has been critically placed in the realm of postcolonial criticism but English writing in India itself is markedly different from the time of Raja Rao's *Kanthapura,* where the 'alien' language struggled to shape a current India (Rao, 2015, p. v). English is sometimes thought to be as intimately a part of our cultural make-up, and as capable of describing our reality as our native languages. Access to English makes Blyton's England a ghost reality, both understandable and distant – allowing Rohinton Mistry's narrator in *Swimming Lessons* to speak of the imaginary Christmas that he pictured through Blyton's books – while located in Bombay (Mistry, 1990). Writing on the reception of English literature in South Asia, Mukherjee explains: 'this negotiation requires us, on some level, to recuperate and reinstall Austen in our world – or Joyce and Conrad, for that matter' (2014, p. 119). The foundation lies not in negotiating the oppressive language into a native culture, but inscribing the native culture into the world of the oppressive language – to reimagine *England* in an *Indian* tongue, rather than using English to recreate India's postcolonial selfhood.

Blyton's popularity among Indian readers has prevailed for the better part of two generations; her England has become as intrinsic a part of the cultural make-up of Indian childhood as R.K. Narayan's *Swami and Friends.* Since independence, India's relationship with itself and the imperial power that ruled it has changed dramatically. English speaking and reading audiences have increased, while pushes for an Indian identity (more specifically Hindu identity) have been strong, encountering resistance from Southern Indian non-Hindi speakers. Access to English is already part of a complicated network of relationships between caste and class: historically, upper-caste Indians have had more success becoming a part of English institutions with better access to better education. Superle's work on children's literature quotes a variety of critics on the subject:

> Only a small percentage of children had access to English-language books. In fact, access to books remains today a significant challenge for many Indian children, especially those who are poor and/or live in rural areas. Beyond the fact that only approximately half the Indian population is literate, it is also important to note that economic disparity, particularly in rural India, prevents much of the population from owning or even accessing children's books.
>
> (Agarwal, 'Off the Beaten Track' in Superle, 2011, p. 23)

Blyton is thus accessible only to children living in urban or suburban India. In urban India, the spaces provided in the small villages of Blyton's England are impossible to find – particularly since liminal spaces which can be claimed by children are indicative of a wealth of resources and disposable space (large houses, gardens, accessible outdoor space) which allow such leisure to exist. Additionally, urban Indian children lack the freedom of the adventurous children of Blyton's England – beyond a certain boundary, exploration becomes socially, culturally and even religiously impossible. Vagh's reader response from Mumbai expresses this privilege of space:

> Enid Blyton's adventures take place in an adult-free world where children have an other-worldly level of autonomy, from the seaside shenanigans of the *Famous Five* to the dormitory escapades of *Malory Towers*. This must have been heady stuff even when it was first published in the 1940s; but for children of the day, who tend to spend less time outdoors than prisoners, it's a giddy blast of fresh air.
>
> (Vagh, 2020, np)

It is important to see that today's constant interaction with screens and children's lives increasingly spent on-line also make the world of Blyton seem distant and strange.

Blyton's new vernaculars

England's ghostly presence in India – in the form of the convent schools, Lutyens' Delhi (designed by the British Raj architect), Victoria memorial and clock towers – lingers in the way Indian children imagine Blyton's world. Fish's categorization of the 'informed reader' includes having access to the language and the semantic knowledge necessary for literary competence. More interesting to me is how uninformed readers make lexical connections from extremely distinct contexts:

> The idea of textual world presupposes that the reader constructs in imagination a set of language independent objects, using as a guide the textual declarations, but building this always incomplete image into a more vivid representation through the import of information provided by internalized cognitive models, inferential mechanisms, real-life experience, and cultural knowledge, including knowledge derived from other texts.
>
> (Ryan, 2001, p. 91)

When imagining the Blyton world, one makes equivalences for what is not available: I imagined English villages from the architecture around me, and had my own real kids' club to solve mysteries. Using the prevalence of Western media in popular discourse, readers mesh multiple imaginations and contexts together to create an imaginary world: the remnants of colonialism, and the interpretive framework provided by lived experience with its multiple intrusions from other cultures. The framework for the way in which Blyton is read in India exists through a reading community that is familiar with her work, yet willing to reconstruct the knowledge it lacks:

> Interpretive communities are made up of those who share interpretive strategies not for reading but for writing texts, for constituting their properties. In other words, these strategies exist prior to the act of reading and therefore determine the shape of what is read rather than, as is usually assumed, the other way around.
>
> (Fish, 1980, pp. 13–14)

When these middle-class Indian readers themselves become writers, they replicate these tropes. In *When Amma Went Away*, an academic mother leaves the family to enjoy a research period in another city leaving the children to have adventures. The story takes place in a comfortably-off family (with a 'maidservant') but this time the academic is not a man like Quentin Kirrin in the *Famous Five* stories, but a woman, Amma, a successful researcher, supported and admired by her husband:

> 'You should be proud of your mother,' their father had said after Amma had announced the news and had gone to the kitchen to make something special for the occasion. 'She tells me that there were seven people in line for this offer and they selected her as the best of the lot. Isn't that great?'
>
> (Rangachari, 2022, p. 4)

Interestingly, Blyton's ghost still hovers here since Amma appears to be the main cook in the household.

Another example of Blyton-inspired vernacular fiction is *Pandab Goenda* by the Bengali novelist Sasthipada Chattopadhyay. Written in Bengali and inspired by the *Famous Five*, it was first published in 1981 by the New Bengal Press. Similarly, *Tin Goyenda,* a series of juvenile detective novels written by Rakib Hasan and published in Bangladesh by Sheba Prokashoni, is the tale of three teenage investigators and adventurers, one being Georgina Parker, the boyish daughter of famous scientist 'Quentin Parker'.

We see clearly that English is in some ways so culturally intrinsic to the way India negotiates its strange, unwieldy identity, that it can be imagined and recreated in Hindi, Bengali in many other languages. The examples of reading and writing processes I have mentioned reveal the multiple ways in which young readers and later writers make Blyton their own through a form of cultural translation and *bricolage*.

Blyton in Stroud, Gloucestershire

Blyton wrote and spoke in what was once called a 'received', 'standard' or even 'Oxford' or BBC English – terms that are now accepted as reflecting regional and class prejudice. A British child reading Blyton in the 1970s would very likely need to translate her into their own form of English or indeed mother tongue or regional variation (Welsh, Gaelic or a dialect for example). It may simply have meant translating the words used at home in a specific class context not matching Blyton's. Rarely would any reader be entirely fluent or a 'native speaker' of Blytonese. Around our house in Stroud, to which we moved from London in the summer of 1972, we discovered the sound of the West-Country accent, a different vocabulary and the remains of a dialect still spoken by older people ('How beest thee' for 'How are you'). Our house name was Fernbank in Summer Street, opposite a farm that had guinea fowl and chickens running in the yard where we helped the farmer stack the hay bales during those first summers. It was the perfect setting for a Blyton adventure; yet, despite its beauty, the shock of moving from London was great and we were considered outsiders with Southern accents. My brothers and I were in need of fiction to help us either distance or make sense of this new rural reality. My older brother escaped into *Pincher Martin* and *Animal Farm* followed by *Brave New World*, my younger brother *Thomas the Tank Engine*. I encountered *Five on Treasure Island* in the local library: it was easy to read and offered immediate gratification – both escapism and a close-knit group of friends. I was immediately hooked.

In *Five on a Treasure Island*, there was a father in the background (a rather remote authority) and a caring but not overbearing mother who allowed space for adventures. The children had freedom outside of the constraints of adult regimes. There was a strong, daring, independent girl character who was admired by the two boys and only the youngest girl seemed afraid. There was just enough tension (George's father's financial problems) to create suspense and make the discovery of treasure important. As a child, I consented to the fictional universe at once and read uncritically and with huge enjoyment as the children explored the island and its castle, discovered a map within the wreck of a ship washed up by a storm and finally found ingots of gold deep in the castle's dungeon, enough to restore George's family fortunes. Throughout the narrative, they consumed sandwiches and cakes, ginger ale, which I mentally ate and drank with them even though ginger ale or 'pop' was not something I often came across. Their enthusiasm for these rather ordinary foods and the emotional weight they seemed to carry was surprising to me (by the 1970s, there were chocolate bars and other treats so cake and sardines seemed rather ordinary). Yet, I adhered to their affective power: '"Ginger pop for me, thanks" said Julian!' (Blyton, 2012, p. 46) or 'They all felt better when they were eating the sandwiches and drinking the ginger-beer' (p. 57).

Of 'good schools' and 'fisher-boys': forms of consent

My consent to Blyton's narrative was not complete despite the allure of the universe she had set up; there were certain areas of the writing which troubled me even as a child. Antonio Gramsci explains that the adherence of a population to certain norms is a 'consent' manufactured in a variety of ways through education, media and the marginalization of dissenting groups (Gramsci, 1971, 2001). Louis Althusser would later use 'manufacture of consent' to elaborate his theory of 'ideological state apparatus' (1971) which would eventually evolve into the nudges of social media which push us towards shared beliefs (Sharma and Tygstrup, 2015). To suggest that Blyton is part of a state apparatus or machinery of consent at the service of a patriarchal hegemony may seem far-fetched, but consent is clearly solicited within the syntax, metaphors and lexical fields, encouraging readers to accept certain norms. We have been conditioned by our language to think and feel in certain ways:

> the "spontaneous" consent given by the great masses of the population to the general direction imposed on social life by the dominant fundamental group; this consent is "historically" caused by the prestige (and consequent confidence) which the dominant group enjoys because of its position and function in the world of production.
>
> (Gramsci, 1971, p. 54).

An example of this linguistic training, which Raymond Williams addresses in his *Keywords*, is the way we come to accept certain meanings which adhere to a particular term or a phrase which, once they are in current use, appear transparent and 'natural' to us even though they are laden with cultural prejudice. Gramsci evokes a counter-hegemony involving the production of new meanings produced by subaltern sections of the population: the latter may be a reader who can produce counter-hegemonic or 'aberrant decoding', counter to the encoder's original meaning (Eco, 1979, pp. 73–74). One example in Blyton is the word 'good' as used in 'good school', 'good' family or 'good mother'. My own memory of the word came during a sequence in *Five on a Treasure Island* devoted to George's father who is a struggling academic and therefore cannot send his daughter to a 'good' school:

> You see Daddy doesn't make much money with the learned books he writes, and he's always wanting to give mother and me things he can't afford. So that makes him bad-tempered. He wants to send me away to a good school but he hasn't got the money.
>
> (Blyton, 2012, p. 41)

This description became attached in my mind to an incident a few pages later involving the 'fisher-boy' whose name with its hyphen seemed to reduce him to a task or a commodity, a thing, like the 'ginger-beer' consumed by the children. The fisher-boy is useful and reliable but appears only as incidental, at best a helper in the 'actantial narrative schema' (Greimas, 1984) which organizes the narrative quest:

> The first thing was to fetch Tim. He was tied up in the fisher-boy's backyard. The boy himself was there, and grinned at George. "Morning Master George" he said... "Tim's been barking his head off for you".
>
> (Blyton, 2012, p. 46)

The boy is part of the backdrop of Blyton's world, one of the local people: the latter call the children 'Master' or 'Miss' but don't have names themselves; they are known in terms of their function. The system is made to seem natural since 'the fisher-boy' is there to 'fish' but not to go to school. As a child, I thought he perhaps had a school, but knew that it would not be a 'good school' (private and fee-paying like the one George was destined for). Something had been confirmed which I instinctively already knew: once you drop below a certain level in society, you no longer have a name and are visible only if you perform tasks for those in a higher station (taking care of Tim, George's dog – who interestingly has a name). Somehow, in solidarity with the fisher-boy, my consent was withheld. The fisher-boy is further designated as unworthy because he 'grins' – the grin being associated with Tim the dog who is said to grin, showing an almost-human propensity. The fisher-boy would never be admitted to the gang as he would not be allowed into a 'good school'. Yet, I remember thinking he would have been a good member of the team, able to steer the boat in the storm and help the children fight the intruders on the island. I wondered why they did not invite him along.

George's status and the pedigree of her 'good' family, however ill-paid her father's job is, is clearly put before the reader. The family goes back several generations and is an 'old' family: 'I don't know if wrecks belong to the queen or anyone, like lost treasure does ... But after all, the ship did belong to our family' (Blyton, 2012, p. 64). Later, she exclaims: "'they were the initials of my great-great-great grandfather!" said George ... "His name was Henry John Kirrin'". Names are powerful and so is time: objects or traditions kept in the family, the idea of generations going to the same school or living in the same house are all distinct signs of privilege. Yet, Blyton's narratives make clear that it is not enough to have had a once-wealthy grandfather: without a good income one is humbled. Social and economic status is laboured in the narrative: at the end of the story when the family fortunes have been saved, George's father says he will be rich enough 'to give you and your mother all the things I've longed to give you for so many years and couldn't. I've worked hard enough for you but it's not the sort of work that brings in a lot of money' (Blyton, 2012, p. 177). George is allowed to keep Tim and 'could go to a good school' while her academic father '... would be able to go on with the work he loved without feeling he was not earning enough to keep his family in comfort' (Blyton, 2012, p. 179).

Lessons learned at boarding school: class, gender, nation

Any young reader of the boarding school and adventure series would be able to describe the pecking order at work in Blyton's society: fathers are at the top – surgeons, doctors, lawyers, business men, academics (in that order) – then come the mothers (the calm sensible ones before the unreliable and overdressed/overemotional ones), female teachers, governesses foreign people (the French teachers and French and Spanish pupils), cooks, farmers, gardeners, fisher-boys, robbers. Working-class people who move up and infiltrate the system are seemingly not to be trusted: Matron's daughter Eileen, a pupil at St Clare's, is a sneak and reports back to her mother on the doings of her classmates (Blyton, 2016, p. 27). Some members of the working-class can be relied upon – in that case they are dependable like the fisher-boy or the local farmers, Mr and Mrs Sanders, or George's parents' cook in *Five Go Adventuring Again*.

At the same time, being too aristocratic is frowned upon. In *Claudine at St. Clare's*, the reader is introduced to a new girl who looks like a blonde 'angel', with a 'pixie' face and an armorial crest on the car that brings her to school. Honorable Angela Faverleigh is a figure of mockery shown to be too exalted and aristocratic to be taken seriously. A more practical mercantile bourgeoisie seems to be the ideal: the girls tell the snobbish Angela that St. Clare's is deemed to be 'a sensible no-nonsense school... not a swanky one' (Blyton, 2016, p. 12). Angela despises Matron's daughter: 'I don't see why Eileen should be allowed to join the school just because her mother is here as Matron... we shall have the Cook's daughter here next, and the gardener's too! It's bad enough to have Carlotta...' (Blyton, 2016, p. 13). The encoding of Blyton is clear: better not to be too rich, but not too poor. And certainly not plain and poor like the governess at Malory Towers: 'Poor Miss Winter... She was plain and poor and always eager to agree with everyone' (Blyton, 2019, p. 121).

In terms of gender, in *Five on a Treasure Island*, George sees girls as second best to boys. When George apologizes for an emotional outburst she says '"I've been behaving like a girl"... "But I did get an awful shock"' (Blyton, 2012, p. 105) and her father confirms this: '"Your mother is guided by me. You're only a child"' (Blyton, 2012, p. 102). When bedding down for the night: 'George looked as if she didn't want to be put with Anne and classed as a girl' (Blyton, 2012, p.111). Girls are shown to be often decent, sharing, supportive – a certain rebellious streak such as George's refusal of gender conformity is allowed yet always tempered and subsumed into the class-gender system. Victorian values of emulation and improvement are transmitted downwards: accepting authority and being helpful/decent to others is a powerful tool of hegemony and in the end even the most difficult and anti-social girls 'consent' to the system. As Tanvi Chowdhary has already noted in the first part of this chapter, girls are prepared to become 'best wives and mothers'. Headmistress, Miss Grayling, makes a speech on this point at Malory and underlines the importance of being 'loved and trusted':

> I do not count as our successes those who have won scholarships and passed exams, though these are good things to do. I count as our successes those who learn to be good-hearted and kind, sensible and trustable, good, sound women the world can lean on.
>
> (Blyton, 2019, p. 28)

The idea seems to be to avoid the excesses and vanity of upper-class Angela or Gwendoline (whose name is chosen because it has mediaeval and fanciful associations) and to become girls for Empire mirroring the boys in adventure annuals and novels of the nineteenth and twentieth centuries (McClintock, 1995; Burton, 1999; Mangan, 2012). Girls are asked to be ready to take their places not as rulers of the 'world' as the boys are – but as props to be 'leant' on.

In terms of the girls being future mothers, the rules are equally clear. Good mothers are fair, smiling, good 'sorts', decisive, but meek when their husbands are near. They are practical and cheerful, not over emotional like Gwendoline's mother in Malory Towers who weeps when she leaves her daughter at school. Women do not work unless they are foreign (the Mam'zelles) or poorer women (matron, teachers and cooks). Darrell's father is a surgeon: 'Her mother was pretty and amusing, and sensible too – and, as for her father, well *anyone* would trust him on sight, thought Emily, gazing at his determined, good-looking face with its big, dark eyes and intensely black eyebrows' (Blyton, 2019, p. 120). Whereas Gwendoline's mother, 'with bright golden hair like Gwendoline's and a rather babyish, empty face' (Blyton, 2019, p. 121), encourages selfishness and spoilt ways in her daughter, Darrell describes 'a proper mother' as '"the kind that would always love you, however many children she had, or whatever you did"' (Blyton, 2019, p. 157).

First Term at Malory Towers was published post-war and just before Indian independence in 1947, so themes of nationhood and of the British Empire are never far from the surface. This is also true of *Claudine at St. Clare's*, first published in 1944. Blyton's stories might be seen as one of an array of many nation-building tools which posited Englishness as an absolute value within Europe and the fast disintegrating British Empire. If Germany could not be mentioned, both France and Spain appear in Malory Towers and St. Clare's through two pupils, Claudine and Carlotta, and through the French teachers. As George Greenfield observes: 'Enid was very much part of that between-the-wars period middle class which believed that foreigners were untrustworthy or funny or sometimes both' (1995, p. 113). Examples of this abound at Malory Towers where the French teacher Mam'zelle Dupont has 'black and beady' eyes, a black dress, tiny feet, is 'short, fat and round' and uses a 'lorgnette' (Blyton, 2019, p. 26). When a spider trick is played on her she reveals a clichéd French fury: 'Her beady black eyes flashed', the beadiness likening her to an animal 'too plump to enjoy the hot weather' while 'little beads of perspiration shone on her forehead' (Blyton, 2019, p. 92). She is also associated with a childlike vengeance and lack of moral fibre (Blyton, 2019, p. 100). The other 'Mam'zelle', Miss Rougier, is a comic counterpoint to Mam'zelle Dupont: tall and thin, with little solidarity shown to her countrywoman, she despises her weakness and 'sneers' at her plight (Blyton, 2019, p. 101). Such Gallic caricatures were, of course, nothing new and had been common currency over centuries. Blyton would certainly have read Dickens's *A Tale of Two Cities* (1859) and been familiar with the many other novels taking the first French revolution as their setting such as Baroness Orczy's *Scarlet Pimpernel* (1905) and *A Child of the Revolution* (1932) and *Mam'zelle Guillotine* (1940).

Interestingly, outsiders, like Claudine, the niece of the French teacher in *Claudine at St. Clare's* with her rebellious and 'foreign' ways, are often accepted on certain conditions. Carlotta is 'mad in a Spanish way' because her mother was a circus rider but Blyton suggests that there seems to be hope for her since her father was an English gentleman (Blyton, 2016, p. 12). Claudine, on the other hand, is the French relative of Mam'zelle and has 'very un-English ways' (Blyton, 2016, p. 22). She is said to have 'a quick brain', but is often 'lazy' and has a tendency to 'simply copy the answers set down by the girl next to her' (Blyton, 2016, p. 22). The girls exclaim: 'I don't believe she thinks it wrong!' and proceed to educate her: 'Claudine, you mustn't copy from *any*one. I know French people have different ideas from ours – Mam'zelle has for instance...' (Blyton, 2016, p. 23). She also borrows: 'She borrowed pencils, rubbers... anything she happened to want at that moment. And nine times out of ten she didn't give them back' (Blyton, 2016, p. 23). The girls feel certain that she will learn 'English ways before the term is over' (Blyton, 2016, p. 24). Despite hating water and the English obsession with games, Claudine is finally accepted and desires more than anything to gain 'an English sense of honour' (Blyton, 2016, p. 157).

Like Tanvi, I had to negotiate my position within a text that offered a beguilingly smooth surface, inviting the reader to accept the ideology carried within it (Claudine is incomplete because in need of English ways). My struggle with certain words and the injustices that they implied helped me become critical while still enjoying and adhering to Blyton's fictional contract. Blyton became my own through a negotiation between alienation and belonging.

Unbelonging and decolonial ghosts

As we have just seen, historical conjuncture and cultural or class *habitus* inflect the readings of Blyton. A second reading ghosts the first: the children have grown up and have critical tools to understand their first reactions and to analyse the ideological agenda of the stories. It is a complex process which involves remembering being a child visitor once an adult, both a spontaneous consumer and critical reader. We have shown a child's imaginative struggle to reuse and reinvent Blyton's quite rigid moral universes. *When Amma Went Away* is a striking example of the creation of a counter-narrative in another cultural space – albeit with similar class aspirations and hegemonies at play. The boarding school narratives of the *Harry Potter* novels and the many teenage adventure stories that have proliferated all over the world since Blyton's death show that the reader is not entirely subsumed into Blyton's universe, but can withhold energy to playfully rethink the narratives.

Our task as twenty-first century readers looking back at our childhood consumption of these texts is a daunting one and potentially a profoundly political one. As Gurminder Bhambra has said: 'The task, following Spivak, is less about the uncovering of philosophical ground than in "reversing, displacing, and seizing the apparatus of value-coding" itself' (2014, p. 117). Similarly, Walter Mignolo and Catherine Walsh's work help us to see how decoloniality 'undoes, disobeys, delinks' from a colonial matrix of power 'constructing paths and praxis toward an otherwise of thinking, sensing, believing, doing and living' (2018, p. 4). It is not certain that a child can participate in the undoing of the hierarchical structures of race, gender and 'heteropatriarchy' (p. 17) but it is clear that an 'otherwise' (p. 16) of reading is at stake among Blyton's readers.

As child readers, neither one of us felt we really belonged to Blyton's universe and this gave us critical power. Tanvi Chowdhary remembers her reading experience in the following way:

> I am very obviously brown - yet when I imagined myself in these stories, I was more often than not thinking of myself as white. This happened to me with the Harry Potter world the most - so much so that when the original fannish reimagining of Hermione as a black woman began, I did not buy into it. I think something about the story is so inherently white that it was difficult to imagine myself as anything other than white.
>
> (Private correspondence)

Why do children continue to rework Blyton symbols and find ways of converting them? Their sense of never quite belonging means they can truly visit the text as an outsider and haunt it like a spirit. Sara Thornton underlines this:

> We didn't feel part of Blyton's world but wanted to be part of it of course. I could feel the privilege was not my own. I could sense even as a 10 year-old that categorizations and adult power play were at work. Blyton's texts colonized the more impoverished middle and lower middle British

classes: we were pulled into its aspirational world in a powerful way but remained outsiders - critical and wanting.

(Private correspondence)

The reader must haunt the text and drift around it, visit its fractures and fault lines and learn to inhabit them: the trick is to see the strangeness and constructed nature of the world portrayed. There needs to be a distance, an estrangement, a moment of discomfort and a refusal on the part of the reader who must trouble Blyton's writings, create trouble within them, provoke divergences and diversions and encourage them to mean differently.

References

Althusser, L. (1971) 'Ideology and Ideological State Apparatuses', in *Lenin and Philosophy and other Essays*, Translated by B. Brewster. New York: Monthly Review Press, pp. 121–176.

Ashcroft, B., Griffiths, G. and Tiffin, H. (2002) *The Empire Writes Back: Theory and Practice in Post-Colonial Literatures*. London and New York: Routledge.

Bennett, S. (ed.) (1990) *Theatre Audiences: A Theory of Production and Reception*. London and New York: Routledge.

Bhambra, G.K. (2014) 'Postcolonial and Decolonial Dialogues', *Postcolonial Studies*, 17(2), pp. 115–121.

Blyton, E. (1945) *Fifth Formers of St. Clare's*. London: Methuen.

Blyton, E. (1950) *Secret Seven Adventure*. Leicester: Brockhampton Press.

Blyton, E. (2012) *Five on a Treasure Island. The Famous Five*, collection 1. London: Hodder. [First published 1942].

Blyton, E. (2014) *The Mystery of the Burnt Cottage*. London: Hodder. [First published 1943].

Blyton, E. (2016) *Claudine at St. Clare's*. London: Hodder. [First published 1944].

Blyton, E. (2019) *First Term at Malory Towers*. London: Hodder. [First published 1946].

Burton, A. (1999) 'Gender, Sexuality and Colonial Modernities' in Cecire, M.S., Field, H. and Roy, M. (eds.) *Space and Place in Children's Literature, 1789 to the Present*. Surrey: Ashgate, pp. 111–129.

Cecire, M.S., Field, H. and Roy, M. (2015) 'Introduction: Spaces of Power, Places of Play' in Cecire, M.S., Field, H. and Roy, M. (eds.) *Space and Place in Children's Literature, 1789 to the Present*. Surrey: Ashgate, pp. 1–22.

Coats, K. (2004) *Looking Glasses and Neverlands: Lacan, Desire, and Subjectivity in Children's Literature*. Iowa City: University of Iowa Press.

Dwyer, R. (2007) 'Bollywood Bourgeois', *India International Quarterly*, 33(3/4), pp. 222–231.

Eco, U. (1979) *The Role of the Reader: Explorations in the Semiotics of Texts*. Bloomington: Indiana University Press.

Feingold, R. (2015) 'Mapping the Interior: Place, Self and Nation in the *Dreamhunter Duet*' in Cecire, M.S., Field, H. and Roy, M. (eds.) *Space and Place in Children's Literature, 1789 to the Present*. Surrey: Ashgate Publishing Limited, pp. 129–147.

Fish, S. (1980) *Is There a Text in This Class? The Authority of Interpretive Communities*. Cambridge, MA: Harvard University Press.

Gargano, E. (2008) 'Trials of Taste: Ideological "Food Fights" in Madeline L'Engle's *A Wrinkle in Time*' in Keeling, K. and Pollard, S.T. (eds.) *Critical Approaches to Food in Children's Literature*. New York: Taylor and Francis, pp. 207–221.

Gramsci, A. (1971) *Selections from the Prison Notebooks*. London and New York: International Publishers.

Gramsci, A. (2001) 'The Formation of the Intellectuals' in Leitch, V. (ed.) *Norton Anthology of Theory and Criticism*. New York: Norton, pp. 1002–1007.

Greenfield, G. (1995) *A Smattering of Monsters: A Kind of Memoir*. London: Camden House.

Greimas, A.J. (1984) *Structural Semantics: An Attempt at a Method*. Nebraska: University of Nebraska Press. [First published 1966].

Hourihan, M. (2005) *Deconstructing the Hero: Literary Theory and Children's Literature*. New York: Taylor and Francis.

Hunt, J.D. (2004) *The Afterlife of Gardens*. Philadelphia: University of Pennsylvania Press.

Iser, W. (1978) *The Act of Reading: A Theory of Aesthetic Response*. Baltimore, MD: Johns Hopkins University Press.

Jauss, H.R. (1982) *Toward an Aesthetic of Reception*. Translated by T. Bahti. Minneapolis: University of Minnesota Press.

Judy, L.G. (2011) 'Looking Back and Thinking Forward: Bildungsroman, Boarding Schools and National Identity in Charles Dickens' *David Copperfield* and Arguedas' *Los rios profundos*.' Master's thesis. University of Colorado Boulder [online]. Available at: https://scholar.colorado.edu/concern/graduate_thesis_or_dissertations/f4752g966 (Accessed: 3 January 2022).

Keeling, K. and Pollard, S.T. (2009) 'Introduction: Food in Children's Literature' in Keeling, K. and Pollard, S.T. (eds.) *Critical Approaches to Food in Children's Literature*. New York: Taylor and Francis, pp. 3–21.

Mangan, J.A. (2012) *'Manufactured' Masculinity: Making Imperial Manliness, Morality and Militarism*. London: Routledge.

Manlove, C.N. (2003) *From Alice to Harry Potter: Children's Fantasy in England*. Christchurch: Cybereditions.

McClintock, A. (1995) *Imperial Leather: Race, Gender and Sexuality in the Colonial Contest*. London and New York: Routledge.

Mignolo, W. and Walsh, C. (2018) *On Decoloniality*. Durham, NC and London: Duke University Press.

Miller, L. (ed.) (2016) *Literary Wonderlands: A Journey Through the Greatest Fictional Worlds Ever Created*. London: Black Dog and Leventhal.

Mistry, R. (1990) *Swimming Lessons and Other Stories from Firozshah Baag*. London: Penguin.

Mukherjee, A. (2014) *What Is a Classic?* Stanford, CA: Stanford University Press.

Narayan, R.K. (1935) *Swami and Friends*. London: Hamish Hamilton.

Nikolajeva, M. (2012) 'The Development of Children's Fantasy' in James, E. and Mendlesohn, F. (eds.) *The Cambridge Companion to Fantasy Literature*. Cambridge: Cambridge University Press, pp. 50–61.

Orestano, F. (2015) 'The Neapolitan Gouache of a Strong Minded English Lady: "The Little Merchants" by Maria Edgeworth' in Cecire, M.S., Field, H. and Roy, M. (eds.) *Space and Place in Children's Literature, 1789 to the Present*. Surrey: Ashgate Publishing Limited, pp. 57–75.

Rangachari, D. (2002) *When Amma Went Away*. New Delhi: Children's Book Trust.

Rao, R. (2015) *Kanthapura.* New Delhi: Oxford University Press. [First published 1938].

Roy, S. (2019) "Why India Should Claim Enid Blyton as Her Own" in. *Mint,* 12 October [online]. Available at: https://www.livemint.com/mint-lounge/features/why-india-should-claim-enid-blyton-as-her-own-11570782071525.html (Accessed: 14 May 2021).

Ryan, M.-L. (2001) *Narrative as Virtual Reality.* Baltimore, MD: Johns Hopkins University Press.

Saïd, E. (1993) *Culture and imperialism.* London: Vintage.

Sharma, D. and Tygstrup, F. (2015) *Structures of Feeling: Affectivity and the Study of Culture.* Berlin: Walter de Gruyter.

Smith, M.J. (2011) *Empire in British Girls' Literature and Culture.* Hampshire: Palgrave Macmillan.

Superle, M. (2011) *Contemporary English Language Indian Children's Literature: Representations of Nation, Culture and the New Indian Girl.* New York: Taylor and Francis.

Thiel, E. (2008) *The Fantasy of Family: Nineteenth Century Children's Literature and the Myth of the Domestic Ideal.* New York: Routledge.

Thiong'o, N. (1994) *Decolonizing the Mind.* Harare: Zimbabwe Publishing House.

Vagh, Z. (2020) 'The Problematic Writing of The Children's Books Author'. *Feminism in India – Intersectional Feminism – Desi Style!* 5 October. [online]. Available at: https://feminisminindia.com/2020/10/05/enid-blyton-childrens-books-sexism-xenophobia/ (Accessed: 14 June 2021).

Williams, R. (1988) *Keywords: A Vocabulary of Culture and Society.* London: Fontana Press.

11 Decolonial poetics

Ghosts of coloniality, capitalism, and care in contemporary anglophone literature

Fiona McCann

This essay will address these three recently published literary works from a decolonial perspective, focusing in particular on the ways in which the aesthetics they develop expose the mechanisms of the coloniality of power. In other words, I will be suggesting that these three works depict in myriad and yet similar ways the ghosts of colonialism and the latter's impact on bodies, territorial boundaries, and the environment. These novels and poetry record, imagine, expose, and critique the ongoing political consequences of colonialism as it stealthily inscribes itself on, and shapes the existence and identities of, living organisms and the body politic.

Adam Dickinson, Mia Gallagher, and Arundhati Roy, hailing respectively from Canada, Ireland, and India, are all interested in questioning the ways in which identities are constructed in our contemporary world, and the ways in which these identities, always multiple, are shaped by the ghosts of coloniality and capitalism. Canada, Ireland, and India all have a somewhat fraught relationship with postcolonialism, the first two as settler colonies which have now fully embraced their place in Global North economies, and India as a country which, in this century, is not only en route to becoming a global superpower but has also developed domestic policies which mirror those of colonial times (exclusionary, extractive, dehumanising, disempowering). In these contexts, the works of these writers, published between 2016 and 2018, nevertheless engage with thorny questions related to ongoing manifestations of coloniality and the ways in which a poetics of care might function as a rampart against this. All three authors are interested in proposing alternative modes of being which disrupt both identity and literary norms. In his collection *Anatomic* (2018), the non-Indigenous Canadian poet Adam Dickinson makes poetry out of microbiology, colonialism, capitalism, and pollution, foregrounding the inscription on and in his body of physical traces of the Anthropocene, that is to say the current geological age in which human activity has been the dominant influence on both climate and the environment;[1] Indian writer and activist Arundhati Roy in her novel *The Ministry of Utmost Happiness* (2017), despite the title's apparent emphasis on an ethics of care, interweaves contemporary Indian history, ecological catastrophe, and violent territorial disputes in a sprawling

DOI: 10.4324/9781003178040-15

story of India's shift from postcolonial to colonialist state; Irish writer Mia Gallagher turns her attention to shifting European borders, both spatial and temporal, museography, and the legacies of colonialism in her novel *Beautiful Pictures of the Lost Homeland* (2016) whose apparently nostalgic title reveals itself to be highly ironic, homelands in that text showing themselves to be constantly fluctuating entities. In spite of the many differences between them, what unites Canada, India, and Ireland is that they were all colonized in the past by Britain (as well as other empires), and the legacies of colonization are still palpable today: India, Pakistan, and Ireland all bear the violent traces of a messy partition (as Roy's and Gallagher's novels show), while Canada's First Nations and many inhabitants of India continue to undergo economic and political domination and discrimination.

As Aníbal Quijano has amply shown, nation-states, which are 'power structures', always function through a partial or total 'imposition by some (usually a particular small group) over the rest'. Nation-states are therefore 'a product of power', and control of power within many European states was further played out in the process of colonization when 'the nation-state depended on the organization of one centralized state over a conquered space of dominion' (Quijano, 2010, p. 558). Even long after the ostensible end of the colonial era, these same systems of domination continue to thrive in what Quijano has termed the 'coloniality of power', not merely haunting, but actually actively structuring the present.

This chapter will address these three recently published literary works from a decolonial perspective. What I will be suggesting is that these three works depict in myriad and yet similar ways the ghosts of colonialism and the latter's continued impact on bodies, territorial boundaries, and the environment. These novels and poetry record, imagine, expose, and critique the ongoing political consequences of coloniality, and its Siamese twin capitalism, as they stealthily inscribe themselves on, and shape the existence and identities of, living organisms and the body politic, yet the writers also sketch out a poetics of care as a possible mode of resistance to these hegemonic forces.

I will focus in particular on the ways in which the aesthetics they develop present both an 'awareness of the integral relation and interdependence amongst all living organisms (in which humans are only a part) with territory or land and the cosmos' (Mignolo and Walsh, 2018, p. 1) and a means of exposing the Colonial Matrix of Power, which Mignolo and Walsh identify as emerging

> at a particular time and place and under particular circumstances that made possible for a particular assembly of living organisms engaged in languaging to tell themselves and to others a story about their manifest destiny to rule, and destroy if necessary, cultures, and civilizations that they invented as dangerous for their own well-being.
>
> (Mignolo and Walsh, 2018, p. 220)

At this point, it is essential to point out that other voices haunt the theoretical framework of this chapter, voices to which I have limited access for linguistic reasons, yet which are nevertheless central. One of these voices is that of Silvia Rivera Cusicanqui, a Bolivian feminist and sociologist who has been scathing in her criticism of the ways in which certain thinkers, like Mignolo and Walsh, have become 'gurus' of decolonial thinking and have packaged it up, depoliticized it, and sent it mainstream. In particular, she takes them to task for 'creating a jargon, a conceptual apparatus, and forms of reference and counterreference that have isolated academic treatises from any obligation to or dialogue with insurgent social forces' (Rivera Cusicanqui, 2012, p. 98). Bearing in mind these valid criticisms of decolonial *theory*, I would like to suggest that the literary *texts* under scrutiny here nevertheless transcend these limits and contribute in their own way to building 'a lasting cultural fabric' and 'legitimate and stable norms of existence' (Rivera Cusicanqui, 2012, p. 106).

The daring aesthetics these writers cultivate, including the relative hermeneutic resistance of the texts, is part of their political project. By foregrounding in indirect ways the insidious, destructive 'capitalist death project' (Mignolo and Walsh, 2018, p. 35), Dickinson, Gallagher, and Roy all raise essential questions about the manner in which the memory of a turbulent colonial past, and its continued role in modelling identities, haunts the present in negative ways. Their poetics are resolutely political and thus contribute to reshaping the ways in which we think about our collective past as human beings; national(ist) identities reveal themselves to be porous, the categories of colonizer and colonized too, and the impact of colonialist capitalism on every living organism nothing short of catastrophic. And yet, these writers also manage to imagine into being uplifting moments of reconfigurations of care which just might sketch out the contours of a viable future for all. These reconfigurations of care are often predicated upon a rethinking of identities.

Strange bedfellows: Dickinson, Gallagher, and Roy

Quite coincidentally, Indian writer Arundhati Roy published her long-awaited second novel, *The Ministry of Utmost Happiness*, in 2017, just a few short months after Irish author Mia Gallagher published her second novel, *Beautiful Pictures of the Lost Homeland* in 2016. Both novels have as their central character a transgender woman, the hijra Anjum in *Ministry* and Geo, formerly Georgie, in *Beautiful Pictures*. These central characters are however somewhat displaced during the course of each narrative, de-centred as it were (in keeping with the political agendas of the authors), as other characters come to the fore. Both novels are very concerned with State and individual acts of 'terrorism' and with the troubles engendered by territorial land claims. Both novels delight in foregrounding temporal and spatial slippage, making the reader work hard to keep up, and both accentuate liminal spaces, reconfiguring them and rendering them less marginal: graveyards and lanes loom large as improbable sites from which a politics of care emerges.

The Ministry of Utmost Happiness has a complex structure – one might be tempted to reduce it to the stories of Anjum and Tilo, a woman who is involved, through her lover, in Kashmiri resistance, but this would be to miss out on the complexities of the novel. Deliberately unwieldy, the novel is purposefully confusing for the Western, or indeed non-Indian, reader unfamiliar with the intricacies of the history, politics, and economic situation in India. It is much less of a textbook postcolonial novel than Roy's first work of fiction, *The God of Small Things*, and more of a generic anomaly. There is a much more obvious incorporation of practically every single important political and economic event in late twentieth and early twenty-first Century India (the Emergency of the 1970s, the Bhopal Disaster of 1984, where nearly 4,000 people died, the Kashmir conflict from the late 1980s onwards, Gujarat violence in 2002, the Naxalite-Maoist insurgency which spans a period from 1967 to the present, to name but these major events). In fact, the novel packs in so many historical events, and so many characters, that it has been somewhat negatively reviewed, or at the very least has left some reviewers perplexed. Yet, it is clear that this novel is above all a novel of dissensus, so much so that it defies categorization and celebrates its own unwieldiness as alternate strands of stories confuse rather than complement each other. The narrative of contemporary India, Arundhati Roy seems to be saying, defies any teleological drive, or any particular logic, especially that based on a narrative of modernity, and can only be understood as part of a hotchpotch of events structurally related to the coloniality of power.

Mia Gallagher's *Beautiful Pictures of the Lost Homeland* is equally unwieldy, both in terms of its temporal span and the many colliding stories and characters found within, but it is every bit as concerned with the coloniality of power. The novel is mainly set in contemporary Ireland, but considerable parts of it are also set in a *Wunderkammer*, an ambulant museum which exists in a constantly fluctuating and unidentifiable space-time and which offers a total immersion into the past. This *Wunderkammer* retraces the history of shifting borders in Central Europe, linking the consistency and relentlessness of coloniality as it played out in Moravia and Sudetenland to Ireland and its own painful partition. Walter Mignolo and Rolando Vasquez explain the importance of considering coloniality alongside modernity and of seeing the two as intersecting structures:

> The rhetoric of 'modernity', and its continuing promises of salvation; and the logic of 'coloniality,' the continuing hidden process of expropriation, exploitation, pollution, and corruption that underlies the narrative of modernity, as promoted by institutions and actors belonging

to corporations, industrialized nation-states, museums, and research institutions.

(2013, np)

Decoloniality is then understood by them as 'appear[ing] in between modernity/coloniality as an opening, as a possibility of overcoming their completeness. Decoloniality refers to the variegated enunciations springing from global-local histories entangled with the local imperial history of Euro-American modernity, postmodernity, and altermodernity' (2013, np).

Adam Dickinson's work tackles this question from a less narrative and more marginal angle. If Gallagher's and Roy's novels make the reader work hard, then this is even more the case in *Anatomic* in which poetry and science operate in symbiosis to produce a highly original work of art.

Anatomic is a scientific, historico-political and, above all, poetic inquiry into the overlap between what human animals have done to the environment and what that environment is doing in return to us. Dickinson drew blood, collected urine, swabbed bacteria, and tested his faeces in order to measure with precision the chemical and microbial diversity of his body. The results alarmingly showed to what extent our petroculture has been absorbed into bodies. From these tests and their terrifying results, Dickinson has made some powerful poetry. The inextricable link between the metabolic processes of human and non-human bodies and the global metabolism of energy and capital is fully foregrounded in this collection. The corrosive effects of the Monsanto empire and the violence perpetrated against Canada's First Nations inhabitants are just two of many issues broached, dovetailing decolonial and environmental approaches at the heart of his aesthetics. Dickinson in fact obliquely depicts a Canadian society which is haunted by its violent colonial past and which continues to be adversely affected by manufactured toxins. The ghosts in this text are truly spectral in that they are invisible and barely detectable, yet omnipresent.

The limits of the poet's body are presented as porous, his body itself a generous host for a myriad of microbes, and his agency regarding this porosity inexistent. Toying with the very idea of poetry as turned towards interiority, Dickinson does indeed take things down to the most intimate level, but without ever losing sight of the external environment and how it has been affected by humans' hubris and so-called 'progress'. He links his own creative writing to the 'form of biochemical writing' which these organisms enact 'through their integral involvement in the metabolic processes that fuel my life' (Dickinson, 2018, p. 42). Yet, lest his collection appear as an individualistic (egotistical) reflection, his body is presented as interlinked with the bodies of Indigenous Canadians and he specifically identities himself as 'a settler' (Dickinson, 2018, p. 65). The collection as a whole questions a number of hegemonic doxas, and this is reflected in the very form of the work which moves effortlessly between sparse poetry, prose, scientific data, autobiographical elements, and photographs.

As Mignolo and Vasquez point out, '[m]odern aestheTics have played a key role in configuring a canon, a normativity that enabled the disdain and the rejection of other forms of aesthetic practices, or, more precisely, other forms of aestheSis, of sensing and perceiving' (2013, np). As a result,

> [d]ecolonial aestheSis is an option that delivers a radical critique to modern, postmodern, and altermodern aestheTics and, simultaneously, contributes to making visible decolonial subjectivities at the confluence of popular practices of re-existence, artistic installations, theatrical and musical performances, literature and poetry, sculpture and other visual arts.
>
> (2013, np)

Dickinson, Gallagher, and Roy all present works which aim to make visible these decolonial subjectivities, exposing the ongoing spectres of colonialism, and proposing forms of care as a response to them.

Coloniality and embodied resistance

In order to chart the ways in which the physical and epistemological progeny of colonialism continues to haunt and structure the present, all three writers pay specific attention to land and territoriality. A significant part of *Ministry* concerns the brutal territorial war over the Kashmir Valley, while *Beautiful Pictures* devotes considerable attention to the shifting borders around Bohemia and on the island of Ireland from the Middle Ages onwards. All three writers establish strong links between bodies and land and this interest in borders, bodies, and the limits of territories is to be linked to their desire to offer an embodied decolonial perspective on Indian, European, and North American history.

All three texts privilege improbable spaces as central sites. The improbable space of the graveyard and the contested space of the Kashmir Valley in *Ministry* and the even more improbable space of the *Wunderkammer* in *Beautiful Pictures* are all de-centred and marginal and thus a means of exposing how borders function and also how they are evidence, as Thomas Nail would have it, of 'kinopolitics'. For Nail,

> since the border is always in between and in motion, it is a continually changing process. Borders are never done 'including' someone or something. This is the case not only because empirically borders are at the outskirts of society and within it, but because borders regularly change their selection process of inclusion such that anyone might be expelled at any moment.
>
> (Nail, 2016, p. 7)

Dickinson expands this even further in his collection as he highlights the porosity of the boundaries between the individual and the community, between the individual and the surrounding environment, and the limited agency of the Indigenous body when it comes to preventing absorption of human-produced toxins.

Roy's representation of both the Kashmir conflict and the Maoist-Naxalite insurgency occupies a substantial part of the second half of the novel. Roy has commented at length on these insurrections in *Capitalism: A Ghost Story*, but in *Ministry*, she incorporates both of these into the complex narrative of the nation which opens up spaces for dissensus. The territorial dispute over Kashmir is accompanied, even mirrored, by ideological lines: 'As the war went on, in the Valley the soft line gradually hardened, and the hard line further hardened. Each line begot more lines and sub-lines' (2017, p. 321). In using the biblical language of begetting here, Roy draws attention to the ongoing consequences of violent colonial claim-staking which then leads to the incremental radicalization of the citizens of the region, conveyed here through personification of martyrdom and the mobilization of the tropes of fable:

> Martyrdom stole into the Kashmir Valley from across the Line of Control, through moonlit mountain passes manned by soldiers. Night after night it walked on narrow, stony paths wrapped like thread around blue cliffs of ice, across vast glaciers and high meadows of waist-deep snow. It trudged past young boys shot down in snowdrifts, their bodies arranged in eerie, frozen tableaux under the pitiless gaze of the pale moon in the cold night sky, and stars that hung so low you felt you could almost touch them.
>
> (2017, p. 313)

The timelessness of the fable ('night after night') mirrors the stasis of a colonial dispute which continues to engender violence, while the spatial markers which borrow from the sublime ('cliffs of ice', 'vast glaciers') ironically highlight the paradox of boundlessness as the condition for the Kantian sublime in this territorial conflict which has everything to do with borders. It is significant that Roy should elide the exact source of the martyrdom by omitting to specify from which side of the Line of Control it moves into the Valley, since this stresses both the porosity of even the most stringently controlled borders and the tentacular consequences of coloniality. Finally, the constant movement of the personified and spectral martyrdom ('walked', 'trudged'), later in the same passage referred to as a 'pied piper', and the relentlessness implied in its occupation of all available space, deftly conveys the inevitability of political action and self-sacrifice in this zone. Roy takes care to depict the period before martyrdom takes over as a Kashmir full of bounty:

> When it arrived in the Valley it stayed close to the ground and spread through the walnut groves, the saffron fields, the apple, almond and cherry

orchards like a creeping mist. It whispered words of war into the ears of doctors and engineers, students and labourers, tailors and carpenters, weavers and farmers, shepherds, cooks and bards. They listened carefully, and then put down their books and implements, their needles, their chisels, their staffs, their ploughs, their cleavers and their spangled clown costumes.

(2017, p. 313)

Roy borrows from the tropes of the Gothic, both through the 'creeping mist', which suggests contagion, and through ghostly depiction of martyrdom itself. The notion of contagion is further enhanced by the alliteration in /w/ as it 'whispered words of war'. The long list of professions and the equally long list of varied tools which they lay down in order to all take up the same tool – guns – is testimony to the profound shift from cohesive, complementary, and diverse community to dysfunctional war zone. Roy is here describing lives close to the Line of Control separating India and Pakistan, and the metaphor of the mist enhances the porosity of the border in spite of all the attempts to partition and divide. In fact, having just gestured towards the previous relative harmony of the area, Roy then presents the present space as directly murderous:

In remote border areas, near the Line of Control, the speed and regularity with which bodies turned up, and the condition some of them were in, wasn't easy to cope with. Some were delivered in sacks, some in small polythene bags, just pieces of flesh, some hair and teeth.

(2017, p. 314)

The passive constructions here, at odds with the initial agency of the bodies 'turn[ing] up', the various bodily parts functioning as synecdoches for tortured bodies, and the deliberate understatement ('not easy to cope with') all testify to the brutal fallout of territorial disputes and the constant threat of violence (the agents of torture and murder are never identified – they could almost be the mist). Wendy Brown cogently suggests that as

a boundary marker that is also a form of power, sovereignty bears two different faces. These appear in two different dictionary meanings of 'sovereignty,' 'supremacy' and 'autonomy,' and two equally discrepant political usages, as decisive power or rule and as freedom from occupation by another.

(Brown, 2010, p. 64)

The Valley, predominantly Muslim, has only limited autonomy and is very much under the yoke of Indian supremacy, but Roy makes sure not to sugar-coat actions carried out by insurgents either, a fact which also accounts for the elided agents in the passage quoted above.

This same elision of agency is present in the opening chapter of *Beautiful Pictures* which is the description of the moments preceding a suicide bomb attack in the London Underground, told in a first-person plural voice. The proximity of all those squashed into the Tube carriage is conveyed through a series of synecdoches: 'the millimetre-thin membrane between arse and cock, tit and elbow, mouth and forehead. We drink in each other's scent' (Gallagher, 2016, pp. 1–2), thus already announcing the permeability of boundaries which will be explored in so many ways in the novel. There are enough clues present to guess, by the end of the novel, who the individual perpetrator is, but the opening passage privileges a collective, rather than an individual act, inviting us to engage differently with questions of 'terrorism', and to see them in a context of global geo-politics. There are no easily identified binary positions of good and bad here, where border politics are world politics.

The choice of a transgender character as protagonist in the two novels, and the various difficulties they encounter in affirming their gender identity, should not, for all that, be misunderstood as a metaphor for colonial partition (India/Pakistan and Northern Ireland/Republic of Ireland). On the contrary, it is the political situation informing both novels which becomes a metaphor for Anjum's and Geo's fluid gender identity. One of the Hijra, in the liminal space of the Kwagbah where Anjum spends 30 years, explains to her that while other people are made unhappy by external events, they face internal turmoil: 'The riot is *inside* us. The war is *inside* us. Indo-Pak is *inside* us' (Roy, 2017, p. 23). Similarly, Geo's childhood friendship with the malnourished and alienated 'Elaine', who later turns out to be an imaginary friend, and who occupies 'a lane' running behind her house, another liminal space, is a spectral manifestation of her own internal gender conflict. Likewise, the link between her burgeoning rejection of her assigned gender and the sectarian murder in the borderlands of the Catholic neighbours of her grandparents, with whom she spends her holidays playing, is established in such a way that Gallagher seems to be suggesting that the rigid lines of coloniality filter into and affect every aspect of life, even the most intimate. Moreover, in the first pages devoted to the space of the *Wunderkammer*, the links between usurpation of land and abuse of bodies are crudely, yet effectively, established:

If you put your nose to the pages and smell, you get this:

> The bittersweet aroma of pyriodl, the region's cherry jam. The golden warmth of straw. Sweat and secretions. Fear and longing. The metallic taste of rusting ploughshares. The acrid residue of artillery fire. The almond warning of nitroglycerine. The scent of shit. The trace of betrayal. The cheddar-sharp tang of a violated cunt.
> Welcome, meine Damen und Herrn, to Bohemia!
> (Gallagher, 2016, p. 25)

In a similar fashion to Roy's description of the move in the Kashmir valley from bounty and self-sufficiency to war, as a result of colonial claim-staking, Gallagher, strongly placing the emphasis on the olfactory (which is precisely what a 'real' museum, predicated on the visual and the haptic only, can hardly ever recreate), also gradually moves from images of the homely and the comforting, to those of the tools of war, to the embodied traces of that warfare, and in particular sexual assault, all of which sum up the history of Bohemia. The insertion of vernacular vocabulary ('shit', 'cunt'), the recourse to olfactory descriptions, and the flippant welcome in the final line all draw attention to Gallagher's reflection on the politics of museum spaces which often enshrine colonial narratives in safe lexical formulations that depoliticize and over-simplify historical narratives. The *Wunderkammer* itself functions as a somewhat ghostly presence in the novel, popping up sporadically in a seemingly disconnected way from the main diegetic strands. Yet, its strong focus on the violent impact of colonial wars on bodies and identities indicates that our reading of the present is enhanced by an understanding of History. In other words, although the events of the past may not always be immediately obvious in the present, Gallagher suggests that they inevitably underwrite identity construction.

It is precisely this osmosis between coloniality and bodies which Adam Dickinson explores in his collection *Anatomic*. In one particular prose passage, the First Nations inhabitants are never named, simply referred to as 'they' or 'the problem', as he mimics, and subsequently undermines, the racist ideologies which continue to proliferate in Canada. The piece is entitled 'The People of Grassy Don't Have a Mercury Problem, They Have a Drinking Problem' and overturns racialized stereotypes related to alcohol abuse and Indigeneity. It does this by repeating the phrase 'There was talk of' or 'There was talk that', conveying the omnipresent power of the doxa to determine how and what we think, and linking it to the invisibilization of both First Nations inhabitants and the poisonous impact of industrial pollution on their ecosystem:

> There was talk that the bodies were not actually poisoned, and if they were poisoned it was because of what goes into them, the weekends in Kenora, the altered dream-states that break into leaf in this culture, but culture urine and vomit in the streets of that culture ... There was talk how drinking was one long peristaltic protest against colonialism ... And here I have it in my blood talking, a settler methylated by the privilege afforded by the problem's extremities shaking with poorly connected dreams. All this talking and I am beginning to repeat myself. Myself.
>
> (Dickinson, 2018, p. 65)

In this short excerpt, the elision of the poisonous agents in the use of the passive form is what enables industrialists to contest the nature of the pollution, attributing it to excessive consumption of alcohol rather than poisonous industrial waste, just as the nominal and verbal meanings of the word 'culture' allow for the erection of a rhetorical barrier between 'this culture' and 'that culture' (synonymous with grotesque excess and the growth or a 'culture' of waste). That the barrier is indeed only rhetorical is exposed by the speaker in the final sentences as he connects 'all this talking' with the ways in which his own body 'talks' in its own way, through the lesser though still present traces of poison in his own organism, revealing his socio-economic privilege as a 'settler' and its contingency upon exploitation and abuse of both certain humans ('non-grievable lives' in Judith Butler's terminology, 2010) and the ecosystem. 'Drinking' (alcohol), ultimately, in a dig at the deliberate oversimplification of some postcolonial discourses, cannot be understood 'as one long peristaltic protest against colonialism', but rather, if understood as 'drinking' (water), as colonialism's ongoing poisonous legacy. In fact, the genesis of this dates back to the 1970s and specifically concerns Indigenous residents of Grassy Narrows (near the white settlement of Kenora). Dickinson (2018, p. 147) explains:

> The community of Grassy Narrows had been and continues to be poisoned by mercury spilled into the Wabigoon-English River system in the 1960s by a pulp and paper mill in Dryden, Ontario. I found mercury in my blood and it made me think about my connection to the issue of racial injustice as a privileged settler in Southern Ontario.

In these three texts, the ghost of colonialism is omnipresent, even if it is not always obvious, and it is always destructive, both on an individual and a collective level. However, all three authors show that the coloniality of power is predicated not just on colonial structures, but also on the demands of capitalism.

Capitalism and destruction

As Roy points out in her essay *Capitalism: A Ghost Story*, capitalism functions structurally just like colonialism, 'wag[ing] wars and militarily occup[ying] countries in order to put into place free market "democracies"' (Roy, 2015, p. 45) which are favourable to Western states' interests. Dickinson, Gallagher, and Roy establish the nexus of all forms of colonialism (including those which operate within a given state) and capitalist structures and networks.

Throughout the collection *Anatomic*, Dickinson places the focus on the Monsanto empire from both an anti-colonial and anti-capitalist angle. The poem 'Agents Orange, Yellow, and Red' (2018, p. 15) in particular lays out the groundwork for the whole collection in which North American (and, more generally, Global North) imperialism is polluting our cultures, our habitat, and our bodies. The chemical which Dickinson is responding to here is also known as dioxin, which is a pervasive environmental contaminant. It is used to manufacture paper, but also herbicides like Agent Orange, which was used most egregiously by the US army between 1961 and 1971 during the Vietnam War when its spraying over the land resulted in a huge impact on biodiversity, defoliation on immense scale, not to mention evidence of deformities in children, and increased cancers (including among US veterans). Significantly, although not originally developed by Monsanto, Agent Orange has gradually become synonymous with this commercial giant which has produced it abundantly.

This poem functions through a series of oppositions which are so binary that only one of each is possible: an imitation of North American do-or-die doxa. The absurdity of these binaries is emphasized in the use of the second person pronoun (which is reminiscent of war time propaganda posters: 'Your country needs you'). It is both a generic and an individual 'you' here, in an imitation of advertising campaigns and the result is a neat parody of that mixture of telling us what we are to believe and telling us what we already believe. The opening opposition of the poem, 'You are either for chlorine / or for the plague', sets up a ridiculous opposition and a dogma that functions on an either/or basis. In particular, the use of the noun 'plague' is indicative of the alarmist discourse that prevails, engendering a climate of fear which impedes critical thinking. The second opposition, which unfolds over double the number of lines, uses bathos in order to undercut the false dilemma/false dichotomy, a major logical fallacy so often trotted out in North American media: 'Right now is the cleanest / we have ever been, and for this / you must love aerial defoliants / or you love communism'. The choice is stark: either we embrace dangerous chemicals and the injunction to be cleaner than ever, or we are implicitly guilty of vowing allegiance to America's enemies. This line of reasoning fails by limiting the options to two when there are in fact many more options to choose from, and the absurdity of this rhetorical process is highlighted in the tone which parodies the language of totalitarian discourses. Moreover, the full stop after each of these opening oppositions reinforces the way they are used to end, as opposed to nourish, discussions.

However, Dickinson is not just interested in uncovering logical fallacies and mocking them in an absurd way, and the poem goes on to develop a series of metaphors which make a very political statement about these toxins used in chemical warfare and indeed in everyday agriculture, in the context of US imperialism and networks of capitalism. The situation is historicized, as the overt reference to settler colonialism makes clear: 'Through the clearing, freshwater carp / blink past the graves of missionaries / who introduced them to the New World'. What is clearly implied here is that this ecological crisis began, or at least had its genesis, in the upsetting of Indigenous biodiversity by first settlers. Irony is also to be found in the term 'New World', which was only 'new' from the settler perspective, and in the fact that the idyllic discourses buttressing the colonization of Americas and bound up in terms 'new' (as in fresh, virginal, etc.) have literally brought us into a devastating 'new' world era (the Capitalocene).

The specific effects of settler colonialism and the development of capitalism are clearly expressed in the poem when the human-made and the organic are juxtaposed: 'Northern rivers are warmed / by the paper mill's piss, which, / like making the world safe for democracy, / slowly leaked into my childhood, yellowing / the lipophilic paperbacks of my / adipose fat' (15). The equation of the factory's toxic ejections with the body's through the plosive alliterative ('paper mill's piss') appear to conflate the 'natural' or organic, and the synthetic. But the use of 'piss' here seems to suggest a lack of proper form and respect – pissing into the river implies not caring about toxins one excretes, and indeed the 'warm[ing] of the rivers' also gestures to a wider global warming that factories such as this also contribute to, on top of polluting the immediate environment. The association of this leaking piss (dioxins) and the political cliché 'making the world safe for democracy' so often trotted out suggest the power of rhetoric too to distil poison, and reveal that there are two types of toxins at play here, as we have seen from the start of the poem: a material one, and a rhetorical one. The metaphor of the 'paperbacks of my / adipose fat' extends this and underlines that rhetoric, like toxins, is ingurgitated all the time, mostly indirectly. Finally, there is great irony throughout this poem related to whole question of agency we have as humans in this North American either/or society. Agent Orange (and the other chemicals), manufactured by companies like Monsanto with the full collusion of governments, have reduced our agency, right down to the functionings of our bodies, and those of other non-human animals, and any living beings. This is brought home with full force in the final lines of the poem with the ultimatum: 'You are either / for the red or the white blood cells, / the tops of the trees, or the bottoms'. Since we cannot actually have one without the other, and cannot survive without both, this false dilemma in the closing lines frames the poem between two logical fallacies and reveals the extent to which we are effectively trapped in this absurd universe.

Arundhati Roy's depiction of the ravages of capitalism is no less acerbic than Dickinson's, and she too uses the body as a canvas on which to write the devastating changes which it brings in its wake. In the opening pages of the chapter entitled 'Nativity', which deals with the arrival of Miss Jebeen the Second in Anjum's life and the hellish dawn of the city of Delhi as 'supercapital of the world's favourite new superpower' (2017, p. 96), she uses personification as an effective tool with which to highlight the violence inherent in the capitalist makeover of the city. The description begins with a benevolent image of the city as an old, lived in, comfortable 'Grandma's body:

> Old secrets were folded into the furrows of her loose, parchment skin. Each wrinkle was a street, each street a carnival. Each arthritic joint a

crumbling amphitheatre where stories of love and madness, stupidity,
delight and unspeakable cruelty had been played out for centuries.

(2017, p. 96)

The association of different body parts and different experiences, both positive ('love', 'delight') and negative ('cruelty'), and the link between secrets,
stories and the city, all celebrate a slightly decrepit ('loose', 'wrinkle',
'arthritic', 'crumbling') yet historically lively entity. Under 'her new [capi-
talist] masters', the city 'bec[omes] a whore', the vulgarity of which is crassly
laid out as a series of cosmetic changes: 'hide her knobby, varicose veins
under imported fishnet stockings, cram her withered tits into saucy pad-
ded bras' (2017, p. 96). The image of the 'withered tits' which can no longer
provide any nourishment or vitality, and which are now instead overtly
sexualized effectively embodies the obscenity of this transformation which
also involves a frontal attack on the environment: 'Skyscrapers and steel
factories sprang up where forests used to be, rivers were bottled and sold in
supermarkets, fish were tinned, mountains mined' (2017, p. 98). In granting
agency to the human-made structures through the verb 'sprang' and by elid-
ing the agents of the bottling, tinning and mining of natural resources, Roy
underscores simultaneously the seismic changes at work and the difficulty
of holding anyone accountable as capitalist industry insidiously takes hold,
separating 'the surplus people' (98) from the 'people (who counted as people)' (2017, p. 99).

In *Beautiful Pictures*, Gallagher too pinpoints the coloniality of power
and the ways in which capitalist ideologies shape relations of power and
influence the drawing and undrawing of borders. All the characters in
this novel who are committed to undermining capitalism fail. Lotte's twin
brother Andreas blows himself up as Lotte watches, helpless and unaware
of the planned outcome, filming from afar the scene which Andreas naively
hopes will provoke a sea-change. Eoin, her lover and the father of her son,
is condemned to repeat over and over the same Marxist discourse, to such
an extent that his words just become media sound bites – another capitalist
recuperation. This is highlighted when he accepts a job as a photographer
of the Troubles in the North for *The Irish Times*. The gap between Eoin's
principles and his co-optation by the establishment is underscored by Lotte:
'*File*. The Irish for bard. The Gaelic bards, he'd told her when they'd been
fucking, had two functions: to flatter the power and, if crossed, to satirize
it. Since when had he been working for a newspaper?' (2016, p. 275). Eoin's
poetic image of himself, and the fact that he places himself in the lineage of
Celtic bards, is revealed to be a self-justificatory measure designed to make
palatable his capitulation to the capitalist status quo. This is already clear
in the opening pages of the novel where Geo watches media handling of the
suicide bomb in the London Underground and observes Eoin pontificating:
'*Over ten years of bloodshed and rhetoric and nobody's asking why this stuff
is happening, much less who it's benefitting ...* They cut to a book jacket; his

latest coffee-table offering' (2016, p. 17). The juxtaposition of the verb 'ben-efitting' and the image of his book, dismissed as ornamental, suggest that, despite his ostensibly anti-war discourse, he is one of those literally profit-ing from the situation, and that he is very much part of the problem. Lotte underlines this in no uncertain terms: 'Newsflash, poet. The system's fuck-ing everywhere and we're part of it. There's stuff going on all over the world, killing, looting, raping, and you know what? Nobody gives a shit' (2016, p. 281). This understanding of the violence of capitalism does not stop Lotte herself from ultimately becoming a suicide bomber in the London Under-ground, although the agenda behind her actions is, significantly, never spec-ified, thus ensuring that the novel raises more questions than it answers.

Despite the presence of so much destruction and violence, however, and the intense detail in which they are depicted, all three texts also manage to move beyond the endemic brutality of the coloniality of power as it spreads its spectral tendrils to places as diverse as India, Canada, Central Europe, and Ireland, to sketch out new forms of care.

Ministry and caring

Although these three literary texts bring into relief the structural damage to all organisms brought out about by the coloniality of power as it devel-oped in the past and continues to expand its realm in the present, they also present a politics and poetics of care which functions as an effective form of resistance.

In *Ministry*, it is a queer caring reconfiguration of family life which Roy privileges. Anjum falls in love with an abandoned baby girl at the observa-tory in Delhi and when the baby disappears, tracks her to the home of Tilo who has taken her and named her Miss Jebeen the Second in memory of the daughter of her lover (Miss Jebeen the First) who was killed by the Indian army in Kashmir. Anjum convinces Tilo to move in with her at the grave-yard, which she does, and a communal form of parenting emerges. One day, a letter from the biological mother of the baby, Revathy, arrives at the grave-yard, in which she explains that her daughter was conceived from multiple rapes due to her involvement as a Maoist guerrilla fighting on behalf of the Adivasi people (one name for Indigenous peoples of South Asia) against the Indian State and its destructive economic and environmental policies in the Andhra Pradesh region. Revathy is dead by the time the letter reaches the graveyard, so her voice literally ghosts the text, but Anjum and the oth-ers, humorously and ironically referred to as the 'the graveyard Politburu' (2017, p. 426), are able to bestow the baby's original name, Udaya, on her, while keeping her new name, Miss Jebeen the Second. In this way, the baby embodies both conflict and commemoration of caring relationships. Know-ing this story makes all the graveyard inhabitants 'close ranks around [the baby] like a formation of trees, or adult elephants – an impenetrable for-tress in which she, unlike her biological mother, would grow up protected and loved' (2017, p. 426). The association here of other forms of community which are non-human based and the topos of the fortress borrowed from the lexicon of war and fable neatly dovetail Roy's ecological and anti-capitalist agendas, and foreground a narrative predicated upon sharing care. From failure, destruction, and violence, emerges a new collective, gender-fluid, communal, and decidedly queer family configuration premised on collective care where a 'ministry of utmost happiness' can in fact be realized.

Mia Gallagher, for all that her novel deals extensively with nuclear family dysfunctions as resulting from class and colonial differences, also makes some, albeit limited, space for relations of care, also through queer identities, as a mode of resistance to the coloniality of power. It is Geo's caring relationship with her miserable and neglected imaginary friend, Elaine, whom she feeds, clothes, and educates, which eventually helps her comprehend her gender dysphoria, and her recently ended relationship with working class Mar which has accompanied her through her physical transition. As Joan Tronto has pointed out,

> [i]n our present culture there is a great ideological advantage to gain from keeping care from coming into focus. By not noticing how pervasive and central care is to human life, those who are in positions of power and privilege can continue to ignore and to degrade the activities of care and those who give care.
>
> (Tronto, 1994, p. 111)

This is exactly what this novel exposes: Geo's father, an architect, is hung out to dry by the wealthy firm owners he works for after the Central Bank building fiasco, and Gallagher here underlines the absence of duty of care in the workplace at a time when Ireland began to fully embrace capitalist and neo-liberal politics, and clearly the fact that he is a (failed) architect reinforces the idea of the structural failure at the heart of Irish politics and economy; Lotte becomes a substitute parent for young Geo, caring for her physically and emotionally while her mother is dying, and is the first to actually see that Georgie has gender dysphoria; Lotte's mother is rendered vulnerable by her unvoiced experience of rape at the end of the Second World War, figured in the text as a blank space, as borderlines in Central Europe fluctuated once again; and finally, Andreas, Lotte's twin brother, who haunts her throughout the novel, sees no other mechanism for making people care about the horrors of imperialism, fascism, and capitalism than making a 'big bloody statement' in the form of a filmed suicide on the top of a newspaper building. Gallagher refuses any hopeful closure at the end of her novel: Lotte is revealed to be the London suicide bomber and the curator of the *Wunderkammer*, while Geo is awaiting the results of a biopsy which may reveal she has breast cancer. Nevertheless, by exposing the interconnections of imperialist conquest, colonialism, heteropatriarchy, and neo-liberalism and highlighting the spontaneous and unofficial forms of care which can be developed, even if they fail to be sustained, Gallagher signposts the potential for these relations of care to transcend the ugliness of our contemporary world.

Adam Dickinson's whole project in *Anatomic* might be seen as an ambitious illustration of a poetics of care, on an individual and collective level. As he points out in the final pages,

> Being able to read the chemicals and microbes in bodily fluids means being able to read the writing of the Anthropocene in ways we have not been able to do yet, in ways that might illuminate the common crowds we bear and the crowds in common that we are.
>
> (2018, p. 143)

Not only is there a reflection here on the parallel established between reading and writing a text and reading and writing the body but also on the importance of this archaeology of the body which uncovers our intimate connections with history and with our environment. The poet's own body is a synecdoche for the body politic ('crowds in common') and his whole poetic endeavour a perfect embodiment of Joan Tronto's definition of the politics of care:

> *a species activity that includes everything that we do to maintain, continue, and repair our 'world' so that we can live in it as well as possible.* That world included our bodies, our selves, and our environment, all of which we seek to interweave in a complex, life-sustaining web.
>
> (1994, p. 103, italics in original)

It is precisely this 'complex, life-sustaining web' which Dickinson privileges in his collection, often personifying hormones, bacteria, vitamins, and microbes in order to highlight simultaneously the multi-species activity within human bodies, and the important relationality between human colonial history, the narratives we choose to tell, and the unseen traces of the Capitalocene which we 'bear' in our bodies. Relations of care for Dickinson are, however, not idealized: even the passage on his mother breastfeeding him is fraught with allusions to dangerous toxins she unwittingly passes on:

> her milk sent me a postcard from the postwar boom. The message was scrambled. [...] Malignant neoplasms of indefinite dose. [...] My jaw owes its plotlines to my mother's breasts, even as they've been ghost-written by power grids redesigning sensoria from a diaspora of unseasonal thunderheads.
>
> (2018, p. 34)

Just as any new literary production is always ghosted by the texts which have preceded it, so too, Dickinson suggests, are our bodies ghosted by histories of displacement, destructive patterns, and environmental contaminants: 'power grids' here are not just electric; they are also the narratives of power which structure our dysfunctional world.

The three texts under scrutiny here, which emanate from three different continents, all proffer innovative aesthetics which feature varied spectral forms as a means of exploring the fertile possibilities offered by a decolonial poetics. Identities are presented as complex and fluctuating, yet are nevertheless constantly reclaimed, whether in terms of biology, sovereignty, class, gender, or sexuality. All three authors are clearly interested in uncovering the brutality of colonialism and the long shadow it continues to cast on contemporary lives, just as they are moved to relate colonial mechanisms of control to the interests of capitalism. The long, historical view adopted by these writers provides context for contemporary forms of violence and for understanding them as always haunted by the spectres of invasion, partition, usurpation, exploitation, and heteropatriarchy. In this sombre context, these texts suggest, relations of care, which offer the potential for transcending the inequalities and brutality of the coloniality of power, can only ever be sporadic and brief, and yet their very existence, and the act of enshrining them in these literary works, is already a statement of hope.

Note

1 I am using this term, coined by Andreas Malm, for legibility here, but as I will show later in this chapter, Dickinson's poetry and Roy's and Gallagher's novels all show the limits of this very term which, if one is not careful, tends to suggest that all humans have equally contributed to the irremediable damage humans have done to their habitat, the earth. In this respect, Capitalocene is perhaps a better term. For more on this question, see Moore (2016), particularly the introduction.

References

Brown, W. (2010) *Walled States, Waning Sovereignty.* New York: Zone Books.
Butler, J. (2010) *Frames of War: When is Life Grievable?* London: Verso.
Dickinson, A. (2018) *Anatomic.* Toronto: Coach House Books.
Gallagher, M. (2016) *Beautiful Pictures of the Lost Homeland.* Dublin: New Island.
Mignolo, W. and Vasquez, R. (2013). 'Decolonial AestheSis: Colonial Wounds, Decolonial Healings', *Social Text Online.* July. [online]. Available at: https://www.udesc.br/arquivos/ceart/id_cpmenu/5800/Decolonial_Aesthetics__Colonial_Wounds_Decolonial_Healings_____Social_Text_15505156052623_5800.pdf (Accessed: January 4, 2022).
Mignolo, W. and Walsh, C. (2018). *On Decoloniality. Concepts, Analytics, Praxis.* Durham, NC and London: Duke University Press.
Moore, J.W. (ed.) (2016) *Anthropocene or Capitalocene? Nature, History, and the Crisis of Capitalism.* Oakland, CA: PM Press.
Nail, T. (2016) *A Theory of the Border.* Oxford: Oxford University Press.
Quijano, A. (2010) 'Coloniality and Modernity/Rationality', *Cultural Studies*, 21(2), pp. 168–178.

Rivera Cusicanqui, S. (2012) '*Ch'ixinakax utxiwa*: A Reflection on the Practices and Discourses of Decolonization', *The South Atlantic Quarterly*, 111(1), pp. 95–109. DOI: 10.1215/00382876–1472612.

Roy, A. (2015) *Capitalism. A Ghost Story*. London: Verso.

Roy, A. (2017) *The Ministry of Utmost Happiness*. London: Hamish Hamilton.

Tronto, J. (1994) *Moral Boundaries: A Political Argument for and Ethic of Care*. New York and London: Routledge.

Index